# WOND[

## DEDI[

To my old dairies that reminded m                    wife
that put up with me always writing of times gone by, before I ....  .r.

# WONDERLAND
### By
# JIMPER SUTTON

## SYNOPSIS

Preacher, a young lad of the early 1960s falls in love with a young girl. Her parents, of a different social class to Preacher, object strongly to this liaison and obtain a Court Injunction to put an end to their love. This drives them to clandestine meetings and through her best friend there love blossoms until a tragic accident separates them.

Preacher's life goes on with her best friend and she becomes his soul mate, but she knows where his love is yet never tells him. His heartache for his first love never dies and his soul mate leaves him and marries.

35 years later a chance meeting with an old friend leads him to his old soul mate whom is now a widow, only to find out she had stabbed him in the back all those years ago and still has contact with his love one.

Plans are put into place for a reunion that has unexpected repercussions.

# CHAPTER ONE

It was in a small wooden village hall off the main road down a little country lane that I first danced with a pretty girl of fifteen, with dark brown hair. She wore a pair of sling back shoes with two-inch heels, fishnet stockings, a knee length skirt, a white blouse, blue eye shadow and no jewellery. Her slim body was made for dancing; she was developing into a fine woman. With a little nose, she stood two inches short from my grey eyes. Her dark brown eyes had that 'come hither, hold me and dance look.' The smile on her face said more than any words can describe. Her young perfectly shaped legs were made for the Quick step, and somehow it felt right for us to glide across the floor together.

***

For four months that winter, we danced as one. She cocked her head up as we turned the corners with a sweeping movement to say to the world, 'did you notice that movement?' Then she threw her head to look the other way in one sudden graceful arc. We felt right, we were getting the fast movements under control.

***

Always after the night of dancing with that girl, I had a job to sleep, thinking of her. After the evening came to an end, I took her and a friend of hers home, dropping her friend off first and then taking the road across the marsh, headed for the hills in the distance. Halfway along this road, we turned up a lane leading to a small village tucked away in a thickly wooded area, where a large house stood with a hard tennis court alongside. The drive to the house was twenty yards of pristine pea beach raked and swept clean, that I dared not drive on for fear of leaving a mark on the immaculate grit. I knew the house to belong to a somewhat posh aristocrat. The girl said she was the daughter of one of the staff that waited day and night on *'His Lordship.'* But she knew of me. The girls talked of me at school, so she had the whip hand on me. I knew nothing of her at the time. Her mates at school had told her I frequented the village hall and they had planned from the very start for her to meet me, she had seen me on the tractor many times as I passed by her home. We owned land that joined the estate she lived on and she rode her pony across the fields. Many times I had seen the girl on horseback and waved at her, but had taken no more notice. Our family had been feuding with the owner of the big house for as long as I could remember, for reasons I had no knowledge of.

***

The following week, the hall dancing classes held a small social gathering with another class from a bigger village four miles away, so I took five girls, all mates of each other, in my father's estate car. It was a week before Christmas and the huge hall was all dressed up for the occasion. The night was a memorable one, but of all the girls I danced with, nothing felt the same as when I danced with Kay. She was somehow special to me. Later that night, back home, I opened my diary and had a job to write how I felt about the ending of the day.

All I knew was that I must see her again soon. It was to be the start of something I am glad I was never to have missed, a real new adventure, with as many ups, and downs, as you could wish for.

Her mother was a friend of one of the girls I had been seeing along with the others, and the mums talked of tales of me and how I could be trusted with their precious daughters, tales that had been handed down from my early teen days at whist drives by their grandmothers, whom I had once accompanied home on dark winter's nights. *'He was such a nice lad, clean, polite and so helpful No harm would come to them as long as he was responsible for them.'*

\*\*\*

The weeks of January and February led to March, and the spring weather made the evenings draw out. I was busy sowing all the corn As the tractor and I drove those straight lines across the landscape, my mind kept drifting back to that girl. I suppose the old urges of man as in all life at that time of year turns to other things. Something happened to me that spring that has never been repeated in me, because by the end of March, there was I all dressed up at the hall waiting for the girl whom I knew as Kay, to arrive. She came in with Abigail and Josephine, who were also my friends. They left Kay to walk over and say hello as they made themselves scarce out in the cloakroom, as if to signal to Kay, *'Well, there he is again, good luck!'* She needed no luck, I was hopelessly smitten.

"Oh you look so lovely. I'll take you home later," was the only thing I could mutter on greeting her. With that and a smile she fled the floor and vanished into the ladies' room to find her mates, minutes later to appear smiling.

"OK then," is all she said, going to sit down among her escort of friends, leaving me standing alone to ponder at what to do next. This was foreign land to me. Kay was mine and for no one else. Never before had I been here. It had always been, *'Well, let's go,'* and the whole tribe of girls responded. Now it was Kay and I with a lot of giggling schoolgirls. *'Where do I go now?'* I thought to myself. The answer came with Mrs Walsh calling out

"Right, let's start with a Waltz." So I rushed to grab Kay, and that was it, we were away. She could not stop asking questions. The evening came to an end much too soon and I walked her and her mates out to the car to drive them home.

Kay's was the last drop. I stopped, got out and went around and opened her door for her. She swung her long fishnet clad legs out so gracefully and stood up. I walked her all of the twenty yards up the crunchy gravel drive, holding her soft, warm, long fingers lightly in mine. Saying good night I ventured to kiss her on the cheek and the back door opened, to reveal her mother in the light of the kitchen.

"Goodnight then," I said, as I turned on my heels and fled. Boy, I had tried to kiss her, and her mother nearly saw us. So daring!

\*\*\*

The full moon shone as I drove the seven miles back home that night across the moonlit marsh. It was the end of March. I could not leave it here, so I stopped by the bridge over the county border, lit a cigarette and ran the evening's events through my head. Kay really liked me. I was confused where to go from here.

They say you never forget your first love. Well even now, old that I am, just to turn the pages of my diaries over I am instantly back to the relevant scene. Just a few dozen random words written in haste before I put the light out for the night flings me back to the written event forty years ago, right down to all the colour, smells and noise. Certain types of music have that effect on me also and the tune on the cars radio that night on the bridge as I wondered what had happened to me, and how it would end was, *'Only the Lonely,'* by Roy Orbison. Here was I a marsh, and sea boy. She a beautiful Kentish country girl and only fifteen, with a three-year age gap between us. Well, only two and a half years as she soon had a birthday coming up. I had enjoyed tonight, so would send her some flowers to show her how I felt. That seemed a good idea. I drove home in a dream.

***

On Monday morning the flower shop was the only place I wanted to get to. The girl that worked there was the sister of my mate, so I had no problems explaining that a bunch of flowers was to be delivered please, *'To Kay, love the Preacher, for the wonderful evening last Saturday night.'*

"Sure, no problem," came the reply. "What would sir like to send?"

I had to send a dozen red roses, I knew that, then looking at the bunch it seemed so small for what I felt, so I pointed at some yellow carnations,

"Sixteen of those also please, one for each year of her age." The girl smiled at me.

"You have got it bad haven't you? Anything else?" she asked, looking at a now respectable sized bunch.

"Some of them I said and those lovely sweet smelling ones in the bucket."

"The freesias"

"Yes please."

"I think that will be enough," she said. "Any girl would love a bouquet like this. That will be fifty four shillings and four pence."

That was easy, I thought as I left the shop. A week's wages gone and with a trade card of theirs in my hand, and instructions that if I needed their services ever again, all I had to do was phone them and they would take care of it for me. That sounded good to me. Of course I had no idea that Kay's mother would receive this lovely bouquet of flowers later that morning, as Kay was at school.

The arrival of the flowers at their home had the effect a nuclear bomb would have been hard pressed to equal! The phone was hot as word went out to Kay's mother's friends. A huge expensive bunch of flowers had arrived for their daughter, and guess who had sent them, and he only met her last Saturday night? What had she done to deserve them?

Their minds ran riot. Her father rang my father for an explanation. What had his son done with their child on Saturday that deserved such flowers, he wanted to know? Of course dad was at a loss and told him not to be such a stupid old sod.

He never really swore, but got his messages over rather well, too well in fact, so from day one Kay's parents, the father of whom had now turned out to be the big man of the house, were at odds with us again. The old hatred was to be renewed.

***

Kay had purposely not told me who her parents were, fearing I would not like her. My mother, of course knew that nothing had ever happened and what was all the fuss about? They could go boil their heads for all she cared. Poor Kay was at school quite unaware of the turmoil going on at home and this on our first real meeting that meant so much to me.

***

I was working the field down ready to sow with oats, adjoining one of their fields, when I had a visitor. I never saw him coming and looking up from behind me as I disked the earth, to see how close I was to the end of the field, there he was right in front of me with his hand up like a traffic cop.

"Stop." he said. It was either stop or slice him up under the trailing discs.

"Well? What have you got to say for yourself? No good denying it. What do you think you are up to?"

Call me dim if you like, but I had no idea what he was on about!

"Getting a tilth to sow Blenda Oats," said I.

"No. Not that, you fool." 'So fool now was I?

"Those blasted flowers! My wife hit the roof. What have you been up to with our eldest?"

"Nothing," I blurted out, "I just tried to kiss her on the cheek and say goodnight."

"What did you say goodnight with?" He shouted, getting aerated with the passing seconds.

"Now, I'm watching you," and with that he was gone.

I think he was more upset about his wife's carry on over the flowers than anything else. I suppose he was ordered to see me and put me straight by her, as they had only just started to let their daughter go out at nights, and straightaway she had got a bloke. Kay's family thought they were a notch up on us, coming from a military background and having the wife's mother live with them, surrounded by all the silver plate that she had acquired out in India. It now became obvious that their daughter had spoken of me at dancing classes. The fact that my family were scrap merchants, fisherman, then farmers, with so much ready cash, rubbed the wrong way. We always had large estate cars, new every two years, and used them as vans.

This hurt them, to use a new car as cattle, and fish truck, and then at night take *'their'* girl out in it. The fact that fish guts or old iron never abused the front seat mattered not to them. The stigma was enough. The cars had full width bench seats, in real leather, and column gearshifts so made a 'real passion wagon' to their minds. Her father with a passing remark pointed this out one day to me as he turned his back on me to leave, and asked when was I *"going to* get my hair cut young man?" So to oblige him, I had a crew cut. *'There, perhaps he will be happy now,'* I thought, but no, always something was wrong, and I was not going away in a hurry.

***

As time went on, I would call for Kay. One day she was out on her pony. On going over to the stable to wait for her, I met her father in a fluster, clearing out the cowshed. Having nothing else to do, I grabbed the wheelbarrow and said,

*"Right, you load it, I will empty it."*

This meant a journey of twenty yards across the yard, to the manure heap, that with each consecutive load was spreading, as he did not have a board up on which to run the barrow, I found a plank of wood and made a ramp to pile the next load on top of the last load, to compress it down. After about an hour, the job was done, and he thanked me for the help, but could not refrain from saying,

*"You must be tired out."*

*"ME!"* I said in a defiant mood, *"I could push a barrow of dung for miles."*

*"Bet you can't,"* he said. *"Anyway I suppose you came to see Kay and she's back now from her ride."*

Later that evening, Kay told me her father had said over dinner how I had helped him that morning, but thought I was all in and would not be up to dancing tonight. One thing led to another.

At the time there was a campaign to raise money for the starving in Africa. As I recall I had bet her dad that I could push a wheelbarrow for miles, so the girls at school, who were collecting for a charity to relieve the starving decided to relieve him of some of his money and hatched a plan.

They were going to get, or make, some posters to advertise the event to raise money. The local paper was informed by the girls, and they came up with the idea that I should push from home, to Tenderden on a Saturday, with the barrow full of hot steaming manure and put in pride of place on top, a wind-up gramophone playing the popular tune of the time, *'Harvest of Love,'* by Benny Hill. With a pot of daffodil yellow paint, the old barrow at home took on a new lease of life. The wheel was greased up and the route was painted on the yellow barrow in the form of a map in dark blue paint. I felt so proud of my Kay thinking that I was strong and capable of attempting a journey of this length, up and down hill.

***

This was going to happen in the middle of May. We were having a spell of warm weather so I took a bottle of lemonade with me, placed in the dung on the barrow. My brother and his mate drove in front in a mini to announce my coming with the barrow and the girls with their collecting tins. My brother later admitted he had only driven in front, to make sure I had not cheated. How I was to get a lift with a steaming load of pig dung, I cannot think!

Across the marsh was a doddle. I was fresh and the going was flat. Into Rye we went and the people had turned out to support me. The local paper had done us proud. The money rolled in and with the gramophone wound up, the crowds clapped. Next was the bit I had dreaded, up Rye Hill, but no, that was easy. It's the downhill part that gets interesting and fun. Uphill the handles push onto you, but the other way, the blessed thing tries to run away and with no brakes. By the time you get to the bottom, you find you are doing twenty miles an hour, or it feels like it! Well in four hours I arrived at the crossroads, where I had expected to see Kay's father, but no, he was in hiding, he had heard all about the girls' adventure. Why had he opened his big mouth at dinner and said, 'He'll never do it, don't listen to him?' Well here I was and across the road and down the lane I went. My precise load ended its day's journey under a plum tree, along with all the other trees surrounded by manure, taken there by me in a trailer on the back of a tractor, a much more civilised way to move dung. And as for Kay's dad, thrilled girls bombarded him with collecting tins, after his donation. The event raised thirty-two pounds, nine shillings and seven pence, a fair bit in those days. So another notch of hate was carved in his big stick to beat me with!

***

I did not see Kay for a couple of weeks. Being May, all the dancing classes had stopped for the summer. On the twenty eighth May there was to be a dance at Rye in aid of the St John's Ambulance Brigade, so never missing a chance to twirl the light fantastic, I wrote to Kay asking if she would like to go. I would pick her up at seven forty five. A friend took the letter to the grammar school and that evening I had a reply. *'Yes, she would like to come and could I pick up Abigail at seven thirty on my way to hers?'*

So it was arranged, but sod Abigail, I had intended to split from tradition and just take Kay yet anything to see Kay, and make her happy.

So at seven o clock on the forthcoming Saturday, with the car swept out, away I went, first Abigail's home then over the bridge and up the hill into Kent to Kay's house. *"She had been ready since six,"* one of her sisters said on opening the door to me. Kay appeared more spectacular than the last time I saw her. Her hair was newly done, she wore a black blouse and a black knee length skirt covered in a pattern of red roses. Her legs went down forever in thin fishnet stockings and ended in a new pair of two-inch high heels that brought her little pointed nose level to mine. Wow! Where had they hidden her away from me?

*"Hello,"* is all she said, smiling as she stepped out of the door past me. *"Hi Abby, he picked you up OK then,"* and never stopped nattering as she made herself at home on the back seat. I said goodbye to her young sister, promising not to keep her out too late, and took my place behind the wheel. Hardly a word was spoken to me on the drive of twenty minutes to the dance.

Parking up, the girls took me by an arm each and we walked to the hall, while they chatted across my face, but never to me. I might as well not have been there! We went into the hall and I paid for three, while it was off to the cloakrooms for the girls.

The dance was held in the school hall, so there was no alcohol present and as Kay was now sixteen, I was happy to buy three cokes and sit down at a table, soon to be joined by another of Kay's and Abigail's friends who they had arranged to meet there. It looked to me as if I was still to act as the local taxi to gather the girls up. *'Nothing's changed from the usual then,'* I thought to myself. We had a lovely time and the evening sped by fast. A few boys asked where I had found the glamorous one and remarked on how I always had a flock of girls around me. A few adults said, *"She was a picture in that outfit and be careful of her."* *'She was not made of China,'* I thought. *'I'm always careful.'* I was very dim.

At eleven forty five precisely, the last waltz was played. I failed to get it with Kay and had to step it out with Abigail, a beautiful dancer she was too. Then out to the car and to my delight, Kay got in beside me, with Abby in the back. After we had dropped off and said goodnight to Abigail, we just sat and talked for a while.

"It's early yet," said Kay. "Where actually do you live?"

"Hold tight, I will show you," and turning the car around, I headed home. I pointed my home out as we drove by the farm and carried on to the sea wall. There we parked and got out to listen to all the frogs on the marsh. She had never realised there were so many and all singing at the same time. We then climbed the steps up to the top of the sea wall and gazed out across the bay. The lighthouse flashed out at Dungeness. The horizon was studded with a hundred small lights from all the ships and trawlers. The sea was flat and just rustled and shushed amid the pebbles on the tide line. Alas, the moon was hardly visible. If only it had been the last time, when we first met that night the moon was full. Now the Parish lantern was running out of light. She spoke first.

*"Do you go out on the water very often? It is so romantic."*

"Bloody wet, but beautiful, yes."

*"You have a way with words,"* she said. *"Why spoil it with swearing?"*

"I don't know, that's what it is."

*"Yes, but you said beautiful and bloody in the same context and that contradicts itself."*

*'Oh'! 'She is a grammar school one all right'!* I thought to myself as we stood gazing out to France over the horizon.

*"Do you bring all your girls here to dream? And those pesky frogs! Don't they ever stop?"*

"Not until the sun gets up," I said.

*"That must be so beautiful,"* she said giving me a quizzing sort of look with those brown eyes. She moved closer and laid her head on my chest. *"So perfect,"* she spoke in a soft murmur. *"What did you mean, not until the sun gets up?"*

"The frogs never stop until sunrise."

*"I thought you meant you did not bring your girls here until daylight. You are so funny, you never explain yourself properly!"*

"I try but I don't have your way with words."

*"Nonsense,"* she said, as she stiffened herself up before me. *"You say and do such wonderful things. That's all that matters, but don't spoil it by using swearwords like the other boys."* So that was it, I did not swear. Was that the reason the girls liked to be seen with me? Kay frowned at me. *"What are you*

*thinking of now?"* She spoke in a slow drawn out manner. *"You look as if you are lost, and stop chewing on your false teeth. Take them out. I hate to see you suffer poor thing. What is worrying you now?"*

*"I don't know, I'm sort of confused."*

*"Confused over what? Now that makes you look better,"* she said, as I deposited my teeth into one of my waistcoat pockets. *"Keep them there."* Kay pulled herself close to me, placed her hands on my hips and stared up into my eyes. I felt her relax as she often did after a fast and faultless quickstep. She tiptoed and kissed me on the left cheek.

*"Oh you are rough! When did you last shave?"*

*"Before I came out,"* I said, pulling the back of my hand across my face to feel the roughness of a new growth growing.

*"You will have to shave better than that, if I am to kiss you again,"* she let slip from her lips. 'She was planning to kiss me again,' I thought. Then she broke the spell. *"You are so slow. Don't you know how to kiss a girl?"*

*"Well, I've never done it,"* I said, somehow sensing something in my voice.

*"I'll show you,"* she said and tilting her head slightly to one side, placed her lips on mine. At the same time she closed her eyes and her arms enclosed me completely. I closed my eyes and placed my arms around her. Then for the first time in my life a magical sensation clouded my whole body. So this was what it was about? My arms automatically took her body in their encirclement and drew her to me so tight that she gasped.

*"Not so tight! I can't breathe!"* I was so apologetic. She stopped me.

*"Don't be silly, that was lovely."*

I shall always remember that kiss, it felt so natural to take that feeling from her. The feel of being held so tight, yet so gentle in her arms was a completely new experience to me. Wonderland! I had arrived at last, I was a lucky boy indeed! I wanted to shout and tell everyone and that was to include the lighthouse ten miles away across the shimmering bay! What after all this time made me hold her so tight? Out of all the nice girls I knew, Kay had pressed that 'right button,' wherever it was. We paused, her hands so gently caressing me up and down my back.

*"Will you be my girl?"* I said.

*"There you go again? So slow! I am your girl!"* and with that I was overcome with sensuous pleasure, ready to collapse in a soft mass at her feet. I asked myself what *'happens now?'* I had no plan for this. She looked into my weeping eyes.

*"Don't cry,"* she said. *"It happens to everyone you know."*

We spent two hours on that wall that night. There she taught me how to kiss. At last I said.

*"I must get you home, its two thirty and your parents will be worrying!"*

*"Oh don't bother with them, they will be asleep."*

*"But I promised to get you home on time."*

*"You worry too much, you'll get ulcers. Come on then,"* and we ran down the

steps to the car. I opened her door. Kay stood and stared back at the spot on the wall where we had just stood, as if to take in the moment forever then she gently lowered herself into the car. We sat and she rested her head in my lap, it was so perfect and natural for Kay to do it. She snuggled up and I somehow found our way to her house. At last I had a love, to share my life with.

***

The porch lamp shone out over the gravel drive. This called for a bit of the hunter instinct in me if she was to make the safety of her bed without waking her parents. We parked up further along the lane and walked back with our arms around each other, stopping to gaze into each other's eyes every few steps and kissing. Carefully we negotiated the gatepost, creeping around on the little piece of grass that grew at the bottom of the post, and then crept across the lawn, so avoiding the crunchy gravel.

Quietly, she opened the back door and there by the aga sat her grandmother, with a scowl on her face that would have flattened a forest of oak trees.

*"BED my girl! And you!"* She said, pointing at me in the doorway with her finger. *"Home! Her father will see you tomorrow."*

I left downhearted. I had promised to get her home early and here it was three am, not the sort of time for a young lady to be arriving home from a local hop. I felt ashamed of myself. What had I done? It was my entire fault. They would never let me see her again now. What was I to do?

I crept in at home and retired to bed. Opening my diary to write the day's events down, there was the letter from Kay accepting my invite to the dance. It hit me like a ton brick. Yes, a letter of apology to her parents. Surely that would show that I was sorry. For an hour I pondered over the wording and what to say. Sure as I was Kay would tell them something, but what? There was no way of contacting her to agree a story but as I was taught honesty is the best way and surely Kay would not lie to her parents, I told them it was my fault. I had only taken her to see the sea and hear the frogs. Had they never heard them? If not, I would willingly come and get them one night, so that they also could be mesmerized by it all as we had been. I was sorry there was nothing else to report, we just sat that unreal warm, calm night and stared at the sea. I prayed she would tell them the same, but leave the kissing bit out like I had.

Sure enough that is exactly what she did, although she added that Abigail had been with us all the time. Good old Abby, she was to be a real friend and my salvation in the years to come.

***

That summer came and went. I was busy on the farm and Kay had her schoolwork to occupy her. We met down in our big wood or in the ripening corn when we could. There I tried to help her with her Latin homework. We even had a post-box in the form of a nest box for birds that I nailed to a tree near the school bus stop. No one ever interfered with it, thinking some bird lover no doubt placed it there, but it did sterling stuff for us.

***

That autumn the dancing started and we were off. Kay and her mate Abigail made a perfect combination, one for the slow waltzes, one for the quickstep. That was Kay's scene, along with the exotic tango, jive and twist that had started to come into our dancing. We won many competitions and travelled a lot of England, leaving early in the morning accompanied by one of the girl's mothers or adult friend, always with a chaperone for competitions when far away, as if we would get lost! What were we going to do one hundred miles from home that we could not do next door in a hay field? We never questioned it, we didn't in those days. If your parents said, do this that is precisely what you did. The bra was still king, contraceptive pills had not arrived and Women's Lib was still a few years away from us in our corner of England.

***

We spent a lot of time at Abigail's as she had a boyfriend called John who she was fond of, but he was in the Air Force and seldom home. This year was the last year of the hop-pickers as from now on a machine was to take over. As was the tradition at the end of hop picking, the farmer laid on a party for all the workers, which we kids always looked forward to. At my mate's farm where the huge green monster had been installed, I met his dad and said,

"What a pity, no more Oast parties."

"No more of those Londoners is all right with me," he said, "but if you kids want a party, don't stop having one without me. You know where the Oast is."

That was all we needed to know. So six of us lads got together with the girls and planned a party.

We set to dressing the huge empty room that was used to dry the hops into an enchanted grotto. The hedges around the farm were stripped of ivy, holly and bracken to line the walls and roof. The hair mat that covered the slatted floor in the roundel at the end was rolled up and made an ideal place to have a bar. All slops and bottle tops vanished to the fire room below. Dell was a wizard at sound and electronics and worked in a town not far away where they made TV sets, all valves and wires. So he was in charge of the music and lights.

Invites were given out. We were expecting two hundred friends to attend and being near Christmas by the time hop picking with the machine was over, planned it to be a Christmas party. We had a huge Christmas tree in one corner. Mud was our big problem and I mean mud. Six inches deep of the 'loving' type, you know the sort that won't let go of you. A path of straw was laid down but this soon turned into more mud and we had to resort to a tractor and trailer to ferry everyone from the main road to the steps into the building. Now I had a plan. As it was not very warm this time of year, I was going to light the oil fires up and put the huge fans on to force the hot air up into the party room as if drying hops.

Well the day came. All was well until Dell turned the spotlights on. Then with a bang, all the power went off. It was terminal. The main fuse had blown. A hurried phone call to the electricity company was met with. *"Is it an emergency?"*

"Well yes, in two hours we have two hundred people coming to a party."
"Sorry, can't come until eight am Monday."
"That's torn it," said Dell. "I'll have to do something then."

Dell got a four-inch nail and used that as a main fuse. We had plenty of power for everything.

\*\*\*

I collected Kay from the bus stop at five p.m. and we spent the night together. I operated the bar, as I did not drink. It was fun. We had two eight-gallon barrels of beer, which we had installed a few days previously that had been supplied by the pub we all used. I don't think it is allowed nowadays but we had it then. All the unopened bottles we were able to return without charge, and we made a fair profit from the do. We charged everyone who was not a very close friend ten shillings for a ticket to get in and the drink and food was all free, as much as you wanted. The money left over we ploughed back into another party in the spring.

\*\*\*

Soon our shindigs became well known and in the end we had up to three hundred people at them. Then someone told the Tax Inspectors and Council. They came down on us strong, so we gave most of the cash to the lifeboat and kept enough for a barbecue and called it quits. And anyway the lads were all getting married and no longer had the urge to party the night away. Kay and I stayed and cleared up into the small hours and then cuddled up and slept in each other's arms until the morning. Yes we just cuddled each other, that was good snugly wrapped up in lovely smelling hop pockets. No sex that was not done in our teen years, she was too young. Sex was for married couples and the nineteen seventies.

The heat I supplied for the party. Well, what with the fuse blowing and all that, I forgot to light the fuel jets and filled the room up with diesel fumes, but no one minded. Even Kay never complained we shared each other's breath.

\*\*\*

So the Oast parties have now left the scene, as no one grows hops like that any more, hop-picking parties are now part of our social history. I think we were one of the last to keep them up, even though the hops were picked by machine.

How did we manage a night together? Well that was thanks to Abigail again. Kay was allowed to stay the night at Abby's some weekends, so her parents believed she was safe at Abby's mums. Abigail was the rebel of the pack. She would go far in life I was sure. With a good education, she could sit down and do *'The Telegraph'* crossword in less than an hour, Abby knew more of life than any of us, she was what you might call today *'streetwise'*. I think, she taught the other girls how to kiss and cuddle, but she was silent on that matter with me.

\*\*\*

It was June now and I got word from Kay that there was to be a Strawberry Dance in a local town twenty miles away on the coming Saturday. She was going to be staying with friends whose parents were away and could I take them? Stupid to ask, just try and stop me! The theme of the dance was strawberries and everyone was to be in fancy dress. I went as a tramp with a straw hat, which had a blue ribbon around it that hung three feet down my back. The girls all dressed in fancy dress also. Kay was a country girl who sold strawberries from a small wicker basket she wore a straw hat, the same as mine, but hers had a red ribbon. The only thing out of place was the blue eye shadow she wore on her top eyelids. Otherwise she would pass back easily into the 1880's. We had copied our outfits from a chocolate box top of a country scene that had a cottage and cottagers standing in their front garden among all the flowers.

I arrived that evening to pick the girls up. The house was over half a mile from the main road and it was with luck I found it. If it had been winter and dark, I would have failed to locate it, tucked far off the road up a dirt track, among a small clump of elderly trees. There was Kay with her friend Mary, a girl of nineteen and as lovely as the rest. She had a young sister of fourteen who was dressed up and would pass for sixteen anywhere. We had to take her to the dance with us as her sister said she was too young to stay in the isolated house alone, so Gillian was to come with us. We locked up and drove west into the sun of a June evening. The sky out to the south looked angry and black a nasty thunderstorm was brewing up over the sea.

***

The dance was a great success, but the local lads of the town saw a chance to have a new girl for the night and were always tempting them with drinks. A free gin and orange was not to be missed and as my attentions were elsewhere, the boys were plying my girls liberally. By ten thirty the girls were in no fit state to be aware of their actions. They were only fourteen, sixteen and nineteen years of age and in my care. They kept egging each other on. It was getting out of hand so I rounded them up into the car and returned to the house under the shelter of the wood.

The wind had got up and was blowing a gale, with driving rain, amid lightning and thunder. We ran to the house from the car through the rain to the backdoor and slamming it shut behind us, Mary put the light switch down, nothing happened.

"*A power failure, common around here,*" said Mary and went to a drawer in the sideboard to get a candle out, her young sister Gillian was then promptly sick all over the kitchen table. Kay rushed to get a towel and Mary took her sister off to bed, along with the only candle.

A few minutes later Mary and candle appeared and I suggested a cup of coffee was in order now Kay had tidied the contents up from Gillian's stomach. Mary had a better plan. I had taken a bottle of champagne up with me earlier in the evening to open on our return, but this was not now appropriate. I thought the girls had drunk more than enough, but Mary and Kay thought it was just the thing to round the night off with. What could happen to them?

The thunderstorm raged on as the girls drank, Kay laid on the sofa with me, tucked in one corner, her head in my lap murmuring sweet nothings and the odd remark about what if the parents could see us now.

"Who cares?" said Mary. "I'm out of here in two months, me and Mark are getting married and going to live in South Africa. I'm going to bed now. Be careful young man! You know where you're sleeping Kay, and don't make too much noise and wake Gillian up. We don't want a repeat of earlier."

And with that, Mary was gone into the dark passageway leading to the stairs. Kay wriggled around and put her arm around my neck and we started to kiss passionately. Then she said,

"You can take me to bed."

"I can only just see the door out of here," I said.

"I'll show you the way, you will have to carry me, I'm drunk."

So I got to my feet and with a little trepidation, lifted her slender frame into my arms. She flung her arms around my neck.

"No, not now," I said as she planted her soft warm lips once again on mine. We stepped around the furniture to the bottom of the old steep rickety staircase. The house was already over two hundred years old and showed its age in places, and the staircase was a point. Up and around we went, with Kay clinging around my neck and her shoeless feet flaying the air in gay abandon.

"This way there in that door Ssh, no noise!" I placed Kay carefully down on her feet and she collapsed into a giggling pile on the mat at my feet.

"Get up!" I said.

"I can't, I'm drunk!" she said throwing her arms into the air in a pointless gesture. "You'll have to put me to bed darling."

The bed was a small affair under the window so I did no more than gather her up in my arms and stepped over to the bed.

"Oh bliss!" she said as she sank into the mattress.

"You silly little angel getting so drunk," I said as I went to kiss her goodnight.

"Where do you think you are going?" she said in a dulcet voice.

"Home," I said, "its one thirty in the morning."

"I want undressing and putting properly to bed," she said in a sad sort of way. "You promised Mary you would look after me."

So into very unfamiliar territory I trod, first the blouse, no problem, the arms were a bit tricky for as I got them up, they kept getting entangled around my neck and we ended up kissing. Next was her skirt, which I had to take off by drawing down her legs and over her feet. As I got hold of her waistband and started to pull, her legs found the power to flap up and down as if running up the wall, all the time shouting

"Go on! Pull! Lift me, pull, off with the bugger!"

(This was a fight, which I intended to win!) It was the first time I had heard her use a swear word and I put it down to the drink. At last the confounded garment was in my hands. The job was done.

"Now my bra and knickers she whispered."

"What!" Oh well. The bra was black and made of a lace sort of stuff. My fingers are the hands of a hard working country lad and not used to such finery. The clasp under her body's back as she lay there defied me. With a laugh that was sure to wake the whole house, she said.

"*No, like this,*" and gave it a yank from the front with her thumb. There was a rip and she laid bra-less, her body lit by the starlight that streamed onto the bed now the storm had passed and the sky was cloudless.

"*There, see,*" she said, "*Do you like what you see?*"

I was gob-smacked. All the imagining of what lay within was now revealed.

"*Please darling, cuddle me.*" So I lay on the bed beside her and ran my hands over her young soft body. She guided my fingers with such gentleness and feeling. My mind left my body and floated somewhere unknown to me.

"*It's my first time.*"

"*Mine too,*" I said. She threw her arms behind her head.

"*I love you so much,*" she said and closed her eyes.

That was too much for me. I realised that the liking bit had now gone past its sell by date. I was falling in love, to take advantage of this Kentish sixteen year old, so innocent and intoxicated was going against my upbringing. I longed to satisfy my yearnings and her invitation but I loved her and would never be able to live with myself, so I slipped her knickers off and tucked her into bed. Then kneeling beside the bed, I apologised and kissed her goodnight. Her parting words were, "*I told Abigail you were a real gentleman.*"

I crept out of the house, putting the candle stub out as I passed the kitchen table. The car was wet and shining now in the moonlight, I turned and glanced back at the inviting door I had just passed through and my mind went to the bed with my darling Kay laying in it, bathed now in moonlight. The thought of her soft warm body made a shiver run all over my body, I had to leave if only for her sake.

*\*\*\**

The car purred as I drove along the lane homewards. Just before I made the main road, a fallen tree blocked my way. This had brought the power lines down with it, which accounted for the failure back at the house. There was no more to do but back up into a gateway, turn around and retrace my steps and go the long way round to reach home. Along the lane around the corner, the house was more visible in the moonlight than it had been approaching it from the other way in daylight. I pulled up in front to gaze at the window behind which that naked girl slept.

I put the interior light on to find a fag. I was so happy that Kay was still the girl that I had started out with those hours before. I prayed one day we would marry then I would never leave her alone.

*\*\*\**

The following day I had a call on the phone which mother took. Could I go to Abigail's tonight? It was important and rather urgent. So at eight p.m. I presented myself at Abby's. Her elder sister opened the door and with a wide smile on her face said "*good night last night.*" The news had spread obviously, and I still felt guilty that I had undressed a girl. Who knew or who didn't was uppermost in my mind. Abigail flung her arms around me.

"I'm so glad, you two were made in Heaven for each other. It would have been a shame if you had spoilt it last night. You didn't did you?"

"What?" I said, trying to act the innocent.

"You know. You didn't, with Kay? Please tell me you did not."

"Abigail! No! What do you take me for?"

"I knew it. Only Kay says she must be pregnant, but can't remember, the only thing she is certain of is that her new bra is ruined and she woke up all wet down there," pointing to her groin.

"No, I never" I said. "She was drunk and I put her to bed she ruined her brassiere herself."

"You never touched her then" said Abby

"Well…"

"I knew it! You did, I never thought you would. All the times she has said you never made love, I believed her!"

"No, we just held each other and kissed."

"Didn't she try to get you into her bed? She said you fondled her all over, she remembers that. You had her last night and now she's pregnant!"

"The only time I got near her was with my hand."

"Oh well better luck next time," she said and put her hands up in a gesture of 'you're hopeless.' I told her she was imagining the whole thing,

"Did they really all get drunk?"

"Well sort of."

"Poor old you three girls drunk, want a milky coffee darling?"

## CHAPTER TWO

The sign on the door of the hall next day said it all, *"Closed owing to snow."* It was just after Christmas, Britain had been in an arctic weather flow for weeks. The snow was one foot deep, arriving on Boxing Day and the sky looked as if more was on the way. I had arrived on a tractor as few vehicles could move on the roads. Here I was and the hall was closed. So there was nothing for it but call on Abigail's just up the hill. I parked the tractor in a snowdrift on the grass verge outside her house and went to knock on the door. When it opened there stood Kay.

*"How did you know I was here?*

*"I didn't, I came to go dancing. I hoped you would come later on the usual bus."*

*"There are no buses. They have cancelled them because of the forecast. My dad cannot get down the hill to take me home so we have got to stay here,"* and she threw her arms around my neck and we kissed.

*"Come in,"* shouted a voice from somewhere behind her, *"and shut that door."*

*"I'll get my cushion first,"* and going to the tractor, removed the sack of hay from the iron seat so it didn't get wet. Placing it down inside the lobby I closed the door behind me.

*"Meet Yvonne, Abigail's friend from Sweden, she is working for Mrs Brown along the road as an au pair."*

*"Hello,"* I said, *"Pleased to meet you."* A six-foot tall blonde stood there, from Swedish stock if ever I saw one, dressed in a thick jumper and long skirt. Her curves still announced themselves even under the clothes she wore. She was a big girl for a nineteen year old. Her English put me to shame. The fire was roaring up the chimney and the smell of cooking wafted through the house.

*"Hungry?"* said Abigail. *"We were just going to eat."*

*"What is it?"* I said, *"smells good!"*

*"Goulash or something? Yvonne made it, some Swedish thing or other."*

*"OK, I'll give it a whirl."*

*"Good. Sit down by your girl, it's your lucky day, what with Kay stuck here for the rest of the night and two of us girls to look after you, now food as well, white bread and tea for you OK?"*

*"I suppose that will do,"* I said and hugging Kay I placed a kiss on her lips and she flung her arms around my neck.

*"You can stay can't you darling?"* she said.

*"Of course I have nothing to do till feeding time tomorrow."*

*"Right, sit next to me,"*

*"Yvonne you sit there opposite Abby. I'll sit next to him to keep my eye on you."* With that sorted. Abigail vanished into the kitchen.

*"Where's your mother and father Abigail?"* I asked, as she rattled the plates around and ladled four dollops of steaming food onto them from a pot.

*"They went to stay a week with Mum's sister in Canterbury and are snowed*

in, won't be back for a few more days, and by the look of the snow now falling that may be longer."

I drew the curtain back and a blizzard was raging outside, visibility was down to ten yards.

"*Where's your sister then?*" I said.

"*Over at Brighton with some chap of hers, staying six months. She's got a job over there.*"

Well I was a lucky boy, three lovely girls, a log fire and the whole house to ourselves, Jackpot! Abigail served four plates of steaming hot goulash and sat on my left.

"*Right you can say grace, it's right up your street. You and your Bible,*" said Abigail.

She was right, I always carry my Bible with me. So thanks were given for the food we were about to receive, and a silent one from me to God for stranding me amid the girls tonight. The pudding that followed was ice cream, '*Just the weather for it*' I thought as by now a peep out of the window showed the tractor covered with four inches of snow and it was still coming down in chunks as large as half penny pieces, showing no signs of stopping.

I phoned home and told my brother to let Mum know that I was OK and staying at a mate's, then the girls washed and I wiped the dishes dry. Finishing that we retired to the fire, it was only eight p.m., the gramophone was loaded and turned down low.

"*Let's play Monopoly,*" somebody suggested.

"*Alright, where's the board?*" I said.

"*In that cabinet somewhere,*" said Abby pointing to a cupboard in the corner.

"*I'll get it,*" said Kay.

"*I'll get some glasses and we can have a drink. There's a bottle of egg flip in there with the game,*" Abigail replied. I placed the Monopoly board on the floor, the bottle was opened and the yellow drink filled three glasses. Yvonne eyed it with suspicion, she gave it a sniff, and then tasted it.

"*Needs a kick,*" she said. "*What have you got?*" getting up to investigate the cabinet. "*Ah wolla!*" she said, waving a large bottle of Navy Rum. "*Yiss, the ticket, no?*" she said, grabbing the top and unscrewing the cap. All three glasses were filled to the brim and they all agreed that it was good.

We started to play and after an hour Abigail was bust. Yvonne had no idea what the game was about, and much less how to play, so we packed it away, and then suggested she think of something for us to do.

"*Poker, you have cards Yiss? We play for money yiss?*" And a glint in her eyes told me to be aware.

"*No not in England,*" not wanting to gamble with her! I sensed she knew how to play.

"*Then we play undress poker Yiss?*" That brought a laugh from the three of us.

"*Strip poker you mean?*" said Kay, correcting her English and blushing at the same time. I closed my eyes and I tried to imagine Yvonne with no clothes on.

"Yiss, we play at home in Sweden a lot."

My heart sank as I tried to make a count of the garments I was wearing and mentally note what amount of clothes the girls could shed before I ran out of options.

"More drinks all round," said Abigail, as three more full glasses appeared and the rum bottle began to look empty.

"Seven cards each," said Yvonne.

Now I played three-card brag with the boys for halfpenny pieces. Seven cards was new to me but after it was explained, it seemed easy. I was the first to lose so I took my socks off. Kay was next and wanted to take her shoes off. This had to go to the umpires but she won the argument. Next two hands no one won, we all stacked. The fifth hand was a tie between Abigail and Kay. Yvonne was not a happy girl with this decision so she decided to change the rules.

"Three cards as we do in Sweden King high, ace low." You counted your cards up and the one with the lowest number of spots was the loser. We pondered this for a minute or two. Yvonne filled the glasses to the top again and I noticed that the Rum bottle was empty, a whole bottle, and the egg flip bottle looked pretty sick as well, over half empty. The next hand I lost with eight so off with my tie.

"That was not fair!" they wailed. I had to lose more than that with such a small hand. It was shirt as well! So I lost my shirt to the pile growing on the floor. Next was Yvonne, so off with her thick jumper to reveal a rather small bra for her size, that also joined the pile and she moved closer to the fire. Now the giggling started! I was wearing a string vest and they all agreed that no one wore a vest any more. It was old fashioned but I held out, it was what I started with and I would stay with it. Abigail, who removed her stockings, more for the pile, lost the next hand. The cards were dealt again and this time Abigail lost her skirt, and sat in her knickers among a lot of tittering from the other two girls. Kay was the next loser with nine and two queens. Rotten luck, we all had thirty. She removed her stockings and rolled them up carefully and placed them on the pile. Then I lost and had to remove my vest and trousers after the girls took a vote.

This was getting serious for me. Someone said it called for a drink so Abigail raided the cupboard and obtained a half full bottle of malt whiskey. I went to make a cup of tea in the kitchen wearing my boxer shorts, noticing it was still snowing hard out side through the kitchen window. While I waited for the kettle to boil a squabble broke out among the girls and I had to sort it out.

"Right that's it," I said. "That's as far as we go, you have all had far too much to drink."

"NO!" they all cheered as one. "Deal Yvonne."

Abigail lost so she took her bra off under her jumper and that went onto the pile. Next was Kay, who took her bra off as well. It was getting exciting! Kay was the loser again so she took her pants off from under her skirt. This was looking more promising. Yvonne now dealt two cards then stopped. She did not feel well and was going to the loo very quickly, *"So play on without her."*

"*She can't do that,*" said Abigail. "*She has garments to go like Kay.*" Too late, the drink was making itself felt by the sounds coming from the bathroom.

"*That's it,*" I said.

"*Yes,*" said Kay. "*Come on slow coach, take me to bed darling like you did last time.*" So gathering up our clothes she jumped on my back.

"*Come on big boy I will show you the way again!*"

On reaching the landing I said. "*I have to make a visit to the loo.*"

"*Me first,*" she said, sliding off my back and fumbling with the door, the drink was getting the better of her too. She came out a few minutes later.

"*All yours hurry up,*" I raised the seat and was back out on the landing in less than one minute. Kay sat on the mat with her back leaning against the wall.

"*My legs have gone all wobbly darling you will have to carry me in your strong arms.*"

With her being only seven stone that was easy. We were in Abigail's room in the attic, more stairs, but this night we had electricity and no furniture to negotiate. The bed was ready made and was king size, and I wondered how it was delivered to this small room. Kay put the light out and with her arms crossed across her front, heaved her jumper off, at the same time she dropped her skirt. There she was having lost all at cards. I stood mesmerised, she had no shyness at all.

"*What's the matter? You've seen it all before,*" and promptly switched the light back on. How could she stand like that and not be ashamed? Words failed to come from my gawping mouth.

"*You are so silly, it's only me, your girl, look.*" With that she came closer and placed her warm delicate hands on my shoulders.

"*Go on, look. I'm looking at you and I love what I see. Don't you find me attractive?*" There were the two of us facing each other with only my boxer shorts between us.

With that I burst into tears. She comforted me as no one else had ever done since my mother did when I was a small boy.

"*Sit down here with me. I will make you better. Abigail's given us these for tonight.*" With those words she lay over the bed and produced from under the pillows a packet of some sort and in big letters across the front was printed DUREX. I cried even more. She tried to kiss me to get me to stop, but it was in vain. She spoke so softly and stroked my hair and back.

"*You know what they are don't you they are for us. Abigail put them there before dinner.*"

I stopped blubbering and said, "*What's she got them for?*"

"*Emergencies of course, you never know when you will get lucky.*" That did it! The girls talked like my mates about the boys and like some of my mates kept a few handy. I had never had one in my hand before and the curiosity got the better of me.

"*What are they like those Durex?*" I said.

"*Oh that's easy.*" Abigail showed me and sliding off the bed onto her knees she pulled my boxer pants down and took the packet from my hand and opened it. Inside were three things wrapped in silver paper that looked like milk bottle tops, she tore one open and in doing so put her finger nail right through it.

"*There, engaged!*" she said, twirling the thing around on her finger. "*Let's try another one, that's no good now*" and she undid the second one. Then unrolling it showed me what they looked like and of course could not roll it back up. Two down and one to go! I was amazed how she was not embarrassed by all of this. I was a physical wreck!

There she was, the most perfectly gorgeous girl in the whole world at my feet completely naked playing with Durex, but other than what dear Abigail had shown, and told her, this was all that either of us knew. That's enough, it was time I took charge. She was in tears,

"*I thought it would be nice to make love together to show you how much I love you.*"

"You silly girl, I know that and you know I love you, we don't have to prove it. That's it, bugger Abigail, I've a good mind to put my trousers on and go and give her a piece of my mind."

"*No please darling don't she will drag you into her bed and you won't escape from her.*"

"Forget it," I said, and then at the same time as stooping to gather her up I pulled my pants up, picking her up and placing her on the bed. Then I lay alongside her, we cuddled and kissed.

"*Touch me like last time,*" she pleaded, "*It was lovely,*" so I fumbled my way around and stroked her gently. She heaved a big sigh.

"*Don't, it tickles! It's a funny feeling, it's Heaven!*"

I caressed her breast with my hands and wished they were not as rough as they were. Her skin was warm and as soft as butter, her breasts so soft and tender. They then became firmer and a funny sensation came over me, as I got excited. She lay in a stupor, "*I love you,*" she whispered, then we cuddled and Kay turned her back to me and fell asleep.

What had happened in the last hour or two was way beyond my imagination. I lay behind her and looked out of the little window in the roof, watching the snowflakes as they shot past in the gale outside. I then became aware that we were not exclusively alone in the room.

***

The door was open and a silent form moved across the floor. I froze! A ghostly form came to the side of the bed and climbed in behind me. I lay as stiff as a ramrod. An arm came over my shoulder and a strange voice with a wavering "*Ssh*" told me the visitor was no other than the big blonde from Sweden and naked as well by the feel of her body against my back. Her hand came over my shoulder and crept down my chest until she found the hair that grew in profusion there, then she started to twiddle her fingers as if trying to knit it into a scarf. I turned to stare into her blue eyes.

"*OK. We do this in Sweden to keep warm,*" and with that she somehow fixed her lips to mine and put her tongue into my mouth.

I jabbed Kay with my elbow, at the same time getting my laughing gear free. "*Kay wake up darling, we've got company.*"

As if it had been her mother lying beside me! Never have I seen a naked body move so fast as when she flung herself over me. She cleared me and had the Swede in a full nelson on the floor, with her legs either side of her.

The screaming from both was so loud and piercing that Abigail came in the door like a tornado. Putting the light on she grabbed Kay by the hair.

"*What's going on? Yvonne. Why are you here? You sleep downstairs.*"

"*It's what we do in Sweden.*"

"*I don't care what you Swedes do at home, you don't do it here! Now out. Tomorrow you are no longer welcome!*"

"*But I was, as you say, hot for it.*"

"*I don't care! He's Kay's and if you don't move it, I will show you what hot is!*" Then turning to the two of us she said, "*Sorry*" and slammed the door shut as she left behind her. Kay was in tears.

"*I should have told you they share their boys in Sweden. We were talking about it just before you arrived.*"

I made her put her knickers on before we got back into bed and we cuddled. Next morning Abigail woke us with a tray of tea, toast and marmalade. As she left she remarked that later we must talk. You won't be going anywhere Preacher, there's three feet of snow. Oh and she's gone, you won't see her again."

We ate up and got dressed. I stood and studied the figure of Kay as she stood and faced the little window, slipping her bra on, and before I could offer to do it up, she had it done up and straightened. I stood behind her, put my arms around her and she snuggled back onto me.

"*I love you so much,*" she said. "*You had the chance again last night but you have such brilliant self control. I can trust you, I'm very lucky. I wish my parents knew how good you are.*"

Not another word was spoken till we entered the sitting room where Abigail had the fire going. Outside the snow was up to the bottom of the window. My transport had vanished under a drift. I had to get home. There were pigs and sheep in desperate need of food.

"*Wait, have a cup of milky coffee,*" said Abby.

The beverage arrived nice and sweet, with a lot of sugar in it, just like she knew I liked it.

"*Now, sit down and listen to me.*" She sounded like a schoolteacher, not like a girl a year younger than me. "*Was everything OK last night Preacher?*"

"*I don't talk about things like that, you know me.*"

"*Yes I think I know you by what you do, and others tell me, but you are so green and your Kay has never looked at a boy before. You were careful with her when you made love?*"

"*No we never made love, we are going to wait,*" Kay said.

"You could have done. I put two packets under your pillow."

"You never told me there were two lots. We ruined the first two. They were not easy to get out of the packet."

"What do you mean, you ruined two last night?"

"I put my finger through the first showing him what they looked like, he had never seen one before and then we couldn't roll the second one back up."

"But I demonstrated how to do it the other day with that broom handle, remember?"

"That's enough! Have you no sense of shame?" I said.

"Oh poor boy, he's embarrassed. Look at him."

"Leave him alone Abigail, no wonder he's so green and slow, never talks or reads up about it."

"OK, I believe you, but please do be extra careful, you know you can have a baby by just touching him with your hand then touching yourself."

We three stood there hugging each other. I drank my coffee and put my mug down.

"I must go. I have animals to feed." I put my coat on and got the sack of hay in the lobby, then waded out to where I had left the tractor. Could I find it, and would the engine start? Yes and yes.

\*\*\*

I forced my way home through the deep drifts of snow in one and a half hours, it usually took twenty minutes. I was still in a sort of daze as I fed the animals. I could hardly believe the last twelve hours, if only I could tell the boys, but that was a thing I would never do, they would not believe it anyway! Mother wanted to know where I had spent the night, as they were worried. I told her that I had phoned, as the weather was atrocious. I had stayed at a friend's, which was not a lie. She did not ask whom.

## CHAPTER THREE

The spring of 1963 saw the local hunt having its Annual Ball, at the nearby airport. All were to be there. As I was on the Footsloggers committee, having given up chasing the fox on horseback, I had free tickets so Kay and Abigail were to be my guests. As it was the Hunt Ball, Kay was allowed to come along as long as it was with Abigail, they would be there along with all the landed gentry, it was an ideal place for their girl to be seen.

\*\*\*

On a Friday night in April the ballroom was laid out for a large party with an area for dancing up by the six-piece band on a stage. The dinner got off to a bad start. I had been on the committee that had chosen the menu. The starter was smoked salmon with asparagus tips. The dish arrived with a small wedge of lemon and as I removed the lemon with my fork, I noticed it also removed the smoke colour from the fish, leaving a pale scar.

I was discreet and took this out to the kitchens, for I knew this was not the smoked fish we had ordered but a dyed substitute. The committee had implicitly stated we wanted the real McCoy and had paid extra for it. The women in charge met my enquiry,

"Will you silly little boy just be grateful that you were invited."

Was she talking to me? I had voted for the real stuff, she obviously did not know who I was. I promptly left after getting her name from one of the staff and I was going to make sure a letter followed it up from my committee. I was the Chairman was I not, and I would see to that.

The rest of the meal was good but Kay kept on. *'How had I the nerve to complain?'* She said I was *'embarrassing her among all those noble guests.'* I told her not to be so silly, they just thought they were better than us. The bar at the airport was open to all and some of the local lads had come along for the evening.

After dinner the speeches were read out. All the farmers whose land they kindly let the hunt roam over were thanked, as if it was not for their generosity, there would be no hunt. At the end of the speeches everyone was told they could smoke and the band struck up. It was the signal for Kay and me to start the dancing off with a display of real dancing.

On our arrival the president had approached us and knowing we danced often, suggested to the girls and me that it would be a very good way to get the lazy buggers off their fat bums, just a few turns to show them, and then the floor would be open to the others. This had been as much a shock to Kay and Abby as me, so taking Kay by the hand we made our way to the floor and showed them how the Quick Step should be done. When the clapping subsided a shout went up to 'see a Waltz!' Kay was embarrassed for the second time that night and it showed, so I took her to our table and took Abby's hand.

"Come on," she said *"Let's show the nobs how to do it and we will finish with a two minute Jive like we have been practising."*

As the audience clapped Abigail spoke to the band. Nodding her head, she said, *"Let's go. One, two, three, four,"* and off we went to the tune of *'Who's taking you home tonight?'* I had noticed six army chaps at the bar having a quiet drink while the speeches were in progress. Not so the local lads, they had noted I had two wonderful, beautiful girls to myself. A move was in operation to relieve me of one as I danced. Two sat down at the table with Kay, I could make out as her posture changed that all was not right. She straightened herself up and shook her head. One of the boys tried to hold her hand and another touched her hair. The dance went on, I had to get back to Kay. Would this damn band not stop? We glided around the floor then suddenly without a stop the tempo changed and went into a Jive. A roar went up from the crowd. I twirled Abigail and threw her over my shoulder, with this the whole room stood and advanced to the floor thinking the exhibition was now over.

I took the opportunity as Abby leapt at me and threw her legs around my waist. I clamped my arms around her and walked off the dizzy floor with her legs each side of me, holding her small bum very tight.

*"What's the matter?"* she said. *"Put me down."*

*"Kay, she's got trouble."*

She looked over my shoulder and was off my waist like a greyhound, barging her way against the oncoming traffic saying, *"Bloody hell, come on, let me sort them out."*

*"You keep out of this, I know them, they are bullies from that housing estate in Rye."* The lads turned on Abigail.

*"Aah! The other one, fed up with him too? Has that sweet arse left the girl alone?"*

*"Girl! I'll give you girl."*

*"She looks old enough."*

*"Shut your mouth,"* she said.

*"A girl with spirit, I like girls with a bit of go in them."*

*"Do you?"* She said, slapping his face so hard that it took the wind out of his sails. I arrived at the scene as the boys left to rejoin their two mates.

*"I'm not having them upset you girls,"* I said.

*"Who the hell do they think they are?"* Abigail said.

*"You should have heard what they called you."*

*"I'll get the drinks I don't think I want to know."* I said.

*"Make mine a large whisky and make Kay's a large gin and orange, we need them."*

The bar was busy, I squeezed in a gap by the army boys.

*"Bit of trouble you're having brother? Don't forget you've got us if need be."*

They had mistaken me for one of them, it was always happening for I now kept Kay's father's crew cut that most army chaps sported.

*"Nothing I can't handle."* He looked at me.

*"Nor that bird your sister's with."*

*"They're just good friends,"* I said.

*"Double gin and orange, and a scotch and water please,"* as the barman asked

what he could get me.

"Five and four please, thank you." I paid and was gone, to look after Kay. Every time two of us had a dance, one of the local lads tried to make a move. By eleven o clock all four came over and the language got coarse.

"No need for that sort of talk," I said and one of them turned my chair round with me in it.

"You can't manage two of them."

With that the six soldiers left the bar and came over.

"OK, what's going on then?"

"Nothing to do with you, get lost. Who do you think you are?" said the local. The answer came loud and clear.

"The army boyo! Outside you."

Kay was fast sliding beneath the table but Abby got there first. The local yelled something as the army lad lifted him from the floor and carried him to the exit. Well that was it, we were now becoming an embarrassment to the evening's event. I found the President's wife and explained that the young girls had to be in before midnight and we had to leave. We thanked her for the lovely evening and left with a stinging remark from Abigail.

"Should have warned us you wanted an exhibition to start the dancing off, we could have practised you know!"

\*\*\*

We got in the car and left. Kay laid her head in my lap as usual. The airport is one mile from the main road, with a few twists and turns to stop traffic speeding. Going round one of the bends our headlights shone across the field, and there were two lads running after each other. The Army was on manoeuvres and looked like getting at least one prisoner.

Half way round the next corner was an army jeep, half on and half off the road, obviously stopped in a hurry by the angle it was parked. The army was now at war and if I knew them, they would win the war with the locals.

Kay cuddled up nearer to me.

"They were horrible!" she said, "The things they said about you."

"Don't worry my sweetheart, you are safe now, the army will sort them out." Abby chipped in from behind. "I bet he doesn't know half the words they used."

"I hope he never learns them said Kay."

"Don't forget tomorrow night girls, real dancing so when we get back I want you to go straight to bed."

"I wish you would come to my bed then I would sleep well."

"No you wouldn't" said Abby, "we want at least silver tomorrow." I dropped them off and told them I would be up at four pm. Abigail got out and went indoors. Kay and I kissed for five minutes until Abigail called out,

"Cocoa is ready."

Kay and I looked longingly at each other, "good night darling, see you later," I said, letting her hand slide across mine, as she slid out of the car and shut the door. It was as if we wanted to touch each other forever. I drove home thinking of the army lads catching the locals and wishing I were there to see them.

\*\*\*

All the daffodils were out as we drove across Kent to Tunbridge Wells and the large hall that was the venue for the South of England dance championship. We found a place to park and got out. Tonight we had a mate with whom I had shared many adventures, we had known each other from year one and he lived near me. We had a fair bit of luggage, my dance suit of long tails, spare shirt, shoes, ties and jive jacket. The girls wore two dresses each on these occasions now all packed in large hang up dust covers that must not be creased. Two held elegant ball gowns covered in sequins that we had spent nights sewing on with a number five needle and silk thread. The other covers held jive and tango skirts and blouses. Shoes were in boxes, and a dozen pair of assorted stockings was in one of the small cases. It was worth a small fortune.

Maggots, my mate, had come along to take photos, not only of us, but also of the other girls, to get ideas for costumes later back at home where we would try to copy some of them. We three knocked up all the dresses in the evenings. Yards of lace and crinoline went into the petticoats, small lead buttons were sewn in the hems of the Latin and Jive skirts, larger ones into the gowns so they twirled but never left the ground.

Abigail always carried two small boxes, these held rings, necklaces, tiaras, and bows for their hair or rumps. The second box contained a first aid box, powder and puffs, lipsticks, scent and perfume, combs, brushes, hairpins, hairspray, tissues and nail varnish, a real collection. And me I had a wallet with pen, paper, safety and straight, pins, needle and thread and small buttons for suspender belts. I had also added a fishhook as it took up less space than a kitchen sink! We had everything.

The lot was taken to the dressing rooms where we were given a large black card with a big white number, this was to be put on my back so the judges could know who we were.

\*\*\*

The first round and the girls stayed in the same ballroom dresses. Then it was a rush to change into the jive costumes. If we were called to go into the quarterfinals after that, it was a mad scramble to change back in to the large gowns it was all go. I stayed, as I was, my feet killing me at times. The lucky ladies were able to slip their sling backs off at will and let their feet breathe.

The dressing rooms were often crowded. Maggots was not allowed around the back after carrying the gear in but I was. I had to help dress the girls as I had made a lot of the stuff. I knew the wrinkles, and sabotage from other girls was not unknown to happen. The only thing that stayed as it was made was the petticoat. The dress was a case of *'Turn round darling'* and with a tug on the right thread, the whole lot fell to bits. Pieces of that one could be used for another type on future evenings. The bra was sometimes changed from a low cut strapless, to an ordinary normal strap, black or white. This operation I was not involved in! Some girls wore a body corset but that was cheating in our young eyes, any tummy tuck that was needed could be made in the gown with a lace up bodice.

*\*\*\**

We were called for the quarterfinals, eighteen down and eighteen to go. In the mid evening interval, every one went for a drink. It was now getting serious and table and chairs were re-arranged round the dance floor. Maggots bagged us one in the far corner, while the girls changed. They arrived back looking lovely. Some of the other couples did not bother but we knew it did matter. Not only were your feet under scrutiny, your whole body was. The judges noticed these things, even a different type of shoe on the lady was seen as if you cared and you could score extra points.

Well we won that round, we were now in the finale show off. Kay felt sick, so many folk were now watching, and only eight couples on the floor with a spotlight that kept following you around. At the last minute, before we were called to the floor, Kay had to go for a pee. That was a two-person job in her waltzing gown as every one was out of the dressing rooms by now. Girls have to sit down on the job and the gown had to be held out on both sides. Last minute and this! They made it back as the compere called *'number eight.'* We were on. *"Come on Kay!"* She was shivering with fright but a hug from me and she steadied up. We did a faultless round, never getting in the way of anyone. We returned to our table and were confident we had done well. Then the Latin couples were called.

*"Come on"* said Abby, *"Let's show them we can do it in our far away neck of the woods."*

*"Changing my jacket,"* I said, *"Don't forget a good high back kick! Show them your knickers! You have got those red ones on haven't you?"*

*"Stop it, you'll make me forget the steps!"*

She was great. I went wrong on one foot but no one noticed, only Abby. She covered it up by doing a slide under me then a leap over my head from behind. The audience went mad, it's a very chancy move to make. The final result was silver for Kay and a bronze for Abby. The girls cried, it was the seventh time we had won a medal but were to go on to win sixty-eight in our years together. All that practising paid off.

*\*\*\**

On our way home, Kay's head was again in my lap. She was fast asleep, we had a journey of over forty miles. It was windy, wet and very dark. The road curved to the left. I was travelling at fifty miles per hour, when I stood on the brakes and came to a shuddering halt in a cloud of white smoke from father's tyres.

*"What's up?"* asked Maggots and Abby in the back and Kay awoke.

*"What's the matter?"*

*"I don't know, something said 'STOP' to me."* We started again and around the corner, right across the road, was an oil tanker blocking the whole width of the carriageway. A man ran up to us.

"Thank God you saw me!"

"But I didn't," I said. "Something just told me to stop."

"You must have seen me, I heard you coming and got out of the way."

"But there was no way I could have seen you from around that corner." I repeated. "I did not see you, someone in my head said 'STOP.'"

"It was not any of us," the girls and Maggots chimed.

"Oh Good Lord! Sixth sense" the lorry driver said. "He's looking over you lot tonight, isn't he? Won't be a minute, stay there with your lights on and I will try to move."

How or what he was doing there across the whole road, we never knew. All I can say is someone did tell me to stop. Everyone, including Kay, sat bolt upright. Kay was kissing her gold cross she wore around her neck and it made me uneasy. Abigail wanted a fag. I said,

"I think there is one of those that you like in the glove compartment," so Kay investigated and found a nearly full packet of Roulette cigarettes.

"What colour do you want?" she said to Abby. "Blue, green or yellow?" Roulette was all different colour papers with a gold tip.

"Any," said Abigail, "I need a fag. Got a light darling?"

Her pet name for me so I pushed the lighter in its socket and a few seconds later it went *'click.'* I removed it and passed it back behind me as I drove. Kay had put the packet back and was kissing her crucifix again. I felt something touch the lighter so let go of it thinking Abby had got hold of it in her hand. Instead she had leaned over to get a light off the red-hot end.

By letting go of it, the red hot metal lighter fell into her cleavage. With the blood-curdling scream from Abby, Kay nearly swallowed her cross, and I jammed the brakes on hard again, for the second time in three miles. I was leaving a lot of rubber on this three-mile stretch of road. Poor Abby was in agony.

I jumped out of my door and snatched the back door open. Abby told us in no uncertain fashion what the matter was! I pushed my hand among the soft no-go area for boys. I burned my thumb but at least it was me and not her again. She really was in agony.

Maggots got out and took the front seat, as Kay got the box of tricks of cotton wool, and sticking plasters, and administered first aid. We still had twenty miles to go. The wind howled and the rain sheeted down. I had to drive with care.

\*\*\*

The moment we arrived home at Abby's the girls were out and in the house. Maggots and I started to unload the dresses and cases when Kay called me.

"I think you should look at this."

I entered and followed her to the bathroom where Abby stood with her head hanging over the sink.

"Turn around, let him have a look, don't go coy on me."

Abby slowly turned. She had been splashing water on her breasts, there in the middle of her cleavage was a raw, red ring where she had been burned. Her left breast had a nasty bruise from where I had plunged my hand.

"I don't like it said Kay, I think she should go to hospital and get it dressed."

"It's alright, the pain isn't too bad, all the bruising is where he grabbed me with those bloody great claws of his!" Then Maggots called out,

"That's the last one," as he finished unloading the dresses and Abby slung the towel around herself.

"You take him home and we will see you tomorrow, thank you for the lovely night," and she smudged her lips across mine. How she could say thanks for the lovely night, I thought to myself, as I left. A scary incident on the road, and I tried to burn her to death!

Kay flung her arms around me and tiptoed to kiss me goodnight.

"I'll look after her take care my precious, and you Maggots."

On the way home I told him it looked bad, I doubted it would heal and was worried it might leave a scar for life.

"Burns like that do." I said. "We mark our cattle with a branding iron and it never grows out."

"You can add her to your herd then!" He spoke more in fun than in earnest but I was not amused. I dropped him at his gate in a deluge secretly hoping he would get wet looking for the door key and having only one eye, he could never find the brick he left it under in the dark.

*\*\*

So home to write up the day's events and pray for Abby to heal quickly although I thought she would never wear a strapless bra again, but she did and called it *'my mark,'* to this day, every night she has a *'keepsake'* that God looked after us.

## CHAPTER FOUR

The summer was a good one, we boys decided to have a party and spend the profit from the Oast parties of other years. We chose the day and everything would be free, no charge this time.

John had found the very location, a hundred feet up a very steep bank, that was wooded its whole length around his father's farm. It was ancient sea cliff from Roman days, now the sea was four miles away across the green, knee high corn and sheep pasture. Facing east, it was sheltered from the winter gales and the trees grew high to reach the sun, situated where they were. By midday the top of the hill left them in shadow. More years ago than I care to think, the cliff had a landslide and a plateau was formed half way up. It was on this one-acre flat area that the party-cum-barbecue was to take place, but first we had to clear the ground. For over a week ten of us slaved away, hacking elderberry and bramble until at last the ground was clear. All the low branches of overhanging trees were lopped off to at least ten feet high.

\*\*\*

The day chosen was Saturday the twenty fourth of July. It would be a full moon, and with luck, the night would not be too dark. For a week, ten of us had scrambled up the cliff to our large size arena. Then on Friday night, one of the lads brought his girlfriend along who had volunteered to be in charge of the barbecue. She was a wonderful looking lass of good farming stock, and although dressed in a pair of jeans, no way was she going to risk her neck and body by scrambling up the steep bank. We must have steps.

"Steps?" said John. "We can't build steps."

"Yes you can, dig them out of the bank."

"That will take ages, we have the party tomorrow?"

The whole gang was now of the same opinion. If she couldn't, or was not willing, to clamber up the hill, the other girls in dresses and skirts definitely won't. Why had none of us thought of it? The answer was simple. We were outside boys, and not used to such refinements on farms. Dirt banks and hills were taken in our stride, no matter if wet or dry.

A gang soon got to work with spades to cut the earth out. Now it is not a thing you can do all as one. First the course of the flight has to be chosen and a hundred feet up a very steep bank is a long way, especially in a heavily wooded area. There was no way to go at it in a gang, each had to start in a different spot until we all joined up.

\*\*\*

So the task was begun. As the evening drew on, night came early on the east side of the cliff-like bank, but we had to press on, tomorrow we had a lot still to do. Digging in the dark around large trees that all have roots growing into each other was a job. The axe was in constant use, until it got lost in the jungle of growth on the side of the steps. Some decided to go around to the left of a certain tree while others chose the other side. The path of stairs up the face of the wood was anything but straight. At one am a halt was called. We would finish the steps in the morning.

***

Next day in daylight the site of the entry point to our chosen arena looked like a battlefield. Those digging at the top had thrown the dirt from their step away downhill. It had in places completely filled the steps below that had been cut further down. The ground was rock hard and very pliable. As one trod on a step, so it collapsed. Some form of riser was called for so two guys set to with bow saws to cut four feet logs. Another with a billhook went after some straight pegs to hold the logs in place. Soon the hillside rang to the laughter of youths working.

***

The drink started to arrive after closing time at two thirty and it all had to be lugged up the now winding steps. How could we not have thought of them before? More planning and we were sure to have done so. Anyway the job was now done and it made life easier. My mind went back to Tuesday evening when three had got two eight-gallon barrels of beer up the mountain. That the two barrels were now in place was the only good thing about it. We had had a shower in the late noon and the way we took to reach the area was straight up through all the brambles, dead bluebells, and green bracken. The struggle we had on the second trip up was not worth thinking about. We lost the keg at about fifty feet. Its half hour journey up with us lads pulling and shoving was a lifetime in comparison to its trip back down that sodding bank! How it failed to explode I'll never know! It flattened the undergrowth in its path striking solid trees with a thud. The bitter was well shaken up and its tour downwards ended up a hundred yards out in the field below, with us all cursing and shouting at it. All that effort and it was farther away now than when we had so carefully unloaded it onto a bale of straw so as not to jar it too much. It was a miracle the bung had not blown out!

So the journey started again and this time we had no fear of moving it roughly we rolled it to the bottom of the hill and then amid a lot of swearing at the thing, we manhandled it up the now very familiar slope. At the top we put it on a trestle alongside the first one and left. The crates of coke were stacked up to the right of the two barrels and we strung a tarpaulin over the bar area. I was to be in charge of the drinks again along with Kay and Abigail, who arrived as the last box of glasses were carried up. Abby was to be in charge of the barrels, having worked in a pub. The first thing she did was to upset all of us.

"This is impossible!" she exclaimed. *"How can I wash the glasses? I need water."*

"Water" Oh no, the nearest tap was way below, in fact two hundred yards away in the barn. It would have to be carried up in buckets. Soon four large empty milk churns were assembled in the back of the bar area, and an assortment of buckets were found for the girls to act as water goddesses to fetch the clear liquid.

Meanwhile Dell had arrived, he was the whiz-kid of electricity among us. He had spent a few evenings putting up fairy lights in the trees around and in the space reserved for the pop group who were coming. These lads were an unknown quantity to us but Bob said they were good, only wanted a drink or two and would play all night. He knew them from work out at the new power station at Dungeness, but they needed a lot of power.

Dell was getting in a bit of a flap as since he was here yesterday, we had now got a staircase of steps up the side of our precarious mountain. He thought it should have some illumination or someone was going to walk into a tree or two, and we did not want the hassle of dealing with bloody noses and skinned shins. Also who was in charge of his power supply? He was going to need quite a bit. We all looked at each other and gasped.

*"You are in charge of the sparks."*
*"No, that's not in my contract."*
*"Contract? There is no contract, we all pull together."*
*"Good, then get me some power, I need to test this little lot out."*
*"Where's John? He chose this spot, John where's the power supply?"*

He turned to look down the bank. We all turned to stare through the trees where far away stood the shed with the power. Time was running out, five hours and it was the off. People would be arriving, the fire was already lit and Charlie had the half cooked pig brought from home on his spit with four light bulbs dangling over his area and no power. The stampede down the hill was like a gold rush, as every boy set forth to find cable to reach the two hundred yards between the plug in the shed and Dell's bare wires that were protruding from a collection of connection boxes. The search on the farm below produced one hundred feet of assorted wire, we were five hundred feet short. At least we agreed, now there was a rush to motorbikes and cars to go home and raid our farms and homes of wire. Dell, who lived nearest me, had already had all ours at home to hang lights on, so I stayed behind to help him and ponder on what else could go wrong. It was only a barbecue surely! Gypsies cooked and ate this way all the time without all the fuss and palaver we were getting into.

Meanwhile the girls were still traipsing up the steps with half buckets of water, mentioning every time they passed us,

*"I hope the drinkers appreciate this! Abigail could use the empty glass over and over, they would never know."*

Dell was fussing around with a battery-operated thing, testing the wire to make sure there were no breaks in it. He then taped the sections together. Soon one of the lads came back with a few lengths of wire to be added. It was going to take more than this to get up the hill and Dell was having doubts as to the capability of the cable to carry the voltage required. Soon everyone was back, the wire was laid out, but it was still twenty feet or more short. That's when the brains of Harriet came to the fore.

*"If you pulled it up across from the shed, to the top of that tree,"* she said, pointing to the huge oak in the centre of our dancing area, *"you would have plenty, as running along the ground to the bottom of the hill then up, took a lot*

*more wire than if it was suspended in a straight line."* That was it! Let's go! So one of us climbed to the top, and pulled the cable up over the tree, and then the damn joins all started to come adrift.

"*It's no good, it will not support the weight,*" said someone.

"*This gives me an idea,*" said one of the onlookers. "*If we can dispense with having it along the ground, we can have an overhead power line made of wire. Only thing we need is insulation of rubber, we can use tyres for those. Come on Mac, you go and get that new high tensile hop wire from your dad's shed. John, get the ladder and some mini tyres off the silage heap.*"

So for the next two hours, eight of us, rigged three wires up across the gap from the shed, to the oak tree only twenty feet from the bar. Dell somehow put three thick copper welding machine wires into the main fuse box ready to connect to the three high tensile wires, now strained and shining in the evening sun. We only had to use nine tyres, three at the bottom tied to the back of the combine where the wires connected to Dell's welding cables. Three more tyres were used half way up near the top of a large tree that was in the way, and nothing was to touch the bare wires. The top end was connected by Dell to his box of tricks by more welding cables borrowed from his brother's van.

Soon Dell had it connected up and we all held our breath as he pulled the mains switch down in the barn. All seemed OK, no flashes or bangs, so it was quickly back up the well trodden steps, now wet from all the water the girls had slopped, but thankfully now given up using, for the churns were full, as also was the tin bath, which was being used as a sink.

I now need to tell you that we all stood well back! Dell without fear approached his box of tricks and, '*Walla! Light!*"

"*There you are, nothing to it,*" he said. To say we were impressed was not overstating it. "*That's all they are you know,*" he said, pointing to the wires on pylons running across the marsh from the nuclear power station far out in the distance. "*Just plain wire, but don't for God's sake let anyone touch them! At work we have copper bars above our heads and just clip on them to get power.*" He turned a switch and all the lights went out. "*No need to waste it,*" he said full of confidence that all would work on the night. "*Right, I'm going home to have a bath, those bloody tyres stink of silage.*"

And so we tramped back again down those one hundred and four crumbling steps, leaving the pig roasting gang behind to watch over their pride and joy, along with all the booze.

***

At eight pm I was back. Kay arrived soon afterwards with Abigail, with the news that she was allowed to stay at Abigail's for the night. She had told her parents that they were going to see a woman about a typewriter and the woman was not sure if she would be home tonight. If not, she would see them later next morning, as she was seeing someone else first at nine am. To me it sounded a flimsy story but as long as Kay was free until tomorrow, who was I to complain?

The group of musicians arrived soon after with a hell of a lot of gear, great big box-like things that had to be carried up all those steps. Carefully they carried their own cases of instruments, moaning all the time while climbing the steps, but they loved the setting at the top.

The pig cookers were busy peeling onions and the air was full of the smell of them. A land rover arrived below, a bellow from Mike told us he needed a hand to lug the bread rolls in trays up to our height, so down we went, then back up again. I was starting to detest these holes in the ground called steps. My life was the marsh, the only hills we had were molehills and we stepped over them.

***

The place started to fill up later as it got dark. The group played many of the new tunes such as *'Lover let me go,' 'That girl belongs to yesterday'* and many of Cilla Black's hits. They were good, four boys and a girl who, unknown to us then, were to go very far, even having a hit the following year. Now they were playing for us, just for the beer.

The bar was busy and Abigail put a cardboard box out, as so many wanted to make a contribution, it was that good. No one complained about the bitter, it was as clear as any, even after the churning we had given it.

***

It must have been around midnight, when with a flash and bang that made the girls scream, all the lights went out. That was it. As it had been so well lit by Dell, no one had thought of emergency lighting.

It transpired next day that in our over zealous haste to get the wire up to the site, the wire holding the tyres to the tree, had been tightened too much and cut into the wire that supports the tyre rim and being made of steel, had formed a circuit. So when the live wires supplying the energy chafed into the rubber, it had made a short. No amount of fiddling with his box of switches allowed Dell to get power up so the congregation of partygoers started to make their way home.

The poor old steps had been worn smooth, the pegs supporting the logs had long given way with all the traffic on the way up. Now the flow was the other way. In the dark there was no hope of not missing the odd footing and a shout of pain told its own story! A large well tanked-up fellow had missed his mark and went down hill rather rapidly, taking twenty other partygoers with him. By the time I got there, someone was on the way to the farmhouse to call an ambulance. There in the moonlight at the bottom of the now slide was a mass of hysterical humanity. We were lucky, only two broken arms and a leg, a lot of scratches, and a fair bit of blood, a lot of torn shirts, laddered stockings and a few very angry men and crying women.

The ambulance soon cleared the area up and the other more fortunate ones made their way home, unlike the police who had come when the meat wagon was called. Amongst the two Bobbies was one with the spirit to try and scale the now vanished steps to find out what lay at the top of the slide that had attracted so many late night revellers up the cliff.

As he arrived at the top, all was quiet. The band was packing away but the stabbing light of the officer's torch was a revelation to the musicians.

*"Help us pack away mate. All the power's gone down."*

Now this man in blue was no ordinary bloke, that's for sure. Not only had he braved the mountain, but now offered to look at the electrics to see if he could get their power back.

*"Where is it?"* he asked.

*"Don't know, see Dell."*

We were blissfully unaware of doing anything wrong when Dell was questioned. Although we could not see his face, I think the policeman's face went white.

*"You did what? Bare live wires up in trees. My God, you can kill people like that!"* The whole area was soon swarming in coppers. Abigail, the dear, had had the sensible idea that they may not be too pleased to know how much money she had acquired through the night in her cardboard box, so had sunk it into the thick murky water of the tin bath. The notes she tucked in the top of her dress under her bra, making herself look lopsided. Good girl she is one you know, always a street ahead of others. No wonder we all loved her!

The power line was inspected as best they could by the beam of their torches, but the trees were over fifty feet up when you stood in the field at the bottom.

Soon they were gone with the threat that it would have to be reported, but we heard no more of it as it was wired in the correct side of the meter. The boys got all the group's tackle down to the bottom as Abigail said *"Good night,"* and left with the pig cookers. The calm night air was warm, Kay and I snuggled down for a cuddle on an open spot above our now deserted well-trodden earth arena.

We lay on a ledge of sand stone jutting out where once the sea had lapped the shore and talked as only lovers do. The sky to the east in front of us began to lose that intense black and the moonlight slowly grew fainter. The birds began to celebrate another safe night. A rook cawed and Kay and I kissed. Then an air of wind talked its way through the leaves up above. We were in our little part of Paradise.

The next thing I remember is Dell calling my name and a sudden pain in my right arm as Kay stirred. She had slept in my embrace on my arm. We must have been tired, or at least I was. It was all those bloody steps! We kissed each other good morning, brushed the dust from our clothes and then went to find Dell.

# CHAPTER FIVE

I was halfway through cutting eight acres of a heavy hay crop when the news came. Alan, a friend of ours, had been killed on the M1 while going to Liverpool with a group of his mates on their scooters. It was all the rage in 1964, to join a gang and burn up some road on a Lambretta or Vespa.

\*\*\*

The sixties was a dramatic decade for change. The Mods rode around in numbers. Only two weeks ago, the police had flown extra coppers in from Northolt, to the local airport to calm things down in the nearby town of Hastings. It seemed that now the Mods had been going north to the capital of the Beatles, to *'have fun'* as they called it, with the police up there.

Alan had been in a crash and died instantly. My girls needed me as they were very fond of him and his sister was a real friend of theirs. The family had lived next door to Abigail but had moved away a couple of years ago, after the death of his Grandfather, to run the family farm.

I finished mowing but left the rough headland and went up Abigail's. She had not received the news and asked if it was really true.

"Yes, Guy told me, he was told by Richard, who is a Rocker. Two were killed. *It was a hell of a smash and five scooters were written off."*

Abigail went to the phone, thumbed through the address book, and then dialled. She put her hand out for me to draw closer. I held her hand as she spoke to them. She hung up and burst into tears.

*"Oh it is true! It happened on Friday night, they are having him brought home tomorrow. We will have to go to the funeral. Can you take us, I know Kay will want to go?"* And she hugged me and cried.

Being Abigail, she soon pulled herself together. *"I must let Kay know,"* and picked the white phone up again.

I heard her tell Kay's mother and she hung up. Coffee was made and we sat in the kitchen and talked. Abigail looked terrible. The news had hit hard.

*"Alan was such a nice boy,"* she said. *"Why he had to be a Mod and buy that scooter with all those mirrors and bits of rag dangling off the handle bars he called trophies, useless things, beats me. The other week he was in a skirmish with the local police. Did you see it in The Telegraph? They had to fly police reinforcements into Lydd."*

*"It's all right Abigail, you cry, it will be good for you."* I could not think of anything to say.

An hour later the phone rang. It was Kay and the tears started to flow again and, by the sound of it, at both ends of the phone.

*"Poor you,"* said Abigail. *"I have got your love here to hug me."* And she pulled me close to her. *"You my dear are alone,"* and it went on and on. At long last Abigail put the phone down and wiping her eyes hugged me.

*"I must go now, there's hay to cut,"* I said. I finished the mowing as it got dark and heavy dew was falling. I thought of Alan as the sun snuggled behind the

trees on the distant hills for the night.

***

The funeral service was arranged for Friday next at ten am, so an early start had to be made as we had a journey of seventy miles to the North West of London. Kay had taken the day off school and her parents knew I was driving Abigail and her up, but for some reason had no objection so Abigail and I were going to be able to pick her up from her home. Abigail was dressed all in black. She had overdone it with a veil and prayer book, I thought to myself as she got in beside me,

"*I'll sit in the front then they, meaning Kay's parents, will be happy if Kay is in the back.*"

As we stopped at Kay's her father came out.

"*She's just coming.*"

Kay appeared in the doorway and my heart skipped a throb. She looked gorgeous, even in black. The hat was a small pillbox kind that stayed somehow at a dainty tilt forward, slanting to one side. She wore a black jacket and white blouse that fitted all the right places. She shone out as someone special. Her skirt was knee-length showing her curvy legs all in black silk, ending in a polished pair of lace up shoes with a little heel. Her father opened the door at the back and Abigail got out the front, forgetting the plan she had made fifteen minutes earlier, and said

"*I'll sit in the back.*" Kay's father looked at her and exploded.

"*My girl is not getting in the front. If that is the way you planned it, you can forget the blasted funeral. She is not riding with you in the front. If you think that, you can think again!*"

His eyes bulged as he looked at the ground between Abigail and him. He ranted on. He had '*given Kay the benefit of going with her friend and not him,*' moving his eyes up to stare at me cowering behind the wheel.

"*You knew he was driving us and had no objection. What has changed so suddenly?*"

"*The way he stared at her the moment she came out of the door. I'm not daft, it's written all over both their faces. What do you take me for?*" He was now spluttering and was having a job to stand. He leaned on the door with both hands and poked his head in side.

"*Look here young man. I was your age once and know what you are after.*"

With that, Kay, who had stood there silent and elegant, said,

"*Dad what did you do when you were our age that you are frightened of?*" He was lost for words and stared at the ground.

"*Never you mind he knows,*" shaking his fist at me. "*You are too young for all this.*"

"*What did you do then dad,*" she asked in her soft exciting voice.

"*Never you mind.*"

"*We must go,*" quipped in Abigail, seeing that we were getting nowhere fast and pushing him aside sat back in the front. Kay sat in the back and swung her long legs in, as a lady does. He slammed the doors shut and we left. I made a point of driving away slowly up the gravel drive to show him I was going to be careful of his daughter on the road, and not mark his nice beach drive. As soon as we had gone a mile, we stopped and the girls swapped places. I gave Kay a kiss and said,

"What was wrong with your dad? He is always angry with me."

"When we were little he used to hit us and mother would cry, but he has been better in the last five years. It is as if something snaps."

We spent a pleasant time on the journey, the girls discussing the meaning of Kay's father's comments of, *'I was young once.'* They went through all the scenarios of the things that he could possibly have done and Abigail came to the conclusion that marrying a battle-axe like his wife, he was now jealous of his beautiful daughter in her first years of adulthood. I agreed but still wondered what did he do to be so ashamed of?

*** 

We found the village and church in time, having to walk approximately one mile after finding space to park. The roads were narrow and congested with the other drivers wishing to show their last respects. He had been a popular boy even here. In the two years the family had lived in this small village they had made a lot of friends. Both the parents' families had originated from the area and this was the family church, a Norman building standing out in the countryside amid a lot of big elms and old thorn trees.

Over three hundred Mods had arrived on their scooters and the roads were jammed. The service seemed to take an age and the two girls stood either side of me, holding my hands. I felt a little under-dressed, having only black shoes, socks, white shirts, waistcoat and suit. The internment was a solemn affair and Abigail was glad to see the flowers we had sent were on top of the coffin, along with two other wreathes.

*** 

We were asked back to the house. The girls went with the sister of Alan, I took a relation with me to show me the way to their farm. It was a lovely house tucked up under a hill facing west and as we drove up, I noticed a large field nearby that had recently been hayed, but the four acres or so of uncut grass in the middle stood out like a sore thumb. The uncle noticed my head looking inquisitively at the scene and spoke.

*"That was the place where my brother got the news of Alan's accident and he never got the entire field cut."*

"Funny," I replied. *"That is exactly what I was up to when I heard."*

*"Here. In here,"* he said, and we turned up a track and parked in a yard alongside a trailer of hay bales. The house was huge. Not many people had come back and I felt out of my depth. This was the first funeral I had attended but my thoughts were soon trained on other things as Kay and Abigail, saw me meeting with Jenny, Alan's sister, who was first to speak.

*"You handsome devil you must be the preacher,"* then started to sob. *"Alan*

*often spoke of you and the time you got stuck up that holly bush."* Then she turned the waterworks on and that started the other two off, so there I was with three beautiful young ladies crying and trying to hug me for comfort. That is how Alan's mother found me, smothered in females. What did she think? She was very nice.

"*Poor young man, leave him alone. He is embarrassed. You knew Alan when did you last see him?*"

"About April, no May. All the rooks had flown their nests and the marsh was full of the young, pestering to be fed by their elders, a real racket they were knocking up."

"Oh yes," he said he had been down that way. Have you seen George? He has something to ask you."

"No, not yet, but I will in a moment."

"*I'll get my husband,*" and she vanished into the next room.

Kay came up to me and put her arm around my waist. George appeared, said hello to Kay and thanked us so much for coming. He knew so few of Alan's so-called mates that had turned up on those noisy things, "*I now wish I'd not let him have one, but as we live so far from anywhere, it seemed only right he should have some fun He was a good lad and worked all hours. He loved the farm but if only he had not got in with that crowd. Oh well we cannot do anything about that now, but I can do something that he would have wished. Come with me young man. I understand you hunt a bit.*"

"Well I have at times you know."

"*Good. Come on. It's not muddy my dear,*" looking at Kay's feet with a wicked twinkle in his eye. Into the back yard we walked as Kay stepped cautiously over the odd piece of dirt that had fallen from some implement while in transit. We stopped at a row of stables and he gestured to us to look into a loose box. A head of a fine fifteen and a half hand chestnut hunter appeared over the door and snorting a greeting to us.

"*There you are, he likes you already.*"

As I put my hand around his neck and blew into his ear, he flicked his head up and down as if to say, 'don't do that!' Kay was now stroking his neck as George delivered his bombshell.

"*All yours, it was Alan's. He would have liked you to have him, hasn't ridden him at all this year, never will now,*" as a watery eye looked at Kay with her arms slung around the animal.

"*He's all yours.*"

"I don't know," I said. "*It's a fine horse. You cannot just give it away like that.*"

"*Yes I can. I bought it for my boy last year. He never liked it, too much to do on scooters to be bothered with a horse.*"

With that Kay let the hunter go and threw her arms around me.

"*Go on darling, buy him buy him for me!*"

"No. I don't want money for it, just a good home and a bit of work. He *deserves that, got a bit of spirit in him though, needs a firm hand."*

*"Oh go on darling, have him. I will ride him home."* Kay knew a good bit of horseflesh when she saw it, and that was it. She would hate me forever if I refused.

\*\*\*

So four days later a horsebox arrived at her father's farm with a rather fine horse for her to ride, a gift from me. Her parents were pleased to have a creature like him on the farm, but not too happy that it was because of me.

\*\*\*

The following days I learned from Abigail that Kay had taken up riding all around the farm, jumping hedges whenever needs be. They were made for each other and I made sure I had plenty of work to do on the farm away from home. I loved to see her over the hedge on her farm, sweeping down the hill into the bottom meadow, all her clothes flapping. Her skirt billowed along the flanks of *'Trafalgar,'* as he was called. She turned him with grace, not leaning over at all. It was as if he needed to please her, then as she followed the hedge around the boundary of the two farms, with the dirt flying from his shining hooves, the pair would vanished over the next hedge. All you heard was the thump of his hooves, the creak of leather of that bloody sidesaddle, and the rhythmic pant of his breath. Alan was still making someone happy.

\*\*\*

Poor old Abigail came up on the Sunday to watch the charger *'fly'*, as Kay put it. I saw the two as I haytered one of our orchards and could not help feeling sorry for her. She had also been a part of Alan, yet had nothing, so I bought her a three-piece green trouser outfit I knew she had an eye on. That was the wrong thing to do as I soon found out. Kay was jealous. The horse was an unwanted gift to me, which she gave a home to. I bought clothes for Abigail. What was going on behind her back? She was determined to know. The green monster had raised its ugly head. To diffuse the situation I had to do something.

\*\*\*

The following week was Kay's young sister's birthday. She was only fourteen but a proper madam. Abigail decided as usual to hold a pow-wow and sort things out with Kay, and what better than a restaurant that we used, to take her young sister as a birthday treat along with us. *'I could pay.'* The table was booked, the usual at the back of the room against the wall. Kay's parents made no objections. How could they? It was their two girls, the youngest one only fourteen, along with Abigail, and I was paying. The birthday girl could be relied on to tell them everything about the night.

\*\*\*

I picked Abigail up and we proceeded to Kay's. I stayed in the car as Abigail gathered up the other two, and then off we went. The atmosphere was, to say the least, tense. Kay's first words to Abby on getting in the car were,

*"I see you are not wearing your new suit then."*

To me that sounded like fighting talk and I began to wonder if I had made the right decision to take them all out. Kay's young sister sort of kept things alive, it was as well, for Abigail sat in the front.

"*That is not her place,*" Kay said. "*I should be beside him.*"

Not fast enough for me we arrived and entered the restaurant. The head waiter saw us coming and had swiftly picked up the flowers I had arranged for Kay and her sister, to be given on our arrival (another one of Abigail's brilliant ideas. She was always spending my money!) Then he ushered Kay to her seat.

"*Your usual and your young man ordered your favourite wine, a 60 Gancia. I hope it is to your liking.*" Holding her chair, he sat Kay down. That did the trick. Kay saw I was making an effort for her attentions and Abigail was second, where she in her mind belonged.

Poor little sister was completely enthralled by all of this. She had heard the waiter say, "*Your usual madam?*" How often did her sister and I come here?

The waiter took their flowers away till after the meal. The wine I had ordered was Kay's favourite by name and year. Her fourteen-year-old sister's brain was in overdrive. I whispered in Kay's ear as we looked at the menu.

"*You darling are the only one for me. I'm sorry that the gift to Abigail upset you, but it's you I love, not Abigail.*" She turned to me and kissed me most tenderly.

"*I know,*" she said. "*It was sweet of you. She is kind to us, the best of friends.*"

Kay's sister was nearly standing up by now in amazement at her sister kissing me in public.

"*I'll tell mum,*" she blurted out.

"*No you won't. I'll kill you!*"

"*No you won't!*"

"*Yes she will,*" chipped in Abigail. "*Now look, make the most of this evening. You will not get many chances like this to come and dine in a five star hotel, so you shut up and sit down properly.*"

All the way through the meal Kay kept rubbing her leg up mine. Her little sister started to get annoyed as we looked into each other's eyes. Then Kay giggled as I squeezed the top of her leg with my hand. The young party girl had to find out the mysteries of '*under the tablecloth,*' and tucked her head under while at the same time lifting the edge up. Abigail was more than a match for a fourteen year old and kicked her leg over to mine for the benefit of her to see. She came out from under the cloth with a look of utter disbelief and stared at Kay.

"*They are playing footsies under the table. He was, I saw them, and he's your boyfriend!*"

"*Sis, it's all right. Don't get upset, we all love him.*"

"*Mum told me you did.*"

"*It's not like mum and dad say, we are just very good friends.*"

That seemed to calm her down and she sat all through the desserts in silence.

We returned to the lounge for coffee and the flowers were returned. I sat with the sister and made a bit of a fuss over her, teasing her about what type of drink she could have to round the night off with, and what her mother would say to the bouquet a boy had given her. She hugged them to her body, and smelt them,

"These are the first any boy has ever given me."

The maid waiting at our table said she had a special drink for her but she was not to tell anyone because it was for grown-ups, and parents did not approve. That was just what she wanted, to be treated as one of us away from mum, and dad. She was *'grown up now at fourteen.'*

It was a sort of cocktail with all the trimmings but a wink from the girl who brought it to our table said *"It's OK, no alcohol."* Sis was delighted, a big flat glass with orange, lemon and lime with a sprig of mint and floating in the middle a lump of blue ice.

\*\*\*

All was going well until we were nearly home, when the birthday girl, who I had sitting in the front with me, declared

*"Wait till I tell mum and Gran where we went, and how you kissed Kay."* I nearly lost control of the car.

*"No, you must not tell them I kissed your sister! They will get the wrong idea, tell them everything else but not that and you'd better forget that drink you had or you will be in trouble."*

*"Was it real? I thought I was a bit squiffy."*

The night's events had gone to the young girl's head, at that age everything was possible in her mind. I took Kay and her to their door while Abigail quickly transferred to the front. Her mother opened the door and the little sister started to jabber on how posh it was and what she'd had to eat.

*"I had lobster,"* she said. *"And look at these 'specially' for me!"* holding the flowers out to show her mother.

*"That was nice, you shouldn't have. Thank you for taking them out,"* and with that she slammed the door in my face. The scowl on Abigail's face was ample to show me that her hate for the woman had gone up another notch.

## CHAPTER SIX

It came in the first post unexpected, my mother had had to sign for it. A brown envelope addressed to my mother and father that contained a court order from a Kent Magistrates court forbidding me to have anything to do with Kay. It was the first any of us knew that her family had felt quite that strongly at our relationship, but obviously they did not like me big time! The reason given was that I was three years older and more mature. Her schoolwork was suffering and she was infatuated by the older boy, ME! I was not to write or phone. Even talking to her was forbidden! My mother was in tears, whereas my father took himself off to sea none too pleased.

\*\*\*

I met Abigail that evening outside the bread shop she worked in and took her to her home. It had turned into a filthy day. The rain lashed the autumn leaves to the ground and I thought of poor old dad fighting the seas. The wind was gusting to a good gale force eight. He had not intended to go to sea today, as he did not like the look of the weather that morning, but this letter was affecting all of us. Abigail was amazed and took no time in phoning Kay, only to get her father.

"Sorry no, you cannot speak to Kay and please do not try to phone again." Abigail slammed the phone down and threw her head back in disgust.

"Who do they think they are? She is seventeen for God's sake. I'm sorry. I know you'd hate me taking His name in vain but it's enough to make you spit! Right the battle is on! You love Kay and she loves you, so let's see how they cope with us. We'll beat them. Going to a solicitor, all that fuss, it's the sixties for God's sake! There I go again sorry, but I'm angry right, coffee. You are stopping?"

"Well, no. I just had to tell you, I knew you finished at four thirty and with all this rain..."

"You are coming up later? Please." She was now pleading in her softest voice. "We've got to help Kay. I'll get my mother to phone when she gets in and find out what they are up to."

With that, I left.

\*\*\*

Father was home when I got there, not too pleased with the day in general. No fish, a lot of sea and a run-in on the phone with Kay's mother.

"No more vegetables or fresh fish for them," he said. "They can buy their own fish, and you keep away from that girl, there's plenty more."

I grabbed a piece of bread and corned beef that was on a plate by mother's side, as she was cutting the other slice of the loaf to go on top of dad's sandwich and left. 'Sod them, now they're telling me what to do,' I thought to myself, and went back where I was more welcome, up Abigail's.

"That didn't take long," she said as I entered the back door without knocking like usual.

"Now my parents are telling me to find another girl."

"Rubbish! Kay's mum has phoned mum and they reckon that in a little while you will find a girl and they will let Kay out. Meanwhile she is grounded for one year."

I sat down on the old sofa and looked at Abby.

"So my dear, a new girl for you and it has got to look good. Of course I don't mean a real girl friend," and she looked at me with a smile, just someone to look as if you care for each other.

"Who do we know for the part? And you have got to flash it about for people to speak of, so Kay's parents know. Now, have you any ideas? Let's make a list."

We sat and talked for hours over pots of coffee. Many hours and pots of coffee later, we had concocted a plan to keep Kay and me together.

"Kay's not going to like me out with another girl. Look how she got green eyes when I bought you that suit."

"Don't worry, you will get ulcers! I'll get word to Kay of what we are planning. Now are these all the girls you know?"

The list only contained the twins I danced with years ago, and neither would be interested, I was sure, that was the lot. Kay had been mine, other girls did not interest me. Then it hit me like a ton brick.

"Hazel!"

"Who the hell is she?" Said Abigail in a startled sort of way? "Hazel where the hell does she come from how do you know her? You've kept her in the dark. I've never heard of her."

"No, you wouldn't. She works in the café her father owns. We have known each other for two years. She is a blonde and Kay knows I would never fancy a blonde, I hate that colour hair."

"Will she do it?"

"I will have to see her tomorrow and ask her. I have a coffee in their place every morning when I do the lookering. She's always asking me to take her out just for fun. She has a boyfriend in London or somewhere, he only comes down on odd days. Look at the time! You let me know what's going on. I am going home."

Abigail gathered the mugs and cups up as I kissed her on her cheek and left.

***

The next morning found the tractor outside the café, and me in deep conversation with Hazel, a six-foot girl of eighteen with long golden hair half way down her back. Black eye shadow, a thin face and a big nose, earrings made of plastic and paste, a string of coloured beads, no sleeve blouse, and slacks. Her wrists were full of bangles and her fingers were hidden under numerous silver rings, she looked a real tart. Not my type of girl at all, but she was up for it. I explained to her my problem and her eyes lit up.

"For the fun of it," she said. "Just show me the girl's parents and they will be convinced. Let me dress up and let's go!"

"No not now, at the next local dance on Saturday."

"OK, but where are you taking me tonight?"

My heart sank. Had she got it mixed up? It was to be pretending. Like a flash

I said

"*Pick you up at seven thirty,*" pushed the empty cup into the middle of the table and charged off.

***

That night at seven thirty, Hazel was ready. Did she look a picture? I just hoped my parents did not get to hear. *'Flower Power'* was not my scene, she was a real Hippy or trying to be.

"*Where we going?*" she enquired, sliding into the seat next to me, and I got the feeling that she was sort of trespassing. That was my darling's place.

"*Where are you taking me?*"

"*You will see, to a mate's of mine,*" and we drove to Abigail's. She was expecting us and heard us pull up.

"*Come on in. You know the way.*" Then when she saw Hazel her eyes stood out as if on flagpoles. She whispered,

"*That "Hazel? God what a find! She will do."*

Abigail and Hazel hit it off straight away. I sat and tried to finish Abigail's Telegraph crossword while she filled the longhaired over-decorated girl in on the plan. Hazel had two things to remember, or Abigail was going to kill her. One, no kissing me on the lips and two, keep her hands off! All this to a girl I hardly knew, other than the one who made me a cup of drink each morning and charged me four pence! I was one of only a few in her age group that she saw. The thrill of adventure was going to her head, she was to meet people of her own age at last. With no transport it had been hard for her to go out, now here we were telling her to lay it on thick all the time, but to remember *'it was going nowhere!'* Who cared? She would meet boys! I sensed trouble, but Abigail said it would be OK. She had got word to Kay at school. She was going to pray for success but had told Abigail to look after me. She was scared this girl would steal me away with her charms.

"*Some hope Hazel's got,*" I told Abigail. "*There is no charm in the girl, not for me.*"

We spent a pleasant evening, the three of us, then I took Hazel home, with the understanding that I would pick her up for the dance at seven thirty on the following Saturday.

***

The day arrived. Hazel was ready and got in the front of the car. We then drove up to Abby's where they had a chat. Afterwards we set off to the hall. Abigail sat in the back to make it look real. Outside the hall Abigail and I gave Hazel one more look over. She had rather overdone it. The skirt is best forgotten. There was not a lot of it and what there was *'only just covered her thighs,'* is how Abigail put it later on when her and I had an inquest on the night's events. I think Hazel had a bath, but in cheap scent. The air behind her as she moved was laden with it!

***

When we arrived at Abigail's, she had mentioned that we should wait until eight thirty before we went in, as we had got to make it look different than other times. We were usually the first to arrive to get an empty dance floor to practice on. Now we had got to appear when everyone was there and make a grand entry and show. The car park was packed as we pulled in so I jammed my car up behind one of my mates, as he never left early. As we went in, Abigail slammed the door shut behind us. Heads turned to see who could not shut a door quietly and there was this girl on my arm. I smiled and acknowledged a couple of friends as if to say, *'Look what I have got.'*

The band knew Abigail and me, so the next dance was a quick step. They always did that when I arrived with Kay. As I swung Hazel round to face me to ask for this dance, she blurted out. *"I can't dance!"* Now the mud hit the floor, everyone was watching, waiting for us to lead the way. I wished the floor would open up and swallow me. Abigail by this time had vanished to the bar and there was just Hazel and I.

"Sorry," I said to the bandleader. *"We will sit this one out."*

He nodded and turned to face his fellow musicians. I went in search of Abigail with Hazel slouching along trying to keep up with me.

*"What are you doing? Everyone is looking. You don't have to go that far. Is something the matter darling? You look terrible."*

"She can't dance!"

*"Don't be silly. Everyone can dance surely"* Abigail turned to square up to Hazel.

"No, never bothered. Silly, I should have," she said.

"Yes you should! Everyone knows he loves dancing, no-one will give him credit for going to a dance with a girl who can't."

"Sorry."

"Stop saying sorry! We must think of something, come on darling. You and I will dance."

Abigail slipped into top gear, but Abigail will be the first to admit she was a waltz dancer, not a fast stepper at the quick step like Kay. We had a whale of a time, then it was onto a Military Two Step. That was our cue to vacate the floor.

Hazel was chatting a few boys up, and I had to nearly drag her over to Abigail with my arm around her. I don't really think she was taking the idea seriously, that it was really only make believe. To her, an arm around the waist meant something completely different to what we had planned. Abigail tried her best all evening to distance herself from us, and Hazel revelled in it. I was not amused, a lot of people asked about Kay and I had to lie.

*"This one,"* nodding at Hazel, *"is more fun than Kay,"* I said as I tried to drive the fact home.

I made a point of leaving early with Hazel on my arm for everyone to see, having arranged to take her home early, then I would return to Abigail's to talk over the evening's events. It was agreed that John, a mate of ours whose car we were parked behind, would take Abby home, and she would explain that now I had found this floozy, I had no time for Kay any more. Telling John to his face was the best way to spread the word to all the boys.

\*\*\*

I was waiting for Abigail, having packed Hazel off home. I parked around the back so no-one knew I was there, for a lot of my mates passed her house on the way back from the dance, and my car parked at Abigail's would not look right with what she had told John. I waited till she was in the doorway before I announced myself and John had driven off.

"I'm here. Hold the door," I said, as she went to shut it. I stepped out from behind the privet hedge alongside the footpath leading past the house.

"You got rid of her fast. How did it go?"

"No trouble at all, only she says we must do it more often!"

"Come in, sit down, I'll put the coffee on."

I must have kept a small village up in the Andes fully employed with all the coffee Abigail made for me. She came into the room with two steaming cuppas of drink, dressed in a pink and white bathrobe that she had changed into while the milk had boiled.

"That's better. Things were starting to stick you know."

I knew only too well how one felt after a night of dancing, and Abigail had done a lot that night with anyone willing, just to keep out of my way.

"Where did we go wrong tonight? I never dreamed of asking Hazel if she could dance," said Abby. "What are we going to do? Everyone expects you to dance. That's it. You don't come I will go on my own, that will make a real impact on everyone. Soon the whole area will know you have a new girl. You stay away, I'll tell them you are too busy with that blonde bird. Kay's mother will soon get the message."

So it was arranged I would stay away from the places that we so often frequented. The nights seemed to drag. There they were all enjoying themselves and I was at home keeping my head down. Then two weeks later, father took a call at one pm from a girl.

"Go now to Rye railway goods yard and meet a girl waiting for you or someone," he said.

Now father had no idea of who it was, but then he never did recognize voices on the phone as he had a job hearing. I hurried to the coal yard to find my darling Kay in her school uniform waiting.

"I knew you would come!"

And in daylight she threw her arms around me and kissed me.

"I love you so much and miss you. It has buzzed around the school that you have a new girl. I so much want to tell them it is all a plan to get mum off our backs. She sounds horrible. How do you stand it? You must love me so much."

"Come on," I said. "We must not let people see us, what are you doing out of school?"

"Oh, that's all right. We had a day out to Brighton on a coach and it broke down this morning, they could not mend it or supply another so the whole lot of us came back. We had lunch and have been given the rest of the day off."

*"Get in, let's go. We must get away from here."*

Kay wrenched the door of the old van open, sat and swung her legs in.

*"Where to"* she said.

*"I know it's only one thirty so the café will be open. It's time you met your stand-in."*

*"OK, but I hope I don't like her or I may get jealous."*

*"You wait until you see her. She's not our type."*

\*\*\*

The café was empty of customers and Kay followed me in. A voice from behind the counter called.

*"Hazel, a couple of friends to see you."*

That was a bad start as her father, the man behind the counter thought that I was there for his daughter. This was starting to get out of hand. Even her parents thought I was courting Hazel. Kay's eyes nearly popped out of her head and she gave a little snigger as Hazel emerged from the kitchen.

*"Is that her? She's awful!"* The words dropped from her mouth. Luckily Hazel had not heard her. She came at me like a blonde tornado. Her arms went up to embrace me as if I was a long lost relation.

*"Steady on,"* I said. *"Meet Kay,"* and Kay stepped out from behind me and held her hand out to shake Hazel's, but the blonde was not that civilised.

*"Is this the one you are trying to keep? Is she your love? She's too young for you, and timid."*

*"Hazel, don't be rude. You're nearly the same age."*

*"She's a school girl, you'll get locked up!"*

If it had not been for the fact that Kay was fascinated in this girl, I think she would have cried. The two girls stood eyeing each other up as cats do before a scrap. I felt uneasy. Hazel's mother came on the scene from out of the kitchen.

*"Hello. Thank you so much for taking Hazel out the other night. She had such a lovely time. We have heard nothing else since, this must be your girlfriend, how sweet."*

Kay hated people calling her sweet. It was a term of affection she associated with little babies, or old heavily scented aunts past the age of helping themselves. But Hazel's mother was a good deal more polite and sensitive than her daughter. We sat at a table and father produced four cups of tea, and then sat with us. The girls chatted and seemed to get on. Kay was fascinated with the way Hazel talked. She knew all the fab words and gossip of pop groups, the names of all the artists and where the next pop festival was to be and if she could possibly get to it. We only stayed an hour, after which I drove to one of our fields out on the marsh, miles from my house and prying eyes, and had a cuddle and kissed. The clocks hour hand quickly moved around on Kay's wristwatch.

*"I must be at school when the school bus comes to go home."*

We drove to Rye and she got out. Her face was red with the crying she had done when starting to leave our field of joy. I promised to see her whenever possible, and then vanished into the traffic collecting the pupils from school.

\*\*\*

News came via Abigail that Kay's mother, had heard the good news. I had not pined long for her daughter as the following week I had already found a more suitable girl. She was over the moon, boasting that they had been right to get a Court Order refraining us from seeing each other and could I come tonight at eight to see her?

\*\*\*

I was sitting on the couch in the front room with a coffee as Abigail talked to someone on the phone, she kept on motioning with her hand at arm's length to me that she was pleased to hear what she was being told. At last she hung up.

*"That was Eileen. She says that Kay's mother may let Kay out soon if you really are no longer interested in Kay. That's what we want to hear so maybe if we can pull another stunt off without too much fuss, just maybe, darling Kay will soon be allowed out, though don't get your hopes up too much yet,"* and Abby put her arms on my shoulders and looked into my eyes. *"Now this Saturday the dance is at Beckley, not a very big affair I admit, but we always go and they have a jolly good floor. So do you think that Hazel will come?"*

*"I'll ask and if last time is anything to go by, I'd say yes!"*

The doorbell interrupted me. Abigail got up and answered it.

*"John. Come in. I suppose you want the Preacher. He's in there,"* pointing to the sitting room door.

*"Ah. Found you. How do you fancy getting your old pick-up out and going after a few rabbits? It's just the evening for it."*

*"I'll come,"* said Abigail. She loved bumping around over fields in the dark after bunnies.

*"Let me go home and change, then we will meet you at your place,"* I said.

*"OK, don't be too long. You are coming Abigail?"*

*"Yes, let me slip into some old clothes."*

\*\*\*

I picked Abigail up adequately clothed for such a foray, and we set out to get John at the farm where we had held the barbeque. John's dad called out to be careful as John and one of his mates left with their twelve bores under their arms. First stop was up at our farm in the orchards. It was not easy as the odd rabbit ran from row to row. Then entering the long field of grass, a flashing torch drew our attention to the person in the adjoining field. It turned out to be the foreman of Kay's dad's farm.

*"Ah good to see it's you, thought we had poachers,"* he said as we drew up to investigate.

I was over the moon with this encounter, for I was sure word would get back to the boss that I was getting on with my life without his daughter and she ought to know that a young girl was hanging around my neck, as on his approach I had mentioned to Abby it was Kay's foreman. Abby laid it on thick for him to see even down to the point of saying.

*"Come on, let's finish this silly game and you and I can get lost."* Then we

moved to John's land that we covered in a short time as a lot of the crops were still uncut, which denied us entry. We then came to the six acres where he said *'had a few.'* The field was laid into grass for it was going to be cut for turf later. Short mown and heavy rolled, it was like a cricket pitch. Along one hedge were twenty rabbits sitting out. We got four of them before they all vanished.

The total for the night was eight, not a bad toll in the early sixties after the plague had all but wiped the cony from the British countryside. Abigail loved to speed across the grass and would not stop saying

*"Over there, there's one. If I was driving we would get more, you never see the ones sitting."*

I told her next time she could drive.

*"Good, but you'll have to teach me first."*

So Abigail wanted to learn to drive. I had the perfect place to teach her, a flat field of nine acres that never lay wet.

\*\*\*

The following day I spent an hour with the tractor and trailer putting out straw bales. This was for an obstacle course for her to drive around. I might as well not have bothered, for that night I collected Abigail and drove her to the field. Pulling in the gate, we stopped and she took her place behind a 1958 Ford car that we used on the farm.

*"Right, I'll show you what the things are for."*

*"Just tell me the clutch, brake, and accelerator." "Right, got that, now make the engine go for me."*

*"Look, you turn the key, that's right, now press that button. Let it go. That's it. First is up there."*

There is not much more to say. The clutch came out with a bang and we went, and how we went! We reached twenty-miles per hour in bottom gear across the field. She was like a little girl, laughing and screaming with joy, this way and that. Unfortunately straight lines held small pleasure for Abigail and we had completely turned around long before the ditch that bordered the field came in sight. Nothing was going to stop this power-crazed lass now. I held on for dear life. Nothing I said did any good. We were moving and she was steering. The bales of straw were the target to hit, not negotiate around! The air was thick with dust and chaff. The whole area was scattered with straw when at last we came to a stalling halt.

With that burst of excitement out of the way she settled down to learn the finer points of driving and within six weeks of having lessons around fields with me in-between dances, I let her drive father's car at night on the country roads if the weather was fine. She never had a licence or learner's plates. I later taught, or tried to teach, two of her friends but never got past starting the engine.

\*\*\*

I crept into bed that night at two am. The sight of that field the next day told its own story. Not two pieces of straw touched each other but lay evenly spread across the grass. Luckily the car was old and showing no marks, but dad wondered what had gone on in the night. Car tracks were too numerous to decipher any pattern of events. The subject was not talked of again.

***

Two nights later the Beckley Village Hall opened its doors to the dance, where only the locals went. Everyone knew everyone else and Abigail, Hazel, and I arrived at eight pm. Abigail, having given Hazel a good talking to on how to behave. We did not wish to draw undue attention to ourselves. As we reached the door Abigail stopped me and stood to face me. Her sparkling eyes looked sad.

*"You poor darling, its Kay isn't it? You are not the same without her. The spring in your step is not there, you walk with a lost look. Now let's have a look at you,"* and placing her hands around my lapels she shook my collar up, then smoothed it, giving a tug on the tail of my jacket. *"There, hold on, your tie is too loose,"* and she pushed the knot up, and then straightened it. *"You'll do. Right Hazel, you just behave. Come on,"* and we were in.

Eyes seemed to follow me around. Hazel tonight did not look the kind of girl to go to village dances on a Saturday night, more like the type you would expect to be running a sideshow at the fairground telling fortunes! Her dress sense was out of place and she moved lazily around. The dignity we all showed to our elders was a mystery to her. Abigail and I danced a few tunes out, and sat at a table with Roger and his girl.

*"What would you prefer, tea or coffee?"* I asked the girls.

*"I'll get them,"* said Hazel, rising to her feet and grabbing the ten-shilling note from my hand. While she was being served, Mike, and Mark came in and sat with us four. Hazel arrived back with a tray of four coffees and a tea for me, along with four fancy cup cakes, and an egg sandwich.

*"Come on, move,"* were her first and only words to Mike and his mate, giving Mike's chair a good kick.

*"Here, steady on,"* he said as the vibrations passed through the chair into his body.

*"You get out of my chair. I'm sitting there now move it."* With that I said,

*"Hazel, quieten down and don't make a scene."*

*"Me!"* she exploded. *"That was my seat. I thought I was to be with you, not them!"* and looking at Mike she tilted the tray down at one end, throwing the tray and contents into my lap.

Every eye in the place turned to look as I got to my feet, tea, coffee, cup and saucers, buns, cakes, and egg falling to the ground. I stood steaming. Abigail was speechless, the two boys roared with glee.

*"You picked a good one there. Hope you can handle her. Wants a good seeing to if you ask me, but for God's sake don't, not here!"*

The faces turned to look the other way and I went to fetch a dustpan and brush from the women coming out of the kitchen door.

*"You poor love. Go out there and Elsie will help to clean you up,"* she said standing aside to allow me into the kitchen, *"I'll see to the mess."* Hazel was quite unperturbed by the entire goings on. Abigail was starting to cry and laugh

at the same time. So much for going to a local dance without too much fuss! A herd of cows in a town centre at mid-day would have made less of its presence known, as Hazel had done in one minute.

Abigail came out the back to see how I was and gave me a hug.

*"You sure know she is in town tonight,"* she said. Elsie asked,

*"Who is she and where did you meet her? It's not like you. Where's Kay?"*

With that a tear formed in my eye. Abigail saved the situation by putting a hand in Elsie's crooked arm and softly said,

*"She's history,"* while giving me a sly wink.

# CHAPTER SEVEN

The corn was ripening. The hay was in and the sheep were shorn. Two months now to the harvest so time to play. On the pier in a large town far from us that Saturday, there was to be a dance, a golden opportunity for us to dance in the summer. Kay could come as she had been warned by me of the forthcoming event and arranged to stay at Abigail's on the night in question. The news of Hazel had reached the ears of Kay's parents, and they were prepared to trust their daughter once again.

The location was far enough away from our home territory that we would not be recognised by anyone, our meeting would remain a secret.

\*\*\*

The evening was an idyllic one as we walked along the pier to the ballroom perched at the very end. Below the sea sparkled through the gaps in the decking. The sun still had that heat in it, as it arched its downward curve for the distant clash with the rim of the earth.

We slowly stepped our way over the joints in the wood, glancing down to the water far below, arm in arm, we were so much in love.

The room was packed with people enjoying themselves, and they tended to flock around the long bar that ran the width of the hall.

A large globe slowly rotated above our heads, covered in small pieces of mirror glass that reflected a pattern of glittering jewels of light all around. No one cared to dance so we had the floor to ourselves. What joy!

The band liked us and took us to their hearts. They started to play music more for our benefit than the hundreds of others gathered around. Kay loved it and so did I? Subconsciously we showed of to them. This was fast becoming our own private show and boy did we pump it for all it was worth!

Never before had we had a ten-piece band to ourselves, and an empty dance floor. She was a beautiful girl of just seventeen and I was only twenty. We had stamina. Nothing was going to get in our way. The sweat poured off me. I hated to think how my darling was coping with it. We must have shed pounds and Kay did not have much to start with.

The group played on and slowly the whole room turned their backs to the bar to watch us. The sequins on her waltz gown that she kept at Abby's dazzled the dark corners of the hall with light. The orchestra hardly let us get our breath back and the crowd went wild. We were the entertainment for the night. We danced as if our lives depended on it, the crowd loving every minute of the show. The odd couple would venture onto the floor to keep up with us, but we left them standing as we negotiated the turns on the corners. A Tango got the better of me and we rested for a break.

The evening flew by. Kay and I never bought a drink. They would suddenly arrive on the table we shared with another couple of elderly folk we did not know. The woman, who was partial to gin, polished the glasses off as they arrived. Kay, along with me, had a coca cola after her first gin, but word spread. *'She drinks*

*Gordon's!'* and so they kept coming. The old lady would smile and say. *"Mustn't let it go to waste!"* and poured it down her throat. The husband wanted to know how long we had been together, and where did we learn to dance like that. In his day his wife and he had always gone dancing up in London, now they were too old, but never had he seen such co-ordination as we had. Kay told him it came naturally and we practised a lot.

A man came up to find out who he should contact to hire us. He thought we were being paid to entertain them tonight! But we took little notice of other people, we were in love and wanted to be on our own.

Now that we had sat down, the tempo changed to twist, and that was not yet our strong point, so we sat them out. The floor filled up to flying arms and twirling sliding bodies. We left early.

\*\*\*

The sky had that blue/black of a summer's night look to it. The sun was far over the Atlantic and we had a perfect night. The glow of the town hid the stars up above. Kay was all in. Her body lay on me as we walked the long way along the pier to dry land and the car park. She said not a word until we had left the town far behind and the stars twinkled in the dark sky.

"Let's find our private place for an hour, it's only eleven now."

In silence with her snuggled up on the seat beside me, resting her head in my lap, we detoured home via the little village of Pett, taking the lane to the marsh into the valley of the little river that drained the surrounding hills.

Turning on to the farm track along the riverbank, we parked under an old overgrown hazel hedge, looking over the stream that was a river in the winter and flowed to the sea. She turned to me as I wound the widow down and said,

"Listen." The night was still after the dance floor. The silent air had no noise to it. Nothing. Then a fox barked up on the bank of the hill, and a heron announced his presence at the water's edge nearby. Then God let the music play. A nightingale close by started to sing to the accompaniment of the running water. Kay pulled her legs up under her side of the seat and snuggled up with such joy in her manner.

*"I'll take my tie, jacket and waistcoat off,"* I said as I opened the door to get out.

She shuffled around and her feet touched a parcel under the bench seat between us where I had placed a purchase the day before from the agricultural merchants. I got back in to ask her,

"What are you doing now?"

She had pulled the brown paper off used to wrap the purchases in, and was examining the twelve inch steel tube in her hands.

"What's this for?" she asked, twisting a length of rubber tube on one end around her finger.

"Leave that alone," I said. "It's not for you."

"It's a surprise for me, I know it is," and gave the tube another turn.

"No. Don't do that," I said as she started to unscrew the end of the four-inch tube with the hose attached.

"*What's inside?*"

"*Darling stop doing that.*"

Of course the more I said no, the more she was determined to do it. We tussled together on the green leather seat that still smelt new. Between our writhing bodies, she had the new grease gun I had bought from Mrs B the day before. '*I would like it filled up if I am to buy it,*' I had told her. "*Of course you do my boy,*" Mrs B had replied, and had got one of the men to fill it with high frequency melting point grease.

With a '*BLOP*' Kay had managed to undo the end. The two pints of red slimy contents exploded into its new freedom from the pressure of its prison. It went everywhere! Somehow a blob of it got on the windscreen but most of all it got us. She let the grease gun slide from her lap then burst out laughing.

"*I think you have overdone the Vaseline job,*" she quipped before she realised how bad it was.

Our clothes were covered and the more you moved, the more it seemed to spread. One drop of the stuff went far. We slid out of the car and stood there. We had to clean ourselves of this vicious jelly. First was get our clothes off, but as we had our hands full of the stuff, it got on everything we touched. Soon our bodies were naked but covered in slime. Kay's hair was plastered. We tried to wipe it off with our hands but only managed to spread it everywhere. We tried grass and looked a real picture as each handful stuck to us. Then we took to the water. That was fun! We lay down and splashed each other. We rolled on each other, hugged and kissed. It was no good, the ruddy stuff was waterproof! At last we got most of it off then the car was the centre of our attention. As we touched the grease, we spread it to anything else. It was terrible. If anyone had seen us, they would have died laughing. To us it was serious. Our clothes were ruined and we had a fight to just hug each other. We slipped all ways. The thought of making love was far away.

"*The only way to remove this is sand and sea water,*" I said, so we slipped, really slipped, naked into the car and I slowly drove to the coast. We could not go fast as the steering wheel was so slippery. I had found an empty sack in the back that Kay wrapped herself in. For once we were in luck. The tide was out and the sand beckoned. The water was warm thank God. We sat and rubbed each other with sand while Kay giggled.

"*Who says we never have any fun?*" she said. Her body felt smooth and soft.

After thirty minutes we were very happy with the results, but her hair was a mess and we both smelt of oil. I put my clean jacket on her and with the empty sack from the back of the car for her to sit on, we managed to negotiate the road to Abigail's.

*** 

Abigail was still waiting up for us and soon had Kay in the bath with lovely smelling bath salts. I stood waiting my turn for the tub, standing on an old newspaper Abby had found, clothed in the smelly sack, with instructions from

Abby *'not to move!'* Kay had the door shut now, her composure had returned with the presence of Abigail. Before, we had both been naked without a thought to it. Now we were more civilized. Kay came out of the door first, wrapped in towels. Abigail followed with the comment.

"It will never catch on, it stinks. You should buy the right stuff if you must use it, now the bath's all yours."

The tap was running to fill the bath as I dropped the well-used sack and entered the glorious warm soapy water. Soon a steaming cup of coffee awaited me in the kitchen, where Kay sat in a blouse and skirt of Abigail's. I had to make do with the bath towel like Tarzan.

"You two had a good night then, but what a pickle you got in! What were you doing with that dangerous thing in the car? It could have killed Kay."

"She would not put it down! It's harmless unless you do something stupid like undo the end when it's full up!"

Kay burst into tears. She was only now realizing the outcome.

"You had better go now, look at the poor girl," said Abby.

I left in my sack to the *'comfort'* of the greasy car and drove home. I crept in and went to bed but could not sleep. The sun was coming up for another lovely day. So I made a start on the car. I had forgotten about the clothes in the back and was glad I had got up early, for if mum had seen Kay's knickers, bra and frock, I hate to think what she would have said! Along with my shirt I hid them in the cupboard out in the cowshed. It was easier now that daylight had come. I could see what I was doing. I now found my trousers in a sticky pile in the back of the car. They, with the aid of a stick, soon found their way to the cupboard. Armed with a lot of gunk that we used to clean oil from engines, I soon had the car grease free. The gun I slung in the workshop, now rather empty, and thought back on last night's fun and games.

***

I made an early start up to Abigail's. I had to return her clothes. The girls were out in the back garden having breakfast as I drew up.

"*Hi. Coffee?*" Abigail shouted for the entire town to hear. "*Come and join us. Kay's been telling me all about last night. You know she was asleep as soon as you went. You will wear the poor thing out at this rate.*"

"*It was rather a good night, but I could have done without the last two hours of it. Look I have got your clothes here,*" throwing a bag down on the patio steps.

"*Careful,*" Kay said. "*That's a new dress.*"

"*Was,*" I said. *You should see it now!*"

"*What am I going to do? Dad will want some answers if he sees that,*" she murmured, peering into the sack. "*Look at these,*" she cried, pulling her bra out and trying to hide it from my view in her embarrassment.

"*You hit the wrong spot,*" said Abigail. "*Grease goes down below!*" Kay dropped her garment back into the bag. "*It's horrid. Look at my hands.*" The sea and sand had made her soft hands very coarse, to say nothing of her long nails.

"*I never want to see grease again in my life.*"

"Don't worry. He will buy you new clothes won't you?" said Abby looking at me.

"Yes, of course," I said, feeling rather smug, as I knew all shops to be closed on a Sunday. *"But you will have to wait until the shops open."*

*"No she can't. I'm too small for her. She's a D cup and I'm a B."* This meant nothing to me. I did not know then that they went in cup size, just big and small was all I knew of such things. *"How much money have you got on you?"* Abigail asked. I produced my wallet and she grabbed it. *"Wow! Look at these fivers!"* she said, and started to count the five pound notes, going on to the one pound and ten shilling notes. *"Well no wonder they say you are a millionaire, look! There's over eighty pounds. Right I know where there are shops open on a Sunday, but we will have to get our skates on. Come on. You're paying."* She jumped to her feet, still clutching my wallet, *"Kay go and get a jumper it could be cold. You get the car turned round London here we come!"*

"Where" I said, as the girls disappeared indoors?

"You heard".

"I hope this car is clean now," she said as she got into the back.

Kay who was getting in the front, gingerly looked under the seat and made her self at home, not caring about the leather seat that now had a good shine to it, as she was wearing Abigail's jeans which were skin tight and hugged her hips.

*"Kay, I've told my dad we are going out for the day so if your parents ring dad they will not worry."*

"Where to" I said.

*"London"* Abigail repeated herself. *"It's that way,"* pointing her finger across my face.

"I know where it is," I said *"but the shops will be closed in the city as well."*

*"It's not the shops we are after, it's new gear for your girl."*

Kay turned to talk over her shoulder.

*"Where do you know of shops that sell clothes on a Sunday?"*

*"Carnaby Street of course you my girl are going to get with it."*

"Where the hell is Carnaby Street?" I asked.

*"You drive. It's far beyond you to know anything like that. You're not with us yet, but Kay will drag you into the twentieth century. We were only saying the other day how slow on the uptake you are. I cannot believe you don't know where it is!"*

"I hope you do," I said.

*"We'll find it, we'll ask someone first Trafalgar Square, that way."*

"I know. I go to London with the fish and scrap sometimes with my brother. I know the way to the Strand and Nelson's Column."

***

When we eventually got there the place was alive, more like an Arabian Bazaar than the capital of Britain. Pop music deafened you and the clothes racks looked more like a jumble sale. The place heaved with the dropouts of society. 'These were the first real hippies I had seen. The girls had no scruples at all. I hoped Kay would behave herself. Abigail was soon at home. So this is where she got it all from, her funny ways and sayings? The Tweed suit I was wearing, right down to the tweed tie around my neck, got a lot of comments from the passing throngs.

"*Way out man!*" and things like that. What really got them was my Deer Stalker hat that I was never without and the way I spoke.

"*Don't mind them,*" Abigail said.

"*Here, that's what you want Kay.*"

I looked away, they were '*women things,*' not to be held up to the light for every one to see, and you could see, '*through them*'.

***

We returned home late in the afternoon with bags and parcels. My wallet was seventy pounds lighter, a small fortune had been spent on the '*right gear,*' and I was not sure that Kay's parents were going to take to the mixed collection she had got. Abigail had accrued three blouses and given me a kiss on the forehead for them.

"*You are a dear,*" she said as I had handed the money over. The problem still remained of the paper bag with all Kay's spoilt clothes now lying out in the garden.

"*Don't worry. We will have them cleaned at the laundry and you can pay the bill,*" Abigail said.

***

As we were enjoying a bit of late tea, Kay's mother turned up to collect her. I hid in the toilet as she came in.

"*You are late. Have you not eaten yet?*"

"*Yes, all finished mother, I'll get my things.*"

Kay rose from her chair and rushed upstairs, I thought to get the clothes she had purchased earlier, and a cold shiver ran down my spine but she reappeared in an instant with all her homework books that she was supposed to have been studying over the weekend. "*See you Abigail*" and she left. I peered out of the door.

"*You can come out now, she's gone,*" said Abigail.

"*Lucky I parked around the back. If she had seen the car, she would have known.*"

"*You worry too much!*" "*As Kay, says, you'll end up with ulcers the way you go on,*" Abby told me.

***

Kay did not take the grease plastered remains or new clothes with her, but instead went home in her school uniform which she had changed into that she had worn from school to Abby's on Friday.

"*Then what was all the hurry for, and the money it cost?*" I asked Abby.

"*Well old bean. You have got to pay for all the fun Kay gives you, and her underwear was ruined. You are a very lucky boy having that girl, she loves you and will do anything for you, so you pay!*"

***

I saw Kay for ten minutes in the following five days, as she got off the school bus. Nothing had been said about the weekend, the parents hadn't suspected a thing, though her mother had said she could not remember seeing her underwear before when she put it in the wash!

***

All seemed quiet on the parent front. That was until the weekend. Then the balloon went up. Abigail phoned in one of her flaps.

"*Come up now! It's urgent! There's a real crisis.*"

There goes Abigail, another panic, I thought.

***

I fed the pigs first, (you have to get these things in priority!) and it was ten thirty am before I arrived at her home.

"*What's up?*" I said.

"*It's all 'up', as you put it!*" she replied. "*Look at this!*" shoving the local weekend paper at me.

There on page three, for the entire world to see, was a lovely clear picture of Kay and me at the dance last Saturday night. On the top was the caption, '*They stole the Show.*'

"That's fucked it!" she said. "*Kay's dad has this every weekend and if he doesn't see it, someone will. Look! It is a wonderful picture of you two. Why did you let them take the photo?*"

"Who" I said. "*I never knew. There was a lot of noise and a lot of people their taking photos. I never dreamed one would be in the paper. What's it got to say? Surely no one knew our names? I'll sue them.*"

"No good doing that now the cat's out of the bag."

"*What do they say?*" Have you read it?

"*Yes. The dance was in aid of a children's home and thanks to two show offs they raised a record amount.*"

"How much?"

"*It doesn't say. Just that they would like to thank you for your support they thought it a wonderful gesture to put a display on especially for them. They are asking anyone that knows you, to contact them.*"

"Gosh! What paper is that? Oh, the Sussex Express. God that paper goes all over Sussex and parts of Kent."

"*Yes and they are sure to hear of it.*"

"Shut up Abigail, let's think."

"*I have and there's nothing we can do now. Everyone's had theirs delivered. You can't buy them all up!*"

"Kay must be warned."

"*That's taken care of stupid! I phoned her first before you, she has stolen the page out of her father's paper. He was out when it came she'll be here on the twelve o clock bus.*"

Kay was in tears when she saw me.

61

"Dad is sure to be told. It is such a nice photo of you. I'm not going home tonight. I don't care what they say. Mum will kill me when she finds out. You will go to prison and it's all my fault."

"Oh Kay, calm down. We'll think something up, if the worst comes to the worst you can stay here, you know that," said Abby.

"Please darling, don't leave me alone tonight," Kay said, clinging to my neck. "Please you must stay all night."

"Ok but I have to get to work now but I will see you at seven darling."

*\*\**

That night I got to Abigail's at a quarter past, a bit late as I hid the car at a mate's and walked just in case anyone saw it parked near the house, and Kay's parents got to hear. The girls could not wait to tell me as I arrived. Abigail had phoned home to be told by my mother that I had left over half an hour before.

"Have I news for you," she said. "Kay's mum and dad know."

Over six people had phoned by two o clock, they could not stop singing praises to them to have such a kind hearted girl to go all that way and to give a display of her graceful dancing for the children's home. Obviously they had brought her up well, no matter who the lad was. He had a good heart as well. So the storm passed her parents knew she was my girl for life, I hoped.

## CHAPTER EIGHT

Abigail had got an invitation to a friend's wedding. She knew the bride very well and had written to her asking if Kay could have one as well. What a cheek that girl had! Kay's arrived within a few days along with *'Please come and bring a friend.'* That was the point of the request as I was to be the taxi and she could not ask me without Kay.

\*\*\*

The wedding was at two pm on a Saturday in August at St Mark's in a small village in West Sussex, a long way from home. Kay's parents agreed she could go as Abigail's guest, not knowing their daughter also had an invitation cleverly sent, care of Abigail, so as not to arouse suspicion. Abigail was anything but crafty and we loved her to bits.

Kay had arrived at Abigail's by the time I got there. She could go as Abby's guest but had to promise her parents that she would not try and see me. *"That had been easy,"* she said because she didn't have to try at all! The trip was uneventful, we arrived at their friend's house to change at twelve forty five, plenty of time for the girls to get out of their jeans into the clothes for the wedding and put all their make-up on. Kay looked as gorgeous as anyone there, dressed in a knee length light blue skirt with a low cut blouse. Her gold cross and chain around her neck showed off her bosom, and she wore light brown stockings and beige two inch heel sling back shoes. She was wearing Stephanotis perfume, had done her eyes with light blue eye shadow and smelt lovely. I stuck to my Brut after-shave. It was arranged that we would stop the night down there with the school friend they knew from their days at boarding school.

\*\*\*

The little church was packed but no one knew who I was and could not make up their minds as to which girl I was with. The reception was held in a large marquee on a field to the back of the bride's house. Around two hundred people were assembled as the speeches were read. An old man took a shine to Kay and would not take no for an answer until Abigail sidled up to him and made a proposition to him about something, after which he left in a hurry! She would not tell us what she had said, but Kay said she knew, anyway it worked!

\*\*\*

The groom was in the Royal Guards and a lot of his mates were there all showing off to their girls. As the evening dragged on a band appeared and started to play our sort of music. There was a wooden floor to dance on so Kay and I got it working. The evening was coming to an end, darkness was approaching, and we were lost in our own private world. Then shouts and screams brought us back to reality as a drunken horseman charged into the tent and attempted to jump one of the long trestle tables. Everything went flying, people were diving under tables and crawling out underneath the sides. It was uproar. The music stopped as the band took cover. The mounted guardsman was revelling in all the attention, with a frightened horse that he had obtained from the paddock next door. He was creating mayhem. We were not the first or last to leave, Abigail was in tears. What would her friend think? It had spoilt her wedding.

***

We arrived at the house we were to stay at for the night to find it locked and empty. We sat talking in the car for half an hour when our hostess, Marion, turned up in a red sports car with her drunken boyfriend.

"*Wow. What a party. You must be Kay's boyfriend, giving me a good look over. Come in Abigail.*" "*You!*" she said to Brian, her intoxicated partner. "*To bed, I'll see you in the morning!*" Then turning to Abby she said "*Come on in, Kay, this must be preacher, handsome bugger! I see what the attraction is! I have heard all about you, it is so unfair the way her parents are treating you pair. No one down this part of the world knows you and there are no newspapers to worry about either. I gather you don't drink, so what can I get you?*"

"*A nice cup of tea,*" I said, stopping Abigail from saying '*he drinks coffee.*' The three girls sat down and I cuddled Kay on the sofa as we talked the day's events over.

"*That bloody yob on that horse has wrecked the place,*" said Marion. "*You should see it now. The only way they could stop him was to pull the tent down. The horse went mad.*" Then looking at us she asked, "*When are you two getting hitched?*" Kay went red. Obviously Abigail had been talking.

"We are going to wait a while," I said.

"*No, go for it, shack up in Brighton or somewhere, it's all the rage now.*"

"When are you getting married?" I asked.

"*Not to that slob, he is rich but not my type really.*" "*You look as if you have a bob or two, that big car is new.*"

"That's his dad's not his," said Kay, "and I love him, not his money."

"*Hmm. You say that now but the old filthy lucre is handy. Abigail, you will have to have the sofa, they can have the spare room.*"

Kay was nearly asleep and Abigail looked all in so I slept downstairs and the girls shared the bed upstairs. Yes I really was that slow and dim! The modern age was rapidly taking over our lives now. The opportunity to hop in and out of bed would not be missed by many and an invitation like that was tempting but unlike today we two were brought up in another age, we respected each other. I loved Kay and the temptation to make love was something I knew deep down could not be suppressed forever, but tonight no. What would our parents say? My mother would whip me then disown me. Her life would be in tatters. We could wait our turn. We had a lot of living to do and bedding a girl only led to trouble. Kay and I had often spoken in about it and had agreed that we could wait as we both shared the same views. Kay hugged me and we lingered that night in a tight embrace out side her bedroom door. Time slipped by so swiftly neither could keep our hands from each other but we both knew we must behave, Abby's call,

"*Are you two going to stand out side that door all night or what? Good night Preacher!*" brought the pair of us back to reality. The door closed behind her and

I made my way down the stairs to the sofa.

\*\*\*

Next morning after breakfast and saying thank you to our host, we left before Brian woke from his drunken sleep. The sun was well up and another hot day was in prospect. Kay had caught the bride's bouquet, and had left it in the car overnight. She wished to place the bouquet on a grave. It was not going to travel very well in this heat so we made tracks back to St Mark's. On finding a grave of a girl only nineteen, our age, she laid the flowers. As we all said a silent prayer for the life that was taken so young, a woman and two men stood and watched us. I was the first to speak.

"*I'm sorry but they would wilt in the car on the way home. My girls thought it only right to place them here, for she was so young.*"

"A sweet idea, that is. Her mother will be so thrilled to know that her friends still think of her." We left the trio in their mistaken knowledge that we were her friends. I mused over in my mind that perhaps God had given Kay the idea and sent the locals there so they told her mother, to give her a little cheer on this bright day to compensate for her sad loss. He does work in mysterious ways. We shall never know who the girl was in that grave.

\*\*\*

On the way home, Abigail got around to the subject discussed last night of weddings, and asked when we going to get engaged. Kay's parents could do nothing to stop us getting engaged, but to marry they would have to give their consent before she was twenty one, the legal age to do so. As she was still only seventeen, it would be all of four years till then. She had cried herself to sleep last night, '*so much in love,*' it wasn't fair. I managed to change the subject by saying how beautiful she had looked in that blue skirt.

"*Did you like my nail varnish? It's new.*" With that the contents of her handbag were shot out on the seat between us. Then she started to line up an array of little bottles of different colour varnish on the dashboard, one at a time to show me. One of the containers fell over, rolled to the windscreen and deposited its contents into the air vent.

"*Put it away, it stinks!*"

"*They all smell the same,*" said Abigail in the back, with her head stuck between us.

We arrived home early, as we did not know the whereabouts of Kay's parents. I left, arranging to see her on Wednesday at the newly formed dressmaking group. The only reason both of us enrolled was that it was another evening Kay would be let out on her own giving us the chance to meet. We were heavy into making our own girl's costumes for dancing. I got the sequins from a shop in Ashford, along with ribbons, lace and the lead buttons for the hems. I also bought the exotic underwear like frilly knickers and strapless bras for Kay and Abby to wear. Kay's mum would have gone mad if she had seen them. It felt safer to do my shopping away from home, as our town was small. Every one knew every one else, and word could have got back to the parent that Kay wore this or that. It was not the case that the girls could not have done that type of shopping, more the case that I paid. The items were kept in a cardboard laundry box with a leather strap around it at Abigail's, only to come out when we danced, away from home.

\*\*\*

On Wednesday Kay and Abigail were already there. I was the only male in the place. The women flocked around me to give advice on how best to do this and that, but there was not much I did not know about sewing as unknown to the teachers, we had been at it for some time and Kay was very handy with a machine. Little did they know it was all a big cover up to see each other?

\*\*\*

We left early and dropped Abigail off at the bottom of Mermaid Street leaving her to climb the cobble stoned hill home, then made our way to a track leading to a wood that we both knew. Secluded and off the beaten way, we came here often. As the last bus to Kay's was at eleven, we could not afford to be late. To tell us to hurry up I had a large brass alarm clock. The bus from the village hall took twenty minutes to her stop where one of her parents would meet her. Our hideaway was only just over one minute to the last stop but one to her home, so if she caught the bus there, she was able to alight in front of her parents. The good old drivers never once asked her for the three pence fare and her parents never asked the driver where their girl had got on, so we had twenty more minutes in each other's arms.

\*\*\*

I kept the two-bell brass alarm clock, under the seat and wound it up each night. This old clock worked well stood outside my door. We only heard the alarm ring and the tick was soft. All was well until one night in the winter after a dance we fell asleep in each other's arms. Kay stirred first and looking at her wristwatch cried. *"Look at the time!"* The timepiece had let us down rather badly, it was twelve thirty! Starting the engine I reversed and there was a crunch. No more was that clock going to tick or tock! In the haste I had forgotten about it.

*"Too late now,"* I said as Kay hurried to rearrange her clothes. *"They will kill me!"* she said. A plan was called for and as Abigail was ill, it was no good saying she was there. Only one thing to do, phone from the box down the road and say you missed the last bus. *"Take your shoes off and ladder your stockings, I'll buy you new ones, and tell them you had to take your shoes off to walk as the high heels were hurting. You tried to phone at the village but the phone was out of order. By the time you got to Josephine's house, all the lights were out and you did not want to wake them up. This is the next phone you passed and could they come and get you?"* It worked like a charm. Their poor girl had to walk five miles in the dark barefoot carrying her shoes on her own. How could they not have come to find her? But they had been sure she was with that *'marsh lad.'* How wrong could they be? They were so sorry that they let her out on Friday night to go to the cinema with a friend, but waited as usual until the girls were in the door before leaving. The friend was no less than Josephine and when she met

Kay still with her mother waiting, she said right on cues,

"*Did I hear you the other night softly calling my name? We were all in bed.*" That was the icing on the cake, thanks to Abigail, who had heard next day all about the flat alarm clock and had a good giggle on us. Josephine had learned her line perfectly. More ammo for our guns and we were to need it later that night as Kay's mothers parting words were *"I'll pick you up at eleven."*

\*\*\*

The girls had no intentions of going to see a film. Josephine went to a friend's house, to talk about tennis, as that is all she ever did. Kay and me had other plans. Earlier I had driven up to our pub where all our mates were playing darts on Friday night as usual. There I swapped cars with Mark and left mine in a conspicuous position that Kay's mother was sure to see on her way to pick Kay up later. I was parked opposite the cinema and as soon as Kay's mother vanished, the two girls came out, having never paid to get in. Then it was to Abigail's for the evening. We parked around the back of the church and entered the kitchen by the back door.

"*In here,*" called Abigail, and her sister held the door open for us as she was just leaving. "*Made it all right then?*" No problems?

"No. Like clockwork."

"*I will see you two lovebirds later,*" she said as she left the house. It was warm and the lamp cast only a glow within the room. Kay and I could not keep our hands off each other. We hugged and petted each other. We had only been at it for ten minutes when the doorbell rang. Abigail's dad, who always sat in his study, answered it.

"*Hello Mrs. Daws.*" "*Come in. I'll get my wife, in here,*" and the door handle turned.

"*Christ! It's your mother. Quick!*" Obviously Abigail's dad did not know we were there, or had the sense not to say anything or he would have been dead meat. As the door opened we gathered up our clothes and dashed to the bay window that had a thick curtain drawn before it. Just in time we made the safety of the space offered there. We heard Kay's mum picking things up and putting them down as she awaited Abigail's mother. "*Looking for dust?*" said Kay in a whisper. I had a job not to laugh but I valued my life! Abigail's mum was also unaware that we were in the room. They started to talk together and what was the top of the agenda? We were! Hiding only ten feet away, we heard it all from Kay's mother's lips. How their poor girl had had to walk home the other night, and that boy! How she hated me. They were so sure that they had control of their daughter, not like some people she could name, but won't, a dig at Abigail's mum if ever I heard one. The virtues of their little girl were above reproach and on hearing that, Kay opened her blouse, which I had unbuttoned on meeting and let her breasts poke out as a silent gesture to her mother. I put my hand in my mouth to stop myself from laughing. Two fingers would have been ample, I thought. How we did not move or make a sound, I'll never know! I think fear of her mother had a lot to do with it!

"*Would you like a cup of coffee?*" Always coffee in that house I mused.

"*Yes please. I'll help you,*" and they both left for the kitchen.

We saw our chance. With Kay's bra and knickers, which I had only just managed to gather up from the floor in our haste to hide, stuffed in my trouser pocket, we peered out of the open door. The parents were busy in the kitchen. The stairs were taken two at a time on our toes.

"*Where's Abigail's room?*" I said as we made the landing.

"*In here,*" and we were safe. Abigail was lying on her bed flat out on her belly with her hands cupping her face and legs bent up at the knees reading.

"*Sorry darlings it's taken,*" looking up in surprise as we shut the door. I flopped on the bed beside her completely exhausted. Kay slumped back against the closed door.

"*Close or what?*" Then I burst out laughing. "*Shut up,*" Kay said in a stiff voice, they will hear.

"*Who?*" Abigail flipped back.

"*My mother she's downstairs with your mum,*" and her voice went up another octave. "*Your dad only ushered her into the room we were in. We lucky we weren't caught. God I could have died!*"

"*Where did you go?*" asked Abigail.

"*Into the alcove of the front window, we hid behind the curtain.*"

"*Gosh, wish I had been there!*"

"*No you don't. You should hear what my mother had to say.*"

"*You heard what they said? Come on, spill it.*"

"*No not now. Keep the noise down.*"

"*I had to smile Kay when your mum said they had you under their control and you were virtuous.*"

"*She's what?*" said Abigail.

"*Virtuous!*" "*And guess what Kay did? Only stuck her tits out at her I nearly died on the spot!*"

"*Well she asked for it. I'm old enough to have some fun I am nearly eighteen.*"

"*Not tonight darling. Keep the noise down I said, or we will all be copped.*"

"*How are we going to get out if my mother stays till its time to pick me up from the cinema?*"

"*Out of the window, we can slide down the roof to the bench in the garden,*" I said. "*It's not very high,*" and that is the way we escaped, down the moss covered roof in the dark, making no noise. Then to Mark's car and down town to the cinema as the folk came out. Kay stood waiting like the virtuous girl until her mother drove up.

"*Good girl. Come on, I'm tired. I called in Abigail's and could not get away, now I wish to go home. Your father will be wondering where I have got to. Abigail is much better now but that woman, I don't know how I can stand her, dust everywhere and that front room, right on the pavement! You could hear a courting couple outside the window. I nearly went to the window to tap on the glass to shoo them away.*"

All this time I was in Mark's car, parked alongside them crouching low behind the wheel. Kay's mother looked behind to make sure it was safe to drive on, and let the clutch out with such a hurry that the car shot forward throwing Kay back into the seat. I followed a long way behind them to the pub where I pulled up and reversed alongside my car and went around the back. The gang was playing cards as I entered.

"*How did my car go then? Nice isn't it plenty of room in the back?*"

"*I wouldn't know,*" I said. "*I never got that far.*"

"*Hope there's no surprises tucked away and she took everything with her. Good was it? With that my hand flashed to my pocket. Yes I still had the small item in my trousers pocket. If only they could see what I fumbled within my fingers.*"

\*\*\*

A few days later I noticed a mark down the roof of Abigail's house. The whole area was covered in moss apart from a strip from her window to the gutter. I later learnt it took Kay an hour to get her bottom clean, as her bare bum had been stained green. The mark showing our getaway was visible for many years to anyone who looked, and is still so, even today. I imagine I can see that scar and my mind snaps back to when we were young. But it only hurts for a little while!

## CHAPTER NINE.

One night Kay and I were in a hurry to get to the bus stop, again ahead of her usual stop where her father would be waiting for her to alight after a night out with a supposed girlfriend. Instead I stood in as always for the friend. Kay on this night was wearing a knee length pleat skirt of tweed made from three yards I had bought two years previously in the mountain land up north on one of my annual forays.

The night was dry and dark, not a ray of light shone from the cloud-laden sky. I forget where we had been, but we were late and I had my foot down in the mini pick up. As we tore along the marsh road, a hare ran out into our path. Kay screamed. *"Don't hit it!"* so I swerved right to miss the creature. Minis in those days had a strap running the width of the door that you pulled to open the door and as I had swerved, her hand inadvertently grabbed this handle. As I swung back to the left side of the road and straightened out the door came open and poor Kay was jettisoned out. I trod on the foot brake, sliding to a noisy halt. I ran back along the road to find my girl lying in a ditch full of water, sobbing her heart out.

*"Look at me. I'm all wet!"*

*"Are you hurt?"*

*"Yes. My knees and elbows, they hurt."* She had hit the road on all fours, then somehow bounced onto the grass verge and slid into the ditch. I offered her my hands and dragged her out. *"Look at me. What happened? My stockings! Look at the blood."*

*"It's all right darling."* I said. *"You can always have more stockings, how are your legs?"*

\*\*\*

She squelched along the road to stand in front of the headlights while I cleaned her knees with my shirt. Luckily the wounds on her arms and legs were no more than grazes. It looked a lot worse than it was. Her tweed skirt had soaked a fair bit of ditch up in it, and she dripped like a miniature waterfall. My poor Kay was in a sorry state. Now there was no hope of overtaking the bus she was supposed to be on. How was she to explain to her parents the state she was in? I shivered with no shirt, as there was no heating to talk of in vans then. A plan had to be hatched and quick. Abigail was away at the time and so she was going to be unable to help. Kay's parents would be on the lookout for her anyway as soon as the bus arrived without her. The pub was the only answer. A mate could be bought perhaps to take her home in this condition and say he found her after she had slipped into a dyke.

I now hurried as fast as the poor little van would go and Kay locked the door for safety. Hares or anything on the way would have to take their chance with our four speeding wheels. Pulling into the car park, I was relieved to see two familiar vehicles. Kay refused to get out in the unladylike looking attire she found herself in. The bar was empty except for my two mates.

"What the hell's happened to you Preacher? Where is your shirt"?
"No time for that now." Who wants to earn some money, fast?"
"What's the catch preacher? How much?"
"Whatever it costs, but now you Wimple you have an old van outside and a bit of stinking ditch water won't go amiss."
"Bloody hell what's the job?"
"It's Kay. We had an accident, she fell out of the van into a Kent ditch and is rather wet. She was supposed to be on the last bus."
"You have got trouble then. One day you are going to get caught."
"Yes, but not now. I want you to take her home and say you rescued her, and if they ask, say I was at whatever pub you like, but not around here, for goodness sake! They may even give you a medal. Now, how much are you going to charge me?"
"Five pounds how's that?" The other lad at the bar chipped in.
"Make it ten and I'll go as well to back his story up."
"All right hurry up. Her father will go by in a minute looking for her if she's not on the bus. I am parked out the front and Kay is inside."
"Come on Alan, leave that!" He was trying to down a pint of bitter in record time and most of it was missing his mouth. Wimple opened the van door. Kay was reluctant to go with them looking as she did. She had removed her stockings to reveal two nasty gravel grazed legs and blood oozed through her torn blouse from her arms. They left with Kay in the passenger seat of Wimple's van and Alan in the back. I parked my mini round the back of the inn and went in the pub to await my mate's return, then as I looked out of the window the late bus went by, running late for a change. I prayed my pals got their story together with Kay. They pulled up as the bus pulled away from the stop, having allowed the bus to overtake them across the marsh. Her father stood anxiously, pondering where his daughter was. Kay got out and ran to her dad as Alan climbed out of the back doors.

"We found her in this state she was run off the road running for that bus."
"Who ran her over?"
"No-one daddy, I slipped."
"All right boys, what's the truth?"
"A car came by close in the dark and she fell in the water."
"Is that right Kay?"
"Yes dad."
"Get in, look at you. Thank you," he said to the lads and walked around his car, got in and drove away.

They came bounding in the pub full of themselves.
"We did it. Where's our money? Come on. Pay up."
I paid up on the nail and hoped to hear no more, but it was not to end there. The time now was ten fifty and time to close but the boys wanted a drink as well as their ten pounds so Gerry, the owner behind the bar, pulled two pints of bitter and locked the door.

Ten minutes later there was a banging on the door. *"POLICE! OPEN UP."*

*"Shit!"* said Alan, slopping half his beer down his front again as Gerry opened up.

*"Have you got the two boys here? Ah, good!"* Wimple physically shrank in his boots.

*"What do you want us for? We've done nothing wrong."*

*"It's all right boys. We're not here to arrest you for drinking after hours. You picked a young girl up earlier and took her home didn't you?" "Her father phoned to report a car being driven dangerously. Now did you see it happen?"*

*"No!"* they both answered together.

*"Can you give us any idea how it happened and could you show us where it happened?"*

*"Not really, it was sort of out on the marsh."* Their faces went deep red.

*"You hiding something are you lad?"* So they told them all and involved me. God I prayed that the police would not remember the court order hanging over me, and tell Kay's dad or I would surely go to prison. As it happened, the officers had been my age once and understood, or at least did not pass my name onto Kay's dad.

***

That Friday the weather was very cold, winter was here with a vengeance. We had been having sharp frosts for three weeks now and we had a dusting of snow, there was no sign of a thaw. Mother had been to Ashford to do her Christmas shopping with a friend. It was late when she returned in the car, with the excuse that the lights had gone out unexpectedly while driving. So she had taken it slow the entire thirty miles home. Father said. *"Of course they had,"* and left it at that. The car was a new light blue, trimmed in chrome, Vauxhall Victor Estate with green leather bench seats and column gearshift, a pretty looking car and fast, easily doing seventy miles per hour.

***

Next day I had use of the car for the whole day. The weather was sunny but cold. That night Kay and I were to go dancing in Brighton with a couple of our friends. We had decided to have the whole day in the town exploring all the lanes and doing a bit of sightseeing at the Pavilion. I drove to Northiam to our friends that Kay had made her way to by bus, and the four of us took the route inland to Brighton away from the busy A259 coast road that I knew well.

***

The morning passed quickly, and I treated everyone to lunch in a restaurant on the seafront. All four of us had fish and chips with bread and butter, on a plate, a real treat, but I made the fatal mistake of letting darling Kay see into my wallet as I paid the waiter.

*"Gosh, look at all the money Preacher's got there!"* That was it, Kay had told Jonathan's girl of my generosity to her and that I could never refuse her. So the girls planned the afternoon shopping, back to the lanes and into every shop. Kay now had control of my wallet as her and Daphne left Jonathan and I outside a

dress shop, for it was considered a woman's environment only, gentlemen were not encouraged into the interior. Now my darling had the chance to count the notes and calculate the amount she and Daphne could reasonably spend without making me bankrupt. From two pm there was no stopping her. A large hug, kiss and a few flashes of her eyelids and I was hers to pay, or at least my wallet was, and for safekeeping, she put it into her handbag and zipped it in. Jonathan and I found an ice cream bar and made ourselves comfortable to await the girls. I had a large Knickerbocker Glory and he had a fruit sundae. We drank cups of espresso coffee from clear glass cups stamped on the bottom with the word 'Durex', which we discussed at length and came to the conclusion that they must be of foreign manufacture, as they obviously did not know that the word had a different meaning in the UK! The girls met up with us again at five pm.

Three hours of my wallet had purchased a considerable amount of bags and boxes so we made our way back to the car to deposit the wares in the boot. On lifting the back door what should greet me but two sacks of barley that father had left in from the night before after feeding the pigs. So if you were ever in Brighton in December that year and saw the pigeons feeding ankle deep in corn as it got light the next morning, that is where we parked, for we emptied and scattered the proctor barley around on the ground. We then used the empty sacks to cover from prying eyes the girls' 'gifts,' as they classed the heap of parcels resting in the back. Now down to the job in hand, the dance.

It was the quarterfinals for the south east of England British Dance School. The girls' frocks and our suits hung from the clothes hooks in the back so grabbing the covers, off we went to the Grand Hotel on the sea front. Over three hundred and sixty people attended and there were fifty-eight couples to compete against.

Half were knocked out quickly and it was nine pm before we took the floor for the third time that night. Jonathan and Daphne had not made it this far. Kay and I danced the waltz, quickstep and foxtrot and got a standing applause for our tango. That was it, we were told that as we had scored top marks, there was no point in us carrying on tonight. We were already through. Kay was thrilled! The next venue was to be Blackpool, the *'top of the pile'* so to speak. I was overjoyed that this girl and I had come so far in the years together and to make matters even better, she and I were in love.

The problem now was how were we to compete all that way away in Lancashire? But that could wait. So many of the competing pairs were neither sweethearts nor married, just good friends that danced together. We were especially lucky. We four left, still dressed in our finery and carried our ordinary dress gear and Kay's Waltz gown in the bags over our shoulders. We strolled along the seafront in couples, leaving our footsteps in the powdery dust now scurrying on the wind that was trying hard to be snow. It was cold and we hugged each other to try and keep warm. Kay remarked that she must be mad to step out in the sling back dancing shoes and short tango skirt she was wearing, for she had a good lace-up pair of stout shoes and skirt in the bag slung over my shoulder. But love and the intoxicated state we were in from winning seemed to take all our self-preservation away!

***

The car was easy to spot as the barley grain shone in the lamplight of the street. Starting the engine, we left Brighton behind with the heater on full blast. As we got further east on our journey home, so the white powder of Brighton turned to real snow. High on top of Beachy Head the wind howled. The snow came in large wet lumps to slide down the windscreen, then Eastbourne lower down, and the shelter of the town. As we drove across Pevensey Marsh it told a story of what to expect back home on Romney Marsh. All was white.

Kay shifted her head from its usual place on my lap and wriggled around in her tango skirt. Daphne was snug in the back with Jonathan hidden under her waltz gown. They looked an odd couple on the back seat all wrapped up in the huge dress, unrecognisable as human beings. Kay was in her short red tango outfit, small blouse and fishnet stockings that stopped at the top to show the suspender strap atop her marvellous legs which were now shoeless. She rested against the doorpost and went to sleep.

***

On reaching Bexhill the road was covered with one inch of the white stuff. We carried onto Hastings where I turned off the A259 for Northiam to return the two girls and Jonathan home. I now knew the road well. I soon took a lane as a short cut, the road dipped down to a little bridge over a stream. As I approached at approximately twenty miles an hour, in one inch of snow, the world turned to darkness.

The car's lights had failed! I felt the car start to ride up the bank on my left where Kay lay slumped against the doorpost fast asleep. I corrected to the right to find the lane, there was a nasty crash and a scaffold pole rushed between a sleeping Kay and me to embed in the back seat alongside the two dozing there.

Kay awoke with a start to find all the lights back on. The impact with the little post and rail fence had halted our progress in a hurry.

"Everyone okay I asked.

"*Yep,*" replied Jonathan in the back and I put the car in reverse to see the black painted pole withdraw the way it came, from the now flattened three foot high white post. I thanked God that Kay had chosen tonight to sleep in the position she had as if she had been in her usual position with her head on my lap, her pretty little body would have received the full force and the iron rail would have penetrated her, maybe fatally. I told them that my mother had said the lights failed yesterday but as the car had only done less than two thousand miles and was new, my father had said that was impossible, now we knew it wasn't!

The rest of the ride was taken very slowly. I had ten minutes alone with Kay before all the luggage had been taken inside Jonathan's house, then Kay and I said goodnight the way I imagine all sweethearts do.

***

I set out on the eight-mile road back home. The snow was still falling and being whipped into little piles behind obstructions in the wind's path. I thought if this carries on for long, we would have drifts to contend with in the morning on the feeding rounds. Luckily, we had ample hay in the barns this winter.

I left the hills and dropped down onto the marsh for the last four miles. There was a bang and something hit the bottom of the car as I ran over it. I stopped and got out to investigate.

The stiff east wind had a clean, cold cut to it. I had been sitting at the wheel for two hours with the heater on, the chill factor was minus five. I soon found the object I had just collided with. I was sure that I had not noticed it in my path and the object proved my thoughts correct, for I had been carrying the thing slung under my bonnet. It was now a very smashed battery. The collision with the pole had entered via the offside headlamp, hitting the battery before entering the car. Now it had let go of the leads that kept it in place. I turned the engine off on getting out solving the mystery.

No way was that car going again tonight! It was Shank's Pony or sleep in the car. I did not relish either but chose the walk across the marsh clad in patent dance shoes and the two sacks Jonathan had left in the back slung over my shoulders. I was soaked and cold and took to my bed quickly, true love never runs smooth and that night it was rough!

\*\*\*

The car was recovered the next morning from a snowdrift by the garage that had supplied it eight weeks before. The visible damage was only the headlight, the internal damage was more severe. Two bench seats, hole in front compartment panel, no battery and a broken carburettor. How it had run was a mystery. Luckily while I had cuddled Kay and said good night I had kept the engine running and the alternator had produced enough power for engine and lights.

\*\*\*

The garage owner listened with a smile to the tale of the lights going out. Young kids always had a reason for crashing dad's car it seemed. But father was adamant, it had to be checked out.

\*\*\*

Four days later the Vauxhall was back with us, with new seats and no mark to reveal the damage. A week later the lights flickered off and on with dad. That was it! Back to the garage and this time, mend it! The garage owner was sorry and would see to it himself. The story told to us later the next day should go down in a book of *'Things Idiots Do.'* All the wiring had been checked, with no faults visible so a spotlight was fitted to the loom of wire and the garage owner himself took it out that night to test it. For three hours he drove with no problems then as he reached sixty miles per hour, all the power to the illuminations, including the spotlight, vanished. The consequential crash wrote the car off and put him in hospital for three weeks. The cause was a loose earth wire in the main loom. We received a brand new Vauxhall.

## CHAPTER TEN.

Even with all the fun I had along with my mates, the fact remained that Kay and I were banned by that court order to see or have any contact with each other. If only Kay and I could hug each other and kiss. She was the first girl I had known that did anything to me, so kind, soft and understanding. I cared for Abigail but she could never replace my Kay?

\*\*\*

Looking back now, after forty-one years, I suppose I was the first boyfriend she also had known, so maybe it was as hard for her as me. We shall never know, maybe it was all a schoolgirl crush for her, but to me it was not. It still hurts and there are times, if the atmosphere is right and I perhaps hear a certain tune, it really tugs at the old heart just to recall those days.

Meanwhile I had Abigail still and I loved her in a different kind of way. She was my soul mate and I saw her at least three times a week, sometimes six.

\*\*\*

Abigail's house was in Rye, opposite the church that stands overlooking Romney Marsh. The house goes back to the fifteenth century with low beams and lower doorways. The leaded lights and windows are old and not double-glazed. The furnishings are in keeping with the whole house. A large couch stands under one of the windows and this was our favourite place to sit and lay.

\*\*\*

This particular evening we sat in the usual place under the window on the soft sofa drinking coffee, always coffee at Abigail's, made with milk. The topic was the same as always, *'Kay.'* Word had got back to Kay's parents that I had a hectic night the other week at a local dance and ended up on the floor with this gypsy girl pouring drink all over me, then she had hit me and I hit her back. That is how it was told in Kay's house. Their daughter was a lucky girl to be rid of me. They painted a very black picture of me.

\*\*\*

Abigail now decided it was the proper time to turn the key in Kay's 'prison door' and release her to society again, or to my arms at least. They were obviously taking a keen interest in what, where and who I was with, so time to give them the *'top of the cream,'* so to speak.

\*\*\*

Abigail had a plan, as she always did. This one was, as she said, *'The tops!'* She would phone the Sussex Express and place an announcement in the engagement column to the effect that I was getting ready to marry someone. But the snag was who to? Now this was in the days when it was still known for the girl to sue the chap for breach of promise so we had to be careful. Abigail wondered if Hazel would mind. Her chap was unlikely to see it and he knew all about our little arrangement anyway.

"*She would not want a lot of money to do it,*" Abby said.

"*Pay her?*"

"Yes, go and see her now, for Kay's sake,"

"You come with me and together she may help," I said, "but phone her first to make sure she's in."

"What's her number?"

"I've no idea, it must be in the book." Abigail jumped to her feet, half ran to the phone in the hall and came back with the phone directory already open at the right page.

"Here it is, go on phone now." The phone was answered the other end by Hazel's mother.

"Oh hello. How are you? I haven't seen you for a week. I hope you are not ill."

"No, no," I said. "Can I talk to your daughter please?"

"I'll get her," and after a pause Hazel came on the line.

"What do you want?"

"You," I said, without thinking of the double meaning of that word to her.

"When," she replied with a trill in her voice.

"Now."

"I'll put the outside light on for you out the front, and hurry up!"

"Right, let's go," said Abigail who was glued to the phone with me. "Come on darling."

\*\*\*

We drove to Hazel's and as we pulled up, Hazel ran from the front door in a great haste with a suitcase.

"Oh!" she said in surprise. "You never said she was coming with us."

"Coming where?" I said.

"Away of course anywhere from here, move it." I started to drive away with Hazel in the back half hanging over the back seat between us in the front.

"What's the rush Hazel?"

"I've left home and am never going back. Where are we going?"

"Left home Hazel? Abby said "whatever for?"

"Him who do you think," she said, putting an arm around my neck.

"Leave that out," Abigail responded, pulling the girl's arm away from me. "He's not interested in you silly girl, you know it is all show for Kay's benefit."

"I don't care. I have had a bellyful of them," meaning her parents. "I've got to get away from them, with him."

"Him!" said Abigail in alarm, "he is not going anywhere with you!"

"Then why did he phone in such a hurry to see me tonight?"

"Ah, I'll explain that if you just give me a chance. We want you to go along with a plan of ours."

"No. If he won't take me away, then you drop me in Rye. I'll catch a train."

"Where are you going at this time of night?"

"To my Dave."

"Where is Dave then?"

"In London he's my boyfriend. You know him Preacher. He works on Radio Caroline in the North Sea. I'll go and live with him, bugger what mum wants. I

77

have left."

"Hang on," said Abigail. "You cannot just run away if they don't want you to."

"You watch me, I'm off now."

"Have a think about it first, we need you."

"You can forget that, he doesn't love me," she said, pointing at me, "you just want to use me. All along you have said so and I thought he was shy."

"Hazel, we told you. Why did you not believe us?"

"No-one tells me the truth, it's all lies."

"Listen, he is in real trouble with his girl and you are the only one who can help him now. He wants to announce his engagement to you so that Kay's parents will let her out."

"What? To me! There you go again, lies, lies, lies. How is a girl to know it's not a trap?"

"You don't, but believe me he is willing to pay you."

"How much I need twenty pounds now, for the train and you will never see me again. Do what you want, I don't care."

"Done," said Abigail, *'spending my money,'* again I thought as I tried to drive with the two girls going at each other as if there was no time to lose.

"Preacher you've got twenty pounds on you haven't you?" Twenty pounds was a lot of money in those days

"Well yes, just about," I said.

"Good, station then and hurry," said Abby. "We'll catch the next London train."

And that was it. We paid, or rather I did. I took her case to the up platform and shook her hand. To this day I have never seen or had contact with the girl to whom I was to be engaged!

*\*\*\**

The following Saturday I was fast asleep having a lie-in as Abigail and I were going dancing that evening, when I was rudely awoken by my mother screaming up the stairs,

*"Get down here now! What is this?"* I was rather slow in responding and father then joined mother.

*"Here, now!"* as if I was a dog out of control. I pulled my trousers on and ran down the wooden hill.

"What's the matter?"

"This!" said mum, throwing the local paper at me. "Read the forthcoming events," and sure enough Abigail, had somehow got them to print the announcement of my engagement to Hazel. The ball was now rolling downhill and out of control.

*\*\*\**

One hour later I had a visitor, Hazel's father in a rage. His daughter and only child had run off with me, they saw it all on the night in question. She had a flaming row with her mother, packed her bags and had not been seen since. The police were not willing to investigate her disappearance as she had so often threatened to do it before, but now he knew where she was, it was in the paper. I was to be her fiancé, so where was I hiding her? I told him that there was some kind of mistake. Abigail and I had only given her a lift to the station, she was going to live on a boat in the North Sea. The paper's announcement was obviously a red herring to put them off the trail. He stood dumbfounded.

"The little bitch," he said, "It could have repercussions on you my boy, wait until I get her home!" And I secretly hoped he never would, for my sake. He left to talk to his wife who was by all accounts in a real state. Later they both paid me a visit, first to say sorry to my parents for all the trouble their girl had caused them, and to say they had contacted the paper, and *'Yes a young girl had placed the advertisement and paid cash.'* They were sorry and would print a disclaimer next week, but he had told the paper to forget it, as he did not wish to let his girl know that he was hot on her trail, or so he thought. I sighed with relief. We had got away with it so far, now for the reactions of Kay's family. It was not long coming.

\*\*\*

That night I picked Abigail up at seven to go dancing. She had one of Kay's school friends with her for the night, a girl of eighteen, five feet nine inches high, made in the shape of a model, long legs, shapely torso, long arms and curly hair, eyes like stars, with a little upturned nose. The voice sounded Scottish, spoken in a soft mellow style. Her whole manner was polite and she always had a tidily widely smile to accompany it.

"You don't mind if Fiona comes along with us do you? She's a boarder at school and has no transport."

"Hi, Fiona nice to meet a friend of Kay's."

"Hop in the back Fiona," said Abby. "I'll sit with him in the front. We've got loads to talk over. Thanks for the phone call this morning." She was glad Hazel's parents were now OK. Abby was over the moon we had achieved our goal. Turning round to face this fresh new face, I introduced myself but was wasting my time, as she knew all about me. It seemed I was the talk of the girls in the dormitories at night. They knew my life and where it was going long before I realised.

\*\*\*

Abigail was full of news. She had got a letter from her boyfriend and he was coming home for five days next week. After two years he was at last coming back to her and she had word for me.

"Come on darling, smile. Two girls for you tonight and my mum has heard from Kay's. They read the paper and guess what? They may, and it is only may, let Kay out again. They had horrid things to say about you. Mum was cross with her and said you were a lovely lad and she felt happy while I was with you and trusted you."

\*\*\*

The dance was at a village six miles from Rye and very well attended. No one questioned me as to where the longhaired hippy was and we danced the night away.

Fiona flirted and enjoyed herself, having an open field with the boys. She was a new face of unknown charm. Together we danced a couple of slow waltzes but I preferred Abigail, as she was a very good mover. I was a lucky lad to have found Kay and Abigail as they were exceptionally good dancers and we were nearly up to gold standards. Now Kay was gone Abigail stepped into all the tunes, but the Twist was still new to us, although we were working hard on it.

***

A new Twist club had been formed in a village near to us and we were among the first to join. Tonight we let our hair down, even Abigail perspired a little. The time passed in a flash, and then Fiona sidled up to us and dropped a bombshell.

*"You've got to get me back to school, I'm late now. Look, its five to twelve I'm supposed to be in at eleven and no later. What am I going to do?"* Why were the two girls looking at me in such a way?

*"Come on darling, your reputation is at stake here,"* said Abigail. We bundled into the car and raced back to Rye as if we could catch and overtake time. We pulled up with the lights out in the drive of the large old house that was the home for all the boarding girls staying in term time. All the lights were out.

*"Come on,"* said Abigail, *"Let's find an open window, but be quiet. You go that way, Fiona and I will try this way,"* pointing to the right. I felt like a burglar must feel as I crept around the wall under all the large sash windows. Suddenly a tap on my shoulder made me jump.

*"We've found one round here."* It was Abigail. I followed her around the back past the kitchens and a smelly fuel tank across a brick paved yard, to be greeted by four half clad eighteen year olds hanging out of a top floor window.

*"Up here,"* the whispered call drifted down to us three on the ground. *"But be careful, the rooms below are the caretaker's and she is a light sleeper,"*

'Oh thanks,' I thought to myself, now what? It was twenty feet up and past the window of her, the light sleeping night watchman.

*"Darling, please."* Abigail implored, *"Fiona has got to get in or she could be expelled like I was."* To Abigail, this brought back memories of younger days. To me, it was a new living nightmare, but a challenge nonetheless! I had never let one of my women down and I had no intentions of doing so now, especially with four observers hanging all their women-hood out of the top window, taking in the situation. The thought of it made me slightly uneasy. Imagine Monday morning at school, the talk among the girls of how I failed a maiden in her hour of need. Kay would never speak to me again, even if she got the chance!

There had to be a way to get Fiona up into that room. We got the message that the girls inside could not get out to open any doors as all the outside entrances and down stairs windows were alarmed, so it was the top window or sleep on the doorstep and take the consequences in the morning. That was out of the question, it was window or nothing. Luckily Fiona was Scottish and made of good stuff, fit, firm, agile and also belying her sexy form, strong and *'could handle herself on mountains,'* as she ladylike put it.

***

So the climb of a lifetime took place. A dustbin was obtained from outside the kitchen door, the contents of which I emptied out in a nasty smelly pile. With the bin upside down against the wall I stood on top. Then Abigail got on my shoulders, nothing ladylike mind you, she just clambered up over me and held onto the window ledge of the *'lightly sleeping caretaker.'* That left a gap for Fiona of approximately six feet to reach her mates.

They got some sheets and hung them out of the window. *"Plenty!"* as Fiona claimed for her to scramble up. Abigail's feet were pushing hard on my shoulders and I was already getting tired balancing on the bin with her on top, but that was nothing to the lassie that flashed before my eyes, fully dressed with dance shoes that I'm sure had crampons fitted to them! She was a real Scottish lass and in a hurry to conquer this particular steep climb.

I held my hands in front of me in a cup position, these she ignored with her feet, instead kicking her toes into my lower belly, looking for a toe hold in my trouser belt as if I were an ice face on a glazier. Her hands found the top of Abigail's dress. As she heaved herself up there was a rip and Abigail swore. That only made the girl kick harder and grab around for a more secure handhold. Then, like a train, she was gone. The whole weight of the pair came on me and I felt the bin threaten to fold under me. Now there was nearly two hundredweight on my shoulders. I know boys that would have collapsed in such a situation but the life of that girl ten feet from the ground was on my shoulders.

As Fiona grabbed for the sheet, she put weight on Abigail and I felt her start to sag. I was fortunate to have such strong girls for company! Then, Heaven! Abigail started to slide down me, her feet looking for the toehold the upward one had used. I was ready for her and put the palms of my hands up to her shoe soles and lowered her down. At one point our faces came level. Those large eyes of hers told their own story and she gave my lips a brush with hers as we passed, the second time our lips had ever touched in all the years I knew her.

Like a flash I jumped down and the bin fell over, rolling and rattling across the yard. We held our breaths. I was bent double with my hands on my knees getting my breath back when a window above went up with a rattle and bang.

"Who's there?" a voice called out. It was the window below the one that had swallowed up the girl, from which no conquering hero's flag flew, thank God! My arse nearly popped. With one movement I leapt backwards to the wall. At the same time the dustbin came to a halt across the brickyard. Luckily it drew the attention away from me crouching at the bottom of the wall. The torch beam lit the yard, bin, and pile of contents up.

*"You Badgers! I'll have you shot!"* The light went out and the window slammed shut.

***

Abigail was at the car when I got there, sitting in the front seat in tears.

*"What's the matter?"* I said, putting a comforting arm around her.

"We got away with it didn't we?"

"Yes, I was thinking, I wish I could have stood back and seen what we looked like up that wall. No-one will ever believe us."

"Who are you thinking of telling?" I said.

"My children one day I was thinking of the things you do for us girls. You should write another of your books about it." After a couple of minutes I drove in reverse out of the drive and put the lights on. It was not far to Abigail's. *"Come on, I need a stiff drink after that,"* she said as she got out. So it was back to the sofa while Abigail made coffee and took her torn dress off. She came out from her bedroom holding the dress in her hands

*"Look at that?"* she said, pointing out the rip in the neckline. *"And look. Go on! This has got to stop! Every time I go with you, my tits suffer!"* She was pulling her jumper down to show the old round scar from the lighter that had left its mark on her breasts. Now there was a nasty scratch and bruise coming up. The scratches were Fiona's fingernail marks and her climbing boots caused the bruise. *"That girl should thank us, she was very lucky to have you with her, other blokes would have run a mile".*

# CHAPTER ELEVEN

I was to go to a solicitor as I had been remembered in my late aunt's Will, according to the letter I had received. The appointment was for three forty five pm so on the day I took Abigail with me. As she said I must have support and she knew her way around these sorts of men. It transpired that I had been left two thousand pounds. Abigail was spellbound.

"All that amount! What are you going to do with it?"

\*\*\*

We left the building and I took her for a meal while the shock sank in. Two thousand pounds! A house only cost one thousand, I could buy two and here I was, with all this money. Over the meal Abigail suggested that we should invest it on the stock market. I loved the *'we bit!* One thousand seven hundred and fifty of it was in shares and I decided to leave them there, as the solicitor had advised. Abigail had plans for the two hundred and fifty cash.

\*\*\*

Abigail was a wise girl but far too young for her brain's way of thinking. She was only eighteen, already played the stock market and seemed to have the eye for it. Her elder sister had a friend who worked in the city for a broker so the information was easy to pass on and obtain shares without a lot of fuss.

\*\*\*

After coffee I bought a box of chocolates for Abigail as a thank you present for coming with me and we drove home. She tucked into the chocolates on our journey home, giving me the occasional one

"Last one," she said, stuffing one in my mouth. As we rode on I got into trouble with the sweet, it was a toffee and stuck to my false teeth. So without a word I removed them, wrapped them in a tissue and tucked them discreetly in the empty box. All the time she was going on about this and that, what was looking good and *'don't want anything to do with those?'* It was stock market talk and not for me. I said goodnight and left as she closed the door.

\*\*\*

Next morning I could not find my teeth or the empty box. So that night I paid a call on Abigail.

"Come in, I'll make a coffee. Sit in that chair, look at this," throwing a pink newspaper at me.

"Abigail. What happened to the chocolate box last night?"

"It was empty, we ate them all."

"I know but where is the box?"

"I threw it out of the window."

"Where?"

"I can't remember. Don't worry darling, it's only paper, it will rot."

"My teeth were in that!" I said.

"Gosh! I threw your dentures away! I am sorry. Haven't you got a spare pair?"

"No, I threw them away in the orchard a long time ago. I bit into an apple and it was sour so I tossed it away. Unfortunately the teeth went with it under the mower. I can't get on with the bloody things any way so won't bother with them any more. You take me as I am or leave me. Even Kay told me to keep them in my waist coat pocket on our first night," and the memory made a tear come to my eye.

"I am sorry darling, what were they doing in the box anyway?"

"A toffee got stuck to them so I put them in the box for safekeeping."

"See anything you fancy?" She said as the milk came to the boil. I was lost.

"What? Where?"

"In the paper" I looked down at the pink sheets. They were all columns of figures and names that meant nothing to me.

"They are the companies and that is the price of the shares. That is what they hope to be next year. See?"

"Nope!"

"Give it here, tell me if any of them ring a bell in your head." She started to read. "BP, Shell, Ford."

"Yes, I know who they are but I don't understand."

"Look," she said "Shipping. That's up your street, you have boats." She started to read out a list of shipping companies.

"I've heard of them, but we have only fishing boats, these are ocean going ships."

"Good." She put a tick with a pencil alongside them and read on with the shipping companies.

"Ah stop!" "I was reading about them the other day, they are the only and oldest steam tugs left in Europe and are being taken over by another firm."

"WHO"? She said excitedly.

"I can't remember"

"Where did you read it? You must know that."

"Of course I do. It was in the Ship Monthly magazine."

"Well get it. We could be onto a killing." Abby would not stop till I returned home and found the relevant magazine and returned.

"Yes," she said after reading the article. "The firm taking over is Smits of Holland and they are listed here. Look. They are at twenty-four shillings and the Steam Tugs at four shillings and going to rocket. Bang, bang, bang." She spent one hundred of my pounds there and then on the phone to her sister's friend, whom I had never heard of or seen. This was madness!

\*\*\*

Six months later we sold those shares for three hundred pounds, a fine profit and I was into the game, reading all the gossip on shipping but only broke even or lost money, so gave it up as a lousy job.

\*\*\*

Life went on. I saw a lot of Abigail that year and we were very happy going out for drinks and to dances whenever the chance came our way. She came to the pub and played darts with the boys but we were just friends. To me, she was not only another girl, she was also my best friend.

## CHAPTER TWELVE

Saturday saw me twenty miles from home on a journey to collect four tons of seed potatoes. I arrived at the farm as agreed and the woman told me there was only the lad to help load them. This was before pallets were in common use, so it was a case of back the trailer up as close as possible then with the boy handing them to me, I stacked the load. The time kept ticking on. I was eager to get home and unload. At eleven I was on my way with a high pile of trays, well tied on the trailer. It seemed to take forever to reach top speed. I juggled with the gears and at last we achieved the dizzy pace of sixteen miles per hour. Eight wheels and two ten-inch drum brakes to stop if need be, not forgetting that was only on two wheels and four tons of cargo pushing along behind you. I prayed nothing was going to get in my way.

The marsh roads were deserted. The plovers hugged the ground in flocks, sheltering from the cold wind and then it started to rain. The water flew off the front wheels and straight into my face. As I pulled into the yard at home, half drowned, dad said,

*"Get them in the shed. They give frost tonight."* My heart sank. I was worn out and wet. It was now one thirty and soon thinking of getting dark. I had to get on the trailer and push the trays to the side, then get down and carry them fifty feet into the shed. By the time I finished it was past five o'clock. I ran into the house shedding my wet work clothes and dived into the bath. Mum said she would put my dinner under the grill to warm back up but I had no time to feed, it was party night! I had got word that maybe, just maybe, my Kay would be there.

In record time, I was on the road again, this time in dad's car. The rain had stopped to reveal a star-studded sky and there was no problem getting up to sixty miles per hour.

*\*\*\**

The party was held in a big historical house that is famous, a long way from home. Then it was owned by some embassy as a holiday retreat for their staff. This weekend it was empty apart for the two girls who worked there and lived in. One was a maid to the cook. She was a local girl so knew the youth of her age and it was she who had arranged the party. Which today I suppose you would now call *'a rave.'* Abby, Kay and this girl had all gone to school together.

The house was an impressive pile of red brick with turrets, gothic windows and a clock tower, hundreds of years old. The drive to it was lined with elm and lime trees. A large stairway led to the front door from a mass of gravel parking area out front amid huge close mown lawns. In the middle sat a statue on a giant stone.

*\*\*\**

The party was in full swing by the time I found somewhere to park around the back, alongside a chain mesh gate that surrounded a large wooden building. I hurried to the tradesman's door as I had been told to. All the other doors were locked and the girl who worked there had no knowledge of the keys, having arranged with the other woman that lived in that she could go home for the weekend.

***

The music was loud with the partygoers revelling in all the plush rooms. As I entered the main hall, Fiona, the Scottish lass I helped in the window and had not seen since, grabbed me.

"*Preacher darling come with me.*" And we ran up the stairs together. Boy she was fit! She led me along a huge corridor where suits of armour stood, and massive portraits hung off long ago owners. She stopped, flung a massive wooden door open and there stood Kay!

"*Here he is Kay. My hero, your man for the evening, don't waste it!*" Turning to leave she said. "*I never had the chance to thank you for that night. I shall never forget it. Now do something memorable tonight. We got here early with John and bagged this room for you. Look, there's even a key in the lock.*"

***

The room was at least thirty feet by thirty feet with a high ceiling all done out in plaster. A painting of angels looked down on us. The curtains were thick, blue and over ten feet long. The walls were a light blue with more huge pictures. The carpet was blue with a floral pattern but my eyes were elsewhere.

We stood and looked at each other then threw our arms around one another, both of us trying to squeeze harder than the other. Kay was in tears.

"*I thought you were gone from me, I love you my darling. Don't leave me, ever. I love you,*" she cried, using all the words of endearment she knew to show how much. She told me to take my tweed jacket off. As I slipped my arms out of the sleeves, she somehow took her slender arms out of her dress straps and it fell on to the blue carpet. "*Put the light out,*" she spoke, with a quiver in her soft voice. "*Take me in your strong arms and hold me tight.*"

My heart was pounding. I silently thanked all my mates, boy and girl, for this night and added a prayer to God for giving her life, and me the strength to stand there. Her arms felt soft but firm as she hugged me. We kissed like never before, so soft and gentle. Then she moved back half a pace and looked at me. I felt her eyes seeing through me like an X-Ray. Then she started to undo my shirt buttons so calmly. I never felt the cotton fabric slide off my shoulders. She tossed my shirt aside and stared at me. My tie hung down loose and crooked, my chest heaved and I stood letting her survey me.

"*You are so strong. I love you. Now off with that,*" and my tie was over my head, still tied in a knot. I remember thinking, '*I never do it like that, I always undo it,*' but this was another time! Kay was undressing me. There she stood in her stockings, pants and bra. I was unable to move, my chest wanted to explode. I had not been expecting this. Then she undid my trousers and they fell to the ground. "*Now you can put me to bed and make love to me. I'll show you what to do.*"

I was not ready for this, I had not put this into my equation for our next meeting. Asking, no begging me, to consecrate our love for each other, I had got nothing with me, I never had. I picked her up, she put her arms around my neck and slowly, so slowly, I walked across the room to the bed. Now I do remember the bed. It was huge, over eight feet by eight feet and covered in a duvet of light blue silk-like material, cool and smooth. I lay her down and she sat up on the edge. She leaned over and kissed my hairy chest then turned her head and snuggled into me. I stood there unable to take it all in. Ten minutes before I was parking the car and now I was in a room made for Royalty, on a bed, the likes of which I had never seen before, with only my pants on and the girl of all my dreams asking me to make love to her!

Now I was not called *'The Preacher'* for nothing, as in the inside pocket of my jacket I always had my Holy Bible and would preach a sermon to my friends, reading Chapter Four from St James, Verse three-seven, just to let them know that *'lust is a sin.'* Now here was I, the high and mighty one of the lads, with the same thoughts as the others at riotous parties. I could not do it to the girl I truly loved, she was so young.

"*Are you on the pill?*" I asked, not knowing where I got the guts.

"*No of course not.*"

"*Well I haven't got anything either.*"

"*That doesn't matter,*" she calmly spoke. "*Just be careful with me. Now come here,*" and she yanked me onto the bed. Her arm went around her back and her bra fell onto the bed to reveal her naked breasts. She lay back and gently said, "*Kiss me there.*" pointing to her breasts, "*and take me with you to Wonderland!*"

I had no knowledge of Wonderland though something told me in the back of my mind how I could get there, but I was not going on that journey tonight. We were in love, yes, but not engaged or married yet.

"*Kay I love you so much, but it is a risk we cannot take,*"

"*It will be all right,*" she said, pulling me even tighter to her near naked torso. She was so soft and warm. Then she started to feel around for the elastic in the top of her knickers and hooking her toe into it she slid them down her legs.

"*No,*" I said, "*leave them on for God's sake, it is dangerous! If I get near you, you could become pregnant.*"

"*Nonsense*" she said. "*You are frightened aren't you? It's all right, you are normal, so am I.*"

"*I know, but I've lambed thousands of sheep and the old ram only has to touch the ewe and we have lambs.*"

"*Come here and don't worry so!*" she said.

"*No!*" I said. "*Let's just cuddle. It is safer and I love you.*" I pulled her knickers up and we turned and lay on our sides, holding each other till we were like one, but her knickers and my pants stayed on!

***

We were making up for lost time. Her fingers had that magic touch like I had never experienced before. She licked my body all over and got a lot of pleasure out of doing so if the gasps and sighs were anything to go by, or was it my finger that pleased her so much? She groaned with satisfaction. Together we cuddled each other in a passionate embrace.

*\*\*\**

I awoke to Guy shouting at us.

"*Wake up, quick there's trouble downstairs, hurry up it's your car!*"

I jumped out of the bed where I had fallen asleep after all the work in the day. I was tired out and the comfort of that bed had overtaken me with the girl of my dreams alongside me. She said I had slept for two hours but she had just lain there and looked at me. Now I was needed downstairs at the car.

"*Hurry up, the ambulance is on its way.*"

"*My car and a bone wagon on its way,*"

"*What's happened?*"

"*I don't know, now hurry up.*" In my haste I noticed that Kay still had her knickers on and that made me feel a lot better, but I needed more sleep. I ran down the quaint staircase two at a time, my shirt flapping in the draught. There was a hell of a balloo going on outside by the wooden building that I was parked alongside. The swimming pool was housed in it, a massive job, like everything else in this place.

A body had been seen floating face down in the pool. My car was blocking the access and could I move it? The keys were in my jacket up in the room so I had to run back up the stairs to get them. As I entered, Kay turned with a startled look that turned to a massive big smile.

"*That was quick big boy ready for another try?*"

"*Can't now,*" I said. Kay was reading the wrong book! I was breathless and gasping because I had run for the keys, not for her beautiful now naked body. The knickers and suspenders were gone, her pubic hair was formed as if cut by the barber and was a different shape from mine. I pondered on this as I ran back down the stairway. I had never noticed her pubic hair's strange form before. Maybe it was because I was further away this time. Still, the car to move! I drove from the gate and had to search for another place to park.

*\*\*\**

The ambulance arrived as I was walking back to see what was happening. A group of people along with the girl, who worked there, were apologising to the first aid men. It was all a prank. Someone had thrown a tailor's dummy in the pool, some other person had seen it and one thing had led to another, they were so sorry.

"*That was all right,*" they said, "*better a false alarm than to leave it too late.*" They were very good about it. Not so the police, who turned up as the ambulance drove away. This house was on their beat, an ambulance had been called and they had it on good authority that only two staff were on duty this weekend. It was then that one of the policemen recognised me standing there in no shoes, just trousers and open shirt.

"*Not like you to be dressed like that,*" he said. "*Got a girl up here have we,*" I did not like the tone of his voice and I remembered the court order, he knew Kay's father as he shot over the land with the Syndicate. Shit! He was sure to tell them he had seen me. Did Kay's parents know of her whereabouts tonight? I had to get back to her quickly. I was gone, not saying a word to the officer. This time I walked, running was wearing me out! I knocked on the door as I was brought up to do. The sound of Heaven said,

"Who's there?"

"Me."

"Come in, don't hang around outside a girl's room, you will get yourself talked about!" The light was now on and there stood the most gorgeous girl of eighteen in her youthful prime. No craftsman in all the ages could have made something so perfect. I stood and looked. "Come here," she said, raising her arms, and then her fingers beckoned me to her. She was still naked. Nothing was so marvellous to behold, the feel of her breasts against my chest were so firm, yet soft. Then she undid my trousers and gave me a big hug. "You love me, and I love you, don't fight it, let it happen." Then the door crashed open.

"SORRY!" and there stood Abigail. "I'm sorry!" and shut the door as she backed out. That was too much for both of us. Kay started to cry.

"It's not meant to happen is it? You do love me don't you?" I hugged her. "Why did Abigail have to come in then?"

This was not my Kay. Was she drunk? I had not detected it before, or was it something else? Perhaps keeping her shut away from me was making her feel she had to do something just to show her parents that she was grown up. Maybe getting pregnant was her idea of getting her own back on them.

"I am still here," said a coy voice from outside the door.

"Christ! What do you want, Abigail?"

"There's something you should see out here Preacher, but put something on first." I pulled my trousers up and Kay slipped her dress on. I picked her bra and knickers up and she grabbed her suspender belt, still with the pair of stockings attached, and threw them on the bed. We then with our arms around each other opened the door to see Abigail pointing at the wall alongside the door.

"Look at that. Who could have spoilt such a lovely wall with that? But I suppose they have a point, it's not every day the Preacher gets caught with his pants down is it!" Kay burst into more tears.

"Nothing happened, it doesn't have to you know!" She stopped as she read what Abby and I were looking at. There, in one-foot high capitals, someone had scrawled along the wall *'THE PREACHER HAD KAY HERE.'*

"It's a lie, it's not true, I'm still a virgin," sobbed Kay.

"I don't care," said Abigail. "It's got to come off. Felicity will get the sack if the owners see that. She is down there now reading the riot act to some gatecrashers. She'll go mad!"

Well have you ever tried to get shoe polish off white plaster? It is made to spread and shine leather and also be waterproof into the bargain. Cloth only spreads it.

John came to help us try to remove it. Some passing unknown-to-us partygoer lent a hand for a few minutes then gave up, with the suggestion that we got petrol or spirits to help shift it. A glass of whisky was obtained, Abigail and John tried it out on a small area while Kay and I polished the glass of the picture that had been written over with boot polish. It came off the glass OK, but John's efforts only made things worse. It thinned the polish and spread it all the more, along with soaking it into the white wall plaster. Abigail called a halt to the work for a pow-wow.

"We are getting nowhere like this and we never will. So let's all concentrate on the words 'Kay' and 'Preacher', and then no one will know who was here. It's a bloody shame but what can we do? I will have to tell Felicity and we will never talk again. Now come on, it's half past ten."

Abigail vanished down the stairs to tell our host the bad news while John and I started on the names. Kay cleaned the frame around the portrait, that was the only easy bit. The frame was dark wood, now stained black, and she got a good shine on it, much more than the other frames along the walls. Felicity came running along the corridor from a different way. There was obviously another stairway up.

"Don't worry about that, it's OK. Just cover the names up with more polish, I'll show you where it is." John looked shocked.

"What! You don't mind? But the owners ..."

"Oh stuff them! They gave me the sack last month and made me work my term of contract out. Did you think I would throw the doors open to a party like this if I worked here still? Come on, this way, it's easier."

Abigail arrived from the lounge stairway as we left by the other way. *"Look after Kay, be back in a jiff,"* I said, and followed Felicity. As we turned the corner of the passage it led to some back stairs down to the basement kitchen where two massive cookers stood alongside racks of plates and dishes. From there we went down through another door into the cellar and found boxes of Kiwi Shoe Polish in all colours.

"Black will be best, it covers everything," said Felicity. So John and I filled our arms up with a dozen tins each and returned the way we had come. Felicity said once again *"Don't worry, I'm off tomorrow and the new owners are taking over, Russian I think. No-one will care."*

\*\*\*

We spent ten minutes painting the wall with black Kiwi, it was a good job well done. We were both proud of it, and then we found the girls. As we entered, Abigail got off the bed where they had been chatting about girly things. The smile and expression on Abigail's face told me everything. Kay had no doubt told her of our night of near passion. She said on leaving,

"It's all right, don't be scared." She gave me a little hug, turned to John and said, *"Come on now, leave them alone,"* and patted me on the cheek as she passed, shutting the door behind her which I now locked. Kay got up, started to hug me and wept soft murmurs in my ear.

"You are so strong willed. I could not help myself, it is the wine. I did, and still do want you so much that it hurts, I could be pregnant now."

"Ssh, don't worry. It's all right," I said, "You'll be OK. Nothing happened and I will always be here for you, but you are silly and don't listen. You remember this my precious, I am yours until I die. I was only breathing until I found you, now I am living, with all your love."

We sank onto the bed and she let her dress slip off once again. She insisted I took my trousers off, and then we both lay together like lovers that we nearly were, with only my pants separating us. Both fondled each other and got immense satisfaction from doing just that. She awoke in me something like a summer sun, and really it has never set.

\*\*\*

We talked that night cuddled in each other's arms, so safe and loving. I asked her to marry me on the day she became twenty-one. Never was a girl so happy, she lay over my body and buried her face in mine, the feeling of solid passion was intense. Yes she swore that no other boy would ever take my place. I was the only one she would ever truly love or marry.

The hours passed by and I was getting worried it was late.

"How are you getting home?" came up in the conversation.

"The same way I got here, by John. Did they not tell you I was coming?"

"No, not really Abigail said maybe, but nothing definite, otherwise I would have been here to meet you. I had to put a load of seed spuds away before I came, that's why I was late. How long were you here before I came?"

"About two hours. I sat on that chair by the window drinking wine, waiting for you."

"You wait until I see Abigail!" I said. We kissed and I suggested she had better see Abigail if she knew where she was, for it was getting rather late, or early, it was now three am.

"John and Abby are in the next room,"

"Come on then my darling, let's be having you. I'll see you again and as soon as it's possible, I will buy you a ring for your finger." I pulled her up by her hands and she flopped into my arms again.

"I don't want to leave, we were born for each other, my parents will never keep us apart."

"Come on," I said. I smacked her little bum and she giggled.

"Put these on do," and I produced her knickers from the bed. "When did you take them off," I said.

"Last night when you were asleep I wanted to get closer to you, to really feel you."

"Kay that is silly of you. Now put them on."

"No, I will not wear them," she said. "I really need a bath."

We found Abby and John in bed together as Kay said they were, and Kay could not help herself from remarking that the pair should be more careful like we had been. They were both naked and our presences made Abby grab the bedclothes and pull it up to cover the pair of them. John agreed that it was time the girls were taken home. We left them to dress. Kay and I stood out side the door and gazed into each other's eyes.

Then the three left and I went in search of our host to thank her for the kindness she had shown Kay before I arrived. She was nowhere to be found so I wandered to the car and left.

\*\*\*

It was nearly four am. I was so tired, not just physically but mentally as well. I had a lot of thinking to do. I was approaching twenty-one and Kay eighteen, we were nearly adults. My twenty-first was in three months time and then I was responsible for my own actions. I could not get my mind around the fact that I was now engaged. But this was the early sixties, we were all brought up to respect our elders and I was not yet one of the older ones. Next time Kay and I got into a bed, would I be able to resist her wickedly women's shape? She had grown from a girl to a woman in front of my eyes over the years I had known her. Now she was ready for the leap into adult womanhood. I would have to pay the chemist a visit. But first the ring, *'one with many diamonds,'* I thought as she gave me so much pleasure in many ways.

I was nearly falling asleep at the wheel as I reached home. The yard gate was open and a frost shone on the turf as I drove in. I crept into the house, crawled up the stairs and mother said *"Goodnight."*

\*\*\*

I awoke next morning at eleven, mother having let me have a lie in. I lay and dreamed the events of the night before over and over again. Had it really happened or was it a dream? It was so unreal. I had known Kay for over three years, three whole years of kissing and hugging and now we had come to this. I thought of all those dances and nights together. Yes, I yearned for her, but this time she was at last ready and it could be magic. What had she said? *'Take me to Wonderland.'* But she was still under her parents' roof so had to do what they said. We both knew they hated me. Anything to offend them, especially like getting their daughter pregnant, would ruin Kay's life forever and then they had the court order to fight me with. A judge did not hand them out like sweets!

The future for Kay was obviously planned out for her, maybe they had hoped I would go away and let their plan work. I did not know. I knew we loved each other but if I got her pregnant by accident, her whole world would be shattered. Nowadays we would *'shack up'* together and sod the parents! But then, no, it was just not the done thing. Even Abigail never came up with that idea.

\*\*\*

My love for Kay and not being able to see her worried me to such an extent I made a sort of shrine to her up in the wood where we used to meet and sit on an old ash stub. I carved her name alongside mine in the bark of a chestnut tree and used to pick posies of wild flowers, placing them in a jam jar of water alongside. It was getting silly. I had to talk to someone. The only person I thought I could relate my feelings to was the local vicar. He had known my family and me for years, he was at my Confirmation in 1950. I saw him regularly, though now I attended church a lot less frequently, and he knew my Kay. We had taken communion together at Christmas Eve Midnight Services, after a night dancing for the last three years.

\*\*\*

The following Sunday saw me at church. I waited until everyone had gone and walked to the door where he stood thanking all who had attended.

*"Can I have a private word with you sir? I have a problem that maybe you can help me with."*

*"Come, come lad."* He put his arm on my shoulder and we entered the church to sit in a pew near the door. *"Now what's the matter? How may I help?"* I did not know where to start so began at the beginning three years before. He looked at his wristwatch as I got to year two. *"I'm sorry young man, but I have another service. You can see the congregation is already arriving. Could we carry on with this fascinating story of yours tonight, perhaps at the vicarage? More time you know,"* and he stood up.

*"OK, see you at seven then…"* and he interrupted. *"I think I can see you have a deep problem. Goodbye and God bless you my son."*

I had started and it had come easily to me to tell him everything but yet the problem I faced was far in the distance. I wondered if I would be able to explain to him the way I felt.

\*\*\*

I went home and got the plough out. I revved the tractor up and wound the depth control round to dig deeper. I felt angry that I could not fathom this out for myself. My feelings were so strong for Kay, yet I did not want to hurt her. Something nagged at my conscience that maybe the other night I had really let her down. This line of thought was out of my league. The vicar was the only hope.

I comforted myself that the sod I was turning over behind the plough looked better for taking an extra two inches of soil. The furrow was crumbling nicely. At least something was going right for me, but Kay, she would not go away from my head. I was planning and scheming all sorts of weird ideas up for how to see her again soon.

\*\*\*

The time came to see the vicar. His wife let me in and showed me to his study. He came in obviously with a mission in mind, swung round and sat in a chair opposite.

*"Now where were we?"*

*"Well …"* I told him everything he should know.

*"My boy, it is a sad tale but you will find a way. The first thing you must do is to stop making altars to her. She is not your God but you are talking as if she is. She is your princess maybe, but not God. You were right to refuse her the lust she has for you."* My mind sprang to my Bible and the passage on lust in St James that I had so often read at parties. *"Now my boy, go home and think of all your weak points, you will find many. Do not be put off by what people have said. You may not think they are important to you, but to others such as the girls'*

*parents, they most definitely are,"* and he placed his hand on my knee. *"I know you and your family, there are many good things, but you, and only you, know of the things you have done that they may wish you had. You love their daughter and that is the one thing they would rather you did not. She is very precious to them and so young. You must show them, not her, your love, as you say. Now, that is all I can tell you, but to show you truly care for them, you will honour their wish."*

He rose to his feet and held the door open for me to leave. I got the message and walked to the front door that I had entered an hour before hoping for a magic cure. His wife appeared from the door opposite.

*"Going so soon? Take care and hope to see you in church on Sunday. Oh, and by the way, why do they call you The Preacher?"* Her husband put his hand on his wife's shoulder and told her,

*"The lad always carries the Lord's book in his pocket."* He was so fast with his explanation to his wife that he had beaten me to it, but as I went out of the garden gate, I thought to myself, 'he at least listened to me but had told me nothing I did not already know.

\*\*\*

The following day I bought an expensive engagement ring for Kay. She had told me her finger size as we had lay in each other's arms that night. I gave it to Abby and she got it passed on to Kay, but she could not wear it in the house for fear of her mother seeing it. Word came that the next time I saw her it was to be placed on her finger by me and bugger her parents! I carried on with my *'altar'* as the vicar put it, putting Kay up for *'Queen God,'* one below the Big Fellow himself. I was not to be outdone by a man in a dog's collar and from that day have seldom gone to church, but still believe in the Lord and his mysterious ways. Then for the rest of the day I was on the tractor again ploughing and I kept thinking where had I gone wrong. We had been seeing each other for thirty-eight months now and were so much in love.

## CHAPTER THIRTEEN

As I drove down the lane a week later on a warm, bright spring morning to our farm, I found her horse loose eating the verge with its reins hanging around its neck. After calling out and getting no answer, I caught and rode it back to the big house. I had never ridden a horse with a sidesaddle like the one that Kay's parents made her use. We trotted into the yard as her mother came out and in an alarming voice said?

"Where is our daughter? She's been gone hours what have you done with her?"

"I don't know. I found Napoleon roaming in the lane."

"Where is Kay?"

"I have not seen her."

"Father" she cried, and with that Kay's dad appeared out of a shed.

"Whatever is the matter?"

"He's just ridden up on Kay's horse, said he found it loose up the lane. Kay's been gone four hours now. She is never that long and she would not let him wander off. Something has happened."

"Here hold him," he said, taking the reins from me "You come with me young man." We clambered into his old land rover and went down the lane to where my tractor was parked.

"That's where I found him," I said.

"Right any idea where she would have gone?"

"Nope," I lied.

"You go that way, I'll go this way," and he drove off down the lane.

I had a good idea that she had come to see if I was down the farm of ours, so took the tractor into the next field and drove over the bank to a place where we left letters hidden. For over eighteen months we had used it, no one else knew of our secret old mustard tin hidden in a hollow cherry tree.

***

As I reached the gully to cross the gill to the orchard, I caught sight of something round and black in the gateway leading to the wood. It was Kay's riding hat! Then I saw an arm move, so drove over. It was Kay, lying where she had fallen trying to unlatch the gate. Her face was covered in dry blood and her lips were blue and cold. She was shivering and could hardly speak.

"Darling I can't feel my legs or move," she sobbed.

"Stay still," I said, taking my shirt off to cover her. I knew shock when I saw it, but did not like the way she had said *'I cannot feel my legs.'*

The tractor had never gone so fast over a field. I had it in fifth gear, flat out at twenty-eight miles an hour, straight through the fence that was the boundary between the Estate Farm and us. The fence I could mend later. It was my Kay who wanted mending now. The fan drawing air through the radiator rattled as I ploughed though the next obstacle. The old thorn hedge never knew what hit it, speed was of the essence and a straight line was the quickest way to get help.

***

On reaching Kay's house I jumped from the tractor while it was still moving. As my feet hit the ground I ran into her mum's kitchen. I grabbed the phone and dialled 999. *"Ambulance please quickly!"* Her mother appeared. *"Get a few blankets now,"* I shouted to her. She got the message the first time.

*"What's the matter?"*

*"It's Kay. She has had a fall."* In silence we ran down the fields to where the shattered body I knew so well lay. We laid the blankets over her and I stroked her cheeks.

*"Get her up,"* said her mother.

*"No, don't move her. She can't feel her legs and could have a neck or back injury."* My first aid was at last paying off.

*"Mum,"* I actually called her mum, *"go back to the house and await the ambulance. No one knows where we are."*

*"Of course"* and she was gone. A large lady in floppy green rubber boots with her long over-size skirt flapping in the air stream, she ran back to the house. I was glad when Kay tried to smile at me. I did not like the signs so ever so carefully, to allow her to breathe more easily, undid her top shirt button. As my fingers fumbled the small button she sort of smiled and whispered, *"Not here,"* and I relaxed a little. For her to think like that obviously meant no head injuries. Then I loosened her belt.

***

I saw her dad in the land rover far away in the distance on the top of a bank, but was powerless to attract his attention.

***

Kay's mum had got a neighbour to stand in the road to stop the emergency services. She came back to her girl, opening the gates on the way. She was so nice to me, almost human.

***

Never have I been so pleased to see a blue flashing light bouncing over a field. The ambulance men were wonderful and told us we had done the right thing. Quickly they put a board under her and placed her on a stretcher. They would not say how bad she was, just, *'let's get her to hospital shall we'?* So slowly they drove back to the road and vanished. Her mother had gone with them, rubber boots and all.

***

I gathered my shirt and blankets up and wandered to her home with a swelling sort of ache in my chest and stomach. How bad was she?

The house was empty and the back door was wide open. I waited for a long time for her father to come home. Luckily I walked out to the road to see if he was coming when a neighbour told me they had seen him over an hour ago, he had driven off after the ambulance. So I told the woman that the house was open. She said she would go in and make sure everything was turned off in case the dinner was cooking. She would lock up and feed the dogs if the parents were not home by evening. It would be all right as she was a good friend of theirs. She also knew who I was and knew my father and where we lived. She hoped I soon had good news of Kay.

\*\*\*

I put my shirt on, which was saturated in blood but as there was a chill in the air I needed something but had nothing else. Then walking over to the tractor that had ended up out on the immaculate lawn, I gently drove onto the superbly raked gravel I had been so fearful of that first time I met Kay, and made my way down to the farm to get a hammer and stakes to mend the fence I had crashed through. After the fence, I had no heart for work. I was sick with worry.

\*\*\*

Later at home I phoned the hospital to get some news but as I was not a close relative they refused to divulge any information whatsoever. I tried to phone Kay's parents but no one answered and I took this to mean that they were still at the hospital. I now wished I knew who the neighbour was as they may have news.

Next I rang Abigail to tell her what had happened. She told me to carry on working and she would take over finding out the news and letting me know the outcome.

\*\*\*

It was the next day that Kay's father came and saw me up at the farm to thank me for my help as I counted the sheep. He thought, as did the hospital, that she would have died within hours if not found. He congratulated me in not moving her for she had a fractured back. He was sorry for the hassle of not being able to see his daughter but his wife had to be taken into account. No one was allowed to see her other than her immediate family at the moment and she was being moved to a special hospital.

\*\*\*

She lay on her back for fifteen weeks far away in Stoke Mandeville Hospital. Then on the sixteenth week she was transferred to a more local hospital in Kent and joy, I was going to be able to see her!

I phoned Abigail and we went up that evening to see her. I took a bouquet, a bottle of champagne and two fluted cut glasses to drink it from. It was a lovely sunny warm day, we were shown into a ward of eight beds. As I entered carrying the flowers and bottle, the whole ward said, *"it's him her boyfriend."* Obviously Kay had tipped them off as her mother had told her earlier that we were coming. The smile on her face was worth all the worry I had gone through. I kissed her very gently and she pulled me onto her face with her arms.

She was soon tired out and was only allowed half a glass of drink, so we gave the rest to the nurses who whisked the bottle swiftly away out of the ward. I told Kay to look after the glasses and get her mother to take them home next time she came, as they were expensive.

*"No more drink then for me,"* she said as she looked into my eyes with those big brown eyes of hers that now looked so tired and dull. I had always known

them as smaller, darker, sparkling objects that sent the whole world a message of *'I'm so happy, come let's play,'* but that was before the accident. Now, after sixteen weeks of being in pain on her back, unable to move, it was starting to show. I smiled,

"Of course there is. I will bring a new glass every time I come and a bottle as well."

I could see that she was tired so left Abigail to talk to her on her own for a few minutes and went in search of someone in the know as to the position of her getting better. I was told the prognosis was not good at the moment. She was paralysed from the waist down but they hoped that as the bruising in her back vanished, the swelling would go down and release the pressure on her spine, though it was too soon to know for certain a conclusion. *'Let's wait and see shall we?'* That was all they would say. So that was it. I returned to the ward and met Abigail in tears outside the door.

"What are we going to do? She is never going to walk or be able to dance again is she? Her whole life is in ruins." Abigail hugged me. "I'm so sorry for you, pray for her tonight won't you?"

"I do every night," I said, "but please Abigail, don't go and leave us now. She wants us around."

"How did you know I was thinking of going away?"

"Oh. I met your older sister the other day when she came back from Brighton to see your mum. She was coming out a shop and I asked her how it was going."

"Great," she said. "I've got a job for Abigail, only for the summer mind, so she'll be back before the dancing starts this winter."

"Hmm. She can stuff that now. I'm with you on this. We must stick together for Kay." We turned and walked to the car.

\*\*\*

I looked back to the hospital and up to the ward part of the building. My mind turned to that poor broken body I loved lying in pain and unable to even sit up. I started the engine, drove out of the entrance onto the street and took the road for home. The forty-minute drive across the marsh was done in silence, each to our own thoughts. The marsh was at its best, the first week of June is the loveliest with everything green and at its peak. Soon the grass would shed its lustre as it goes to seed and turns brown. The whole area will look tired from the heat of the summer sun. The lambs will grow to small sheep. At the same time the old ewes shrink to half their size as their heavy wool fleece is shorn. Abigail was the first to speak as we pulled up at her home.

"You have been unusually quiet. Come on in. We must talk. There is so much to plan, but first I must get out of these jeans, it's so hot and they cut". She vanished up to her room. I put the kettle on. Abigail appeared in a small black skirt.

"What is that? It's only a wide belt. You are not going to wear that out are you?"

"This," she said, trying to pull the hem out to show the length, which only *displayed her white knickers, is the latest fashion.* "Aren't they fab? It's a mini skirt." Her smile changed and she burst into tears. *"Kay will never be able to wear one will she? I forgot. God, it's terrible. What are we going to do?"*

"We must hope and pray, that's what, and be there for her. There is a lot we can do."

"What?"

"I don't know. We can only take it day by day at the moment."

"Her horse, said Abby, what are we going to do with it? You should go and shoot the damn thing."

"Don't be silly Abigail, calm down. It was not the animal's fault."

"I know, but why wasn't she on the new saddle you got her for her birthday? Her parents want shooting, not the horse, for making her ride on that stupid sidesaddle, trying to make out she's a lady. Who do they think they are?"

"I know. Those saddles are so old fashioned but girls like them."

"But Kay so much wanted to ride with her legs over the beast. Do you know they had forbidden her to use that new saddle you got? They said it was too much like a cowboy's and that fawn colour looked new. I think they were jealous because she liked it more than that old side-saddle."

"Don't worry about that Abigail, it's done, we cannot undo it. Let's look forward and hope the news is better soon, and that bit of rag around your waist is useless, it shows all your legs to your bum."

"Great isn't it?"

"No. It's all the rage I know, I have seen it on the telly but I don't have to think its great do I?"

"You are such an old prude. Get into the twentieth century. Where have you been all your life?"

"Well for the last three years with you and Kay, but I really must go now, you know, things to do and that."

\*\*\*

On my way home I mused over Kay and what Abigail had said about doing something for her. Abigail was truly a girl who knew herself. Circumstances had made her grow up before her time. A year younger than me, she knew so much more of life. We both had no idea of what trick fate would pull on each one of us.

\*\*\*

Abigail and I visited Kay every day, always with two glasses and a bottle. Her glass cabinet was growing into quite a collection. Her mother had made it quite plain that I was spending too much money on Kay and the court order was still in place, but I could visit the hospital. She did not understand that I loved Kay, it was as if that was what I was born to do.

\*\*\*

Her condition did not improve and the crunch came one week later on a very hot day. Abigail and I arrived, as usual at four pm, to be called to one side by a nurse, as we were about to enter the ward. She was so sorry but there had been an accident.

That day had been very hot and sunny so the staff had wheeled some of the beds with patients out onto the terrace. Kay had been one of the lucky ones to be allowed out. She had been in a lot of pain earlier in the morning and the drugs they gave her for the pain had made her very sleepy. The staff had not noticed the sun was so hot and as Kay had not said anything, no one worried but she had fallen into a deep sleep and been badly sunburned. She was not responding to the treatment as they hoped. (This was in the early sixties long before anyone thought of suing people for neglect of duty.) Anyway, we were shown to a small dark one bedded room to the side of her normal ward. There was a dull light and there lay Kay, all covered in a gauze bandage. Her eyes showed, she knew I was there. I held her hand and she squeezed it gently. Poor darling she had been through so much now this!

I placed the two glasses on the locker beside her and Abigail put the bottle alongside. There was no more we could do. We were there for only a few minutes when her mother came in.

"What are you two doing here? Please go." So we left so as not to upset Kay. We planned to return as the nurse on duty said we could. Kay was in a side ward and she thought it a good idea if she saw a few young faces. We sat in the car, watched Kay's mother leave after half an hour and then we returned. As we made our way to Kay's room a voice called out.

"Could we come in here?" It was the staff nurse. We entered her office where on her desk stood two glasses and the bottle of champagne.

"I believe these are yours," she said pointing to the collection on her desk.

"In fact," I said, "They are Kay's,"

"She is no longer with us," she said. "She is gone."

"My God what has happened? Don't tell me that Kay has died?"

"No nothing, like that! Her parents have had her removed to a special hospital in Austria or somewhere. Did you not know? Oh dear. I hope I haven't said anything I shouldn't have. I just thought you would know." Abigail pushed herself past me and snatched the glasses and bottle up.

"Come on. Let's go. There's nothing more for us here." A tear swelled in her eye but her expression said much, much more. "That bloody woman," she said, as we entered the corridor. "She could have told me. I'm Kay's oldest friend. I can understand her not letting onto you. She hates your guts."

"Thanks!" I said. "That's nice."

"It's not your fault," she said, putting her arm in mine. "Take me home please. I have a phone call to make."

***

All the way home Abigail kept on about *'that bloody woman!'* If she could get her hands on her and when she next saw her she was going to tell her what she thought.

At blessed last we arrived at Abigail's. She was out of the car like a scolded cat. She slammed the car door and strode up the path, not stopping to shut the front gate in her haste. She was in one of her moods!

By the time I entered the house she stood in the hall with the white phone to her ear. After five minutes she slammed the receiver down.

"Typical," she said, "not answering. That's like them. They know it's me. I bet that sodding staff nurse has tipped them off. I didn't like her attitude did you?"

"No, and I got the idea you didn't when you grabbed the bottle off her desk."

"Well I wasn't going to let you give it to that bitch. She had pleasure telling us Kay was gone, but Austria! Where the hell is she?"

"She will let us know, don't worry."

"Worry! I'm going to find out as soon as I can."

The next day I had a phone call from Abigail at about six o clock. "Guess what? Nothing I have tried all day to get them on the phone and no one has answered. I am worried. Can you come up and get me, and then we can go to Kay's and see them. They will have to come to the door."

\*\*\*

So I went, and we drove to Kay's, then as Abigail was making a racket on the back door a van pulled up and Mr Simpson got out.

"No good you doing that dear," he said, "They have gone away."

"Where have they gone?" Abby said, in a commanding sort of voice.

"Don't know dear. Somewhere on the continent, took their daughter to a special clinic or something. I am to look after the place and animals till they come back."

"How long are they going to be away?"

"Don't know."

"Where are the young daughters?"

"Can't tell you, I don't know. They did not catch the school bus this morning, I know that."

"That's it, come on darling. Can't do anything here he doesn't know. School next. They must know where they are."

"No good us going there now, it's all locked up surely?" I said."

"Well I'm going there first thing tomorrow. Come on, hurry up."

"Where to now?"

"Down the pub someone must know something." So to the pub we went. All the time Abigail was getting more and more riled up. "They can't just spirit her away from you like this. It's not fair on you or her. She loved seeing you it really cheered her up."

\*\*\*

The pub car park was empty as we drew in.

"Hmm, not many here yet still come on, you can get me a large gin, I need it. That bloody woman! We saw her at the hospital and she never said". I got a large double gin and a small bottle of tonic water for Abigail and a coke for myself. The pub was empty. As I was being served she was quizzing the barman to find out if he knew anything. All he knew was that the eldest girl was in a sorry state in hospital. The last he heard, she was up North or somewhere. We sat at a table by the window because Abigail wanted to see anyone coming in, as if she could not see them as they came through the door! I got the distinct impression that Abigail did not like Kay's mum by the way she kept harping on about her!

\*\*\*

Only eight people entered the pub that night and no one knew anything of the whereabouts of the family. We arrived back at Abigail's at midnight. I went in for one of her special coffees made with milk and sprinkled with cocoa powder. I just had to find out what was up with Abigail. She kept on about Kay's mother so I asked her outright.

"Why do you hate her so much? She did not have to tell us they were moving Kay away."

"That bloody woman never has liked me. You know what she once did? Years ago when Kay and I were at boarding school, she told everyone at the WI that I was creeping out of the school at night to sleep with a local boy, and Kay was being made by me to keep it quiet and let me in later." And for the first time in our lives Abby sat on my lap and looking me in the face said, "Someone wrote to the school and it all came out. We both got expelled and worst of all," she put an arm each side of me and placed her hands on my shoulders so I had to look her in the face, "the vicar came and saw my mum and dad to give me a sermon on being virtuous and all that old rot. As if!" And gave me one of her wicked winks 'as if.' "Well Kay got the chop too and it did not go down very well." Her eyes were staring me out and she lowered her voice. "You see it was the same school that our mothers had gone too. They were best mates and the fault was mine, not Kay's. They could not see why she had to go as she was 'made to do it.' Rubbish! It was only a bit of fun." Abby put her arms around my neck and her eyes seemed to say 'you must believe me.' "All the girls did it, but not Kay," trying to make it clear that my girl was not like that. "OK, she smoked a bit of pot and that, but her parents just would not give it up and made a real fuss. Of course it only made things worse and we never went back to that school." Abby then moved on my lap, put an arm around my body and hugged me. "That's when we came back to Rye and met you. I gave up school then. Poor old Kay had to go on to grammar school and they kept her locked up until she was sixteen. Now look where we are. She's eighteen for goodness sake! We've got to find out where she is and how she is. She did not look fit to be carried out and across the sea. I bet she is somewhere near and they have made the story up to fit, and are on some holiday because where are her younger sisters?"

\*\*\*

I wrote every day to Kay at her home 'care of,' hoping the letters would be sent on, but never got a reply. The days turned into a week then Abigail phoned in excitement. The parents were back and her mum had seen Kay's mum. Yes Kay was in hospital on the continent, but she would not tell her where and they did not want either of us to contact Kay. I was to forget her and my letters were not going to be sent on. She was gone. The days dragged by. I was so depressed. Where was my sweetheart?

***

The news came as a shock. The family was moving to Devon and the farm was going on the market. The young daughters had been sent to an aunt's on the day of the accident and from there onto a boarding school, never to return again. Abigail broke the news gently, holding me in her arms and pressing me into her bosom.

"Don't worry, she will write." I kept thinking of all those wonderful times we'd had together, how she glided around the dance floors and held her head up, so proud to be with me. Those little hugs when we pulled off a tricky little corner crowded with other dancers. I remembered how we negotiated all the turns with such ease and she was so graceful, with never a foot wrong. That first kiss and how we had promised each other that when she was able we were to marry. Meanwhile she had said no boy had ever shown such love to any girl. I was so strong to be able to respect her body, not wishing to place her in any position that neither of us wanted yet. That word *'yet'* had to carry me through life till we met and got together. Oh Kay!

***

On a warm sunny morning one day late in October, after ploughing, I sat relaxing and having a bite to eat. I was sitting by the very gatepost with its gate hook that caused her to slip and which was now dangling there, bent out of use where I had hit it with a hammer in my frustration. I cut a piece of oak wood from a tree in the hedge and whittled it into a little two inch high figure with flowing hair and a little pointed nose to represent Kay. I was proud of it, *'rather good for me I thought.'* Its little arms and hands beside its body, two little eyes and long legs, it was a perfect image of Kay. Later I drilled a small hole in its head, put a piece of string through and hung it around my neck. A year later I hung it in the oak tree from where I had cut the wood in view of her old home up on the hill, to keep guard of that gate.

***

That year father sold our farm in Kent, as I was ill. The doctors diagnosed ulcers of the duodenum. It was caused through worry, tractor driving and running one hundred and sixty acres of arable on my own. All this along with another one hundred acres of sheep, pigs and orchards, it was just too much. So again, my world was in turmoil.

***

Father was now eighty plus. Our family had always been in the fishing game and I was going to have a thirty-two foot trawler built, forsaking the land I loved for my third love, the sea. My first love, Kay, was still missing. Later that evening I went and saw Abigail.

"Come in darling. I was just thinking of you."

"Don't worry about me. It's Kay that is number one. I've been thinking," I said. *"You remember a year or so back, that competition she won? I wonder if they would still be interested in her work. She could still use her arms and hands and she will be able to sit up and draw."* The competition had appeared in a girl's magazine and was for a dress designer. You had got to send three sketches away, one of a wedding dress, one for the mother of the bride and another one of your choice. Kay had always played around drawing new designs of clothes on bits of paper and we had chivvied her into doing one for the competition. She had designed her own wedding dress and one for her mother. The third one was for the ex girlfriend of the groom. To everyone's surprise she had won second place and along with it the opportunity to go to Paris and study for a famous fashion house. It would have been followed up with a watertight contract to work for them for life and no one else. Her parents had hit the roof on finding out as she was only just seventeen and still had two years at school. They were not having a girl of theirs going to Paris, or anywhere else, to mix with the sordid fashion business. That was a den of vice! How little did they know of their wayward girl?

"That's a marvellous idea. You always come up with the perfect answer. You really are clever. Now who was the fashion house? Do you remember?"

"Well no, but it will be in my diaries."

"Well go and get them now. Come on, I'll come with you. Hurry up!"

"Steady on old gall. What's the rush?"

"Kay is. Come on."

So we proceeded to the car and drove home. Stopping in the yard Abigail followed me up to my room. It was the first time any girl had seen my room. One wall was lined with books on birds, the feathered kind, the other two were full of fishing and countryside books.

"Good God! Are they all you ever think about?" She said, as she picked up a Farmer's weekly from the pile beside my bed. "Have you no pin-ups of naked girls? And your radio is tuned to Luxembourg, how dull! Have you never listened to Radio Caroline? Where's your so-called diary? Is that it?"

"No Abigail. Not that one. That's current. We want last year's." With that I pulled a large wooden box out from under the bed and lifted the lid.

"Good Lord! Are they all yours? There must be dozens!"

"Yes. There are nineteen of them and that one, pointing to this year's, that's twenty."

"And all this!" she said, holding an empty bottle up. "What's this tied to the bottle?" It was the cork with a date written on it.

"Oh, that is - let's look, fourth June 1961. Yes, I will have to look it up. Yes, that's the power failure one with Mary and Kay."

"This?" she said, holding up a very big garland of dead dry flowers.

"Put that back, it's personal."

"You have got everything in here. Let's look."

"No, it is my life and mine only!"

"Look my name!" As she opened a diary,

"Put that down. Yes Abigail, you are a big part of it. Now when did we enter Kay in that competition?"

"In April."

"Right here it is," and among the pages I had kept the page of the advertisement.

"Thank God you never throw things away. Come on, let's write a letter to them now."

"No, not on that," she said, as I offered her a notepad. "This has got to be posh. We are dealing with class here. Take me home now, I'll get proper scented paper." 'Abigail can be so bossy at times,' I thought, as we went down the stairs and mother called out.

"Did you find what you were looking for?"

"Yes thank you," replied Abigail.

"You're a lucky girl then. I never go into his room. It's full of old junk."

"That's not junk, that's part of his lovely life," and with that she was out of the door.

\*\*\*

Back at Abigail's the coffee was brewed and she produced a wallet of lovely white leather that contained an assortment of coloured paper and envelopes.

"Pink I think," she said, sliding a sheet out and an envelope to go with it. She had a way with words and was soon licking a stamp to put on the letter. *"There"* she said. *"Now we will go together and post it. It's not far to the box at Church Square. Hurry up and finish your drink, you always let it get cold."* So together we strolled arm in arm to the letterbox. Pausing, she said, *"Kiss the letter,"* and *together we will say a little prayer to send it on its way."* With that, I kissed the envelope and wished *'God's Speed'* to get a reply. We ambled back along the pavement, Abigail rested her head on me, both of us deep in thought.

\*\*\*

It was about a week later. We had been dancing in the meantime but it was not the same with Kay so far away, when Abigail phoned. I was far out on the marsh when I saw the white flag flying from its mast. It was a signal to tell me to come home so I walked beside the ditches, lost in a dream, not realising the urgency of the flying flag. As I entered the back door mother said,

*"Abigail's been on the blower, something about a reply. Come up or something whatever that means."* I was gone, no time to wash or change. Pulling the old pigswill van up in the road at Abigail's, she appeared on the doorstep.

*"Where have you been it's come a reply from them!"* I kicked my rubber boots off and entered the front room.

*"Wait a minute,"* she said, as she put an old newspaper on the chair.

*"There, sit on that, you stink of pig shit!"*

*"Sorry,"* I said. *"I can't smell it."*

*"Of course you can't, it's you! Look!"* she said, unfolding a letter on headed notepaper from France. *"They want to see more of Kay's work, but we don't know where she is."*

*"I've got a lot of her old ones at home,"* I said.

*"What, in your room? Clever you come on then"* and she rushed out of the room. *"Come on!"* Always in a rush our Abigail, with her there was never a dull moment.

*"I'm coming!"* I said, as I stumbled to get one of my feet into a boot.

\*\*\*

We arrived at my house in ten minutes. She was in the back door with a *"Hi mum"* and up the stairs with no finesse at all. The second time the girl had gone to my bedroom in one week! What was mother to think? Oh well, I am twenty-one now and starting to get more like the girls every day. Mother said *"she's in a hurry"* as I kicked my boots off once again on the doorstep, *"I think she is upstairs."* I entered my room to find Abigail lying over my bed with her bum in the air, struggling to pull my box out from underneath the bed.

*"No, not in there,"* I said, and pulled a drawer out from the pine dressing table. *"Here you are."* It was full of old notes and yes, two-dozen sketches of Kay's on scraps on paper that she had done at school.

*"Give them here." "They will have to do any more?"*

*"Well only that."* I gestured to a picture Kay had drawn of me on a large piece of stiff card with three photographs of her stapled to it.

*"Marvellous,"* she said, pulling the drawing pins out and rolling it carefully up into a neat roll with the other drawings and photos inside.

*"This will have to do then, but we must not stop saying our prayers at night. Some of these are very old, but they won't know that will they?"*

\*\*\*

We returned downstairs where mother was standing at the bottom.

*"Found what you were looking for?"* giving Abigail a good once over with her eyes, and I could see she was pleased with what she saw. *"Do have a cup of tea and tell me all about yourself. He has talked so much about you. I think by what he has said that you must be Abigail. I hate it when he calls you Abby. Your mother gave you a name, which is what you should use, not corrupt it like he has his. No-one knows his real Christian name, they all call him by his grandfather's name but people seem to love him."* That was a cue for Abigail.

*"Yes, yes, he is adorable, such a treasure, never a bad word for anyone, always so generous and polite. It makes me laugh to see him tip his hat every time he says hello to people."*

*"Of course he does,"* exploded mother. He has manners. This took Abigail by surprise for if nothing else, mother thought that she was a notch up on most women and woe betide anyone that sneered or laughed at her boys. The two of them got on like a house on fire. Mum liked Abigail. That was the first thing to make me happy in the last six months.

\*\*\*

I took Abigail home and we packed the drawings up, we arranged for her to take them to the post office tomorrow, as the roll would not go into a pillar-box without bending. Then it was home to bed and another entry in my diary that only mum, and now Abigail, now knew I kept.

\*\*\*

We got our answer within six days. They were sorry for the delay in answering the last letter. Yes, they would accept Kay and could she meet them in one month's time? Hell! We had no idea where she was or how to contact her, but surely someone must know even if it was only her parents? They must by now see the sense of such a lucrative job for their precious daughter now she was no longer going to be able to walk? Trouble was we didn't know where they were. Abigail had the solution. Place an advert in a reputable national paper, which was read worldwide. An entry would be put in the personal column for anyone who knows the whereabouts of Kay, please contact Abigail, at this address, reward given. This ad ran for one and a half years, costing me a small fortune, but unfortunately we had no replies. So it looked as if Kay was gone forever. The light of my life was somehow slowly ebbing away. Would the tide never turn?

\*\*\*

Our farm at home was at last sold but Kay never left my mind, every day I had her in my head and she would just not go away. Abigail was the only link I had with the memory of my darling. So much had gone before, always with her in the background.

\*\*\*

As time went on I saw a lot of Abigail and became very close to her, she was my best mate. John was out east for ten months at a stretch. I wrote to Kay every day, sending the letters to her old house hoping to get some response. One of our farms had sold very quickly, within five weeks. Kay's parents could not shift theirs. A caretaker was looking after it for them but he could not, or would not, tell anyone the whereabouts of the family. Yes the letters were sent on from him but through an agent in Ashford, and no, they would not divulge the address of the family, for reasons that they were not at liberty to give. Still Kay never wrote to either Abigail or me.

\*\*\*

That winter as my new trawler took shape, Abigail and I went dancing and to folk clubs. There we would stand, tap our feet, slap our sides with our hands and sing all the old favourites. We were enjoying being young. We went out together for a drink and walked in step with our arms around each other, seeming to the entire world like lovers, but we never kissed. It was a truly platonic friendship. We both needed each other at that time in our lives. She had the occasional letter from her John to keep her going but I had no news of Kay, so needed Abigail to help me live. She was my true soul mate. We could speak to each other on any subject and did so. She told me one night as we sat on that old sofa along the window in her front room drinking coffee of the party just before Kay's accident. While John and I had attacked the shoe polish, Kay and her had lay on the bed and Kay had told her all about how she felt, that I had refused to love her, and that we had got engaged. She said Kay was all right, that I had been a saint to her and she was glad. It had proved to her more than words could how much I really did love her. She hoped to marry me and have my babies. Did I understand? She was only waiting for her twenty-first, so she could leave home and marry me, but both of us had no explanation as to the lack of any word from her. I must have been really down that night for Abigail to hug me and tell me all that.

***

I was under the doctor all that first winter with terrible stomach pains. Abigail said it was all the fussing I did over Kay and was glad the farms were gone. Now I would not spend all my time on a tractor bumping across ploughed ground. Perhaps my ulcers would now heal up? But she failed to see the difference going to sea trawling would have what with all the worry of the weather and wrecks I may catch with the trawl and the shipping in the channel. It was the most dangerous job in the world, everyone knew that. Surely it would not help me recover? But I wanted to get away from it all, at least for some of the time, and while I worried about my safety, I would not be thinking of Kay.

"*What are you naming this vessel of yours?*" she asked me one day over one of her cups of coffee, then stopped in full flow as if a voice had spoken to her. "*Oh Lord, you're not are you?*"

"*Why not*" I said sixth sense again for I had not said a word.

"*You will never forget her if you do,*" but I already knew the name it had got to be and so did Abigail even though we had never talked of it before. It was going to make me happy and keep me safe.

So '*Kay*' it was. '*Ann*' was added after the '*Kay*' this was Abigail's idea, which I went along with to please her, and it took the edge off '*Kay*'. Ann was Abby's second name.

"That's good," she said. It is a type of pepper and goes well with fish. Then she started to cry.

"Please don't." I said. Kay was always in tears. "*Come to the launch and come to sea with me sometime.*"

## CHAPTER FOURTEEN

With one of the farms sold and the other rented out, my life took a new turn. It was now two years since I had heard of Kay. Abigail and I were getting on with our lives.

Our advert in the paper produced not one enquiry from all the millions of readers and no longer could I afford to throw money away. I pressed harder for the big fellow above to give me a clue.

*\*\*\**

All the summer I was out trawling from five pm to six am after Dover Sole that only become catch-able in the summer nights, so I saw less of Abigail, but come autumn, the whiting came in huge shoals and the winter season began. This ran from September to Christmas followed by huge shoals of plaice, which can be trawled in the dark or daylight, just in time for when the dances started. The whiting and plaice gave me all the darkness to concentrate on Abigail. All summer she had worked in tearooms. Now with the whiting and frosts at night, the tourist trade slowed down and she was laid off for the coming winter. As the nights drew in, I would collect her and go dancing or meet up with our mates in some pub. Abigail loved a good pint of bitter in a mug, along with good company.

Her boyfriend was still sending the odd letter and on meeting Abigail that night I would immediately know she had heard from him. Her manner stood out like a ray of light.

As we left her house, and not before, no matter how many hours we stayed in, she never told me she had heard from him. But from the very first step we took together from her home she would say.

"I had word from John today or yesterday. He still says he loves me and I am to wait." Then she would turn and hug me. *"You don't mind do you? You do understand you and I are 'only friends' no more. Hug me and say he is still coming for me one day."*

I was so pleased for her, but she never spoke a lot of him, as if she did not wish me to go away. She needed me as much as I needed her. She was the only link with Kay that I had to cling on to. For some reason I think she understood. Then slipping our arms around each other we walked down to town as if we were lovers. In silence we strolled, lost in our thoughts. Me? I always knew mine. Abigail could never replace my Kay.

*\*\*\**

Fridays were special. Abigail and I took Martin and Graham with us to a town fifteen miles away and there, hidden under a pub in the cellars, was a live folk club full of our age group all out to enjoy themselves. Abigail and I joined in with gusto, standing all night for four hours. With our arms around each other we swayed and sang all the old favourites. The odd tear would appear as we both thought of things that might have been when certain words of a song hit the sentimental nerve spot.

Then often, usually at midnight, the four of us would retire over the road from the pub to a lovely Chinese restaurant for a meal that could last at least one and half hours but more often than not usually took two hours.

The drive home was normally accomplished in silence on a full belly with the others dozing after all the ale that they had drunk.

\*\*\*

The following day, being a Saturday, was my day off from sea. There are no fish markets on Sundays so to a dance somewhere or, as on one occasion, a coach was hired and the whole gang from the pub went to the Lees at Folkestone to hear Bob Miller and his Miller Men play at the hall Kay and I had often danced in. That night the place was packed so Abigail and I stood and hummed to the band as we frequently did while dancing.

These nights of music with Abigail somehow got me through the night but how could I forget Kay? If she had died and was wrapped in a shroud, then I could have cried and said her name aloud. I could have grieved and she would be but a dream.

Somehow, for a while, I did manage to put her out of my mind but next morning she would once again haunt me. It was all the uncertainty of not knowing. Every night before I closed my eyes, I marked the page of my diary for tomorrow with the number of days left to her twenty-first birthday. If only I knew she was still alive. For all I knew she could have died from complications but Abigail and I had ruled that out, as surely we would have heard from someone?

I asked Abigail one night if she had heard from Kay but had been afraid to tell me. She denied this and just said, *'I must wait.'* I don't know why I asked, I just got that funny feeling that Abby knew something and was not letting on. If Kay herself had told me it was all over and given me a kiss, I would have been able to handle it. The pain would have been great at the time, but that uncertain feeling would have gone. I could then have got on with my life. All I had to remember her by were her letters to me and the awful memory of that day, now so far away, as she lay in the hospital bed wrapped in bandages with just her eyes, those sad eyes of hers, looking into mine, the way they said, *'It's you darling'* as she squeezed my hand. Then her mother, *'Out you!'*

\*\*\*

One night Abigail dropped a bombshell on me.

"I have been and got a plane ticket to Germany for tomorrow. I cannot go on like this any more. I must leave you." No amount of pleading would change her mind. She said it was best for her and me. She was so sorry but she had to make a clean break.

Abigail was gone and now I was alone. I cried that night, first Kay and now Abby. Why was my world falling apart? Then my life took another turn.

\*\*\*

I could not live and sleep on the water, the weather saw to that, so I found my mate who could play chess and we played every hour we could.

Abigail sent a letter as soon as she got to the hotel where she was to be a chambermaid. I had sent a huge bouquet of flowers by Inter-flora to greet her. They were in her room as she entered and that had upset her. She wrote. *'There you go again, you do know how to get a girl going, and then stop.'* I had no idea of what she was on about, the last bit read so like a telegram. She was so sad and missed me. *'Love Abigail, kiss, kiss, kiss.'* I read and placed the letter back in its envelope, dated it and put it away in my wooden box of keepsakes. It was forty years later that I read it again.

## CHAPTER FIFTEEN

A few days later, while at sea trawling, the dawn broke to reveal a blood red sky as the sun rose over England and the cliffs of France shone in the early morning rays. Above, the little clouds we called postmen, raced across the sky from the S.W, a sure warning of a blow to come. If I left now I could be on my way home in an hour. I had to make a choice now, as it was a three-hour run to home and I had to be there in the next four hours to catch the tide or stay another eight. There was a ground swell but nothing *'Kay Ann'* could not handle. I had fags, milk and five hundred gallons of fuel so was well supplied. Fish were plentiful, I had nothing to go home for. The sun shone and I daydreamed. I was on my fifth haul and the gear was not due up for another hour, then home.

\*\*\*

Suddenly *'Kay Ann'* took a green sea over the side. *'Where did that come from'* I thought. I then noticed the sea had risen considerably in the last twenty minutes so I turned the radio up and called to see if there were any local or Newhaven boats off but the airwaves were silent. Nothing. I was alone again. My thoughts went to Kay and Abigail out on that land mass to my right. I looked up but could not see France any more and I was only fifteen miles off the coast. The sun had now vanished, the little puffs of cloud from earlier had called their dads and mums up along with all their relations. The sky was lowering all the time. I then called up the Dover Coastguard for a forecast, it was not good. I was told that gales were imminent, they already had wind gusting thirty knots. They asked me where I was and what was the sea condition like? I gave them my position, the cloud base and sea state and they signed off saying,

"Go to Channel 16, listen, out."

\*\*\*

I was on the far side of the Bullock Bank, closer to France than home, and inside of me the sea was already getting wild. Maybe if I hauled now and ran, I could make it to France before the weather closed in over the whole Channel. I would be forty miles closer to Kay and Abigail and I could send Abby a post card. There would be no problem getting rid of the hundred odd stone of plaice and ray out on deck ready boxed, as a trawler that is storm bound is allowed to sell his fish in emergencies, even if the skipper had no passport. The boat was registered in Rye and carried the world famous RX letters and numbers.

\*\*\*

Already we were being pooped over the stern by some of the larger waves so I swung to haul the trawl. Laying broadside I had to be easy on the winch and could only haul as she slid down a wave. The deck was awash as good old *'Kay Ann'* slipped her gunwale under a crest falling wave. I shouldn't be here on my own. Why had I not listened to the six o clock forecast on the wireless?

The cod end was washed, more than hauled, over the side. I lashed the doors of the trawl to the gallows and crept back to the dry of the wheelhouse.

*"What's the weather like now with you?"* I asked the man who answered the

radio in Dover.

"*Channel 12 please, going down.*" So I switched to channel 12.

"*That's better,*" he said. "*Must keep 16 open as there is a severe gale warning, the wind is fifty knots here now. Can I help you?*" I gave him my boat's call sign and he immediately said "*Oh yes, you called an hour ago. Where are you now?*" I told him and he said, "*Good luck and be careful, keep on 16.*" I wished him good evening and turned to steam into the heaped up waves now racing towards me with angry hissing white lips.

Poor '*Kay Ann*' had a job to cope as she rose to meet the challenge before her. The water curled over her bows and surged along the deck. I was concerned that the forward hatch could come off then all would be lost so I lay her to the sea and donning a life jacket for the first time in my life, I tied myself to a three quarter inch rope and crawled on my hands and knees. The smock I was wearing came down to the calves of my legs. As I tried to crawl all I did was creep up the inside of my waterproofs and could not advance an inch. After five minutes of playing silly buggers I pulled it up around my waist. Holding four six-inch nails in my mouth and a four-pound club hammer in my right hand, I managed to get to the hatch. It nearly made me cry to drive the nails into that lovely mahogany wood but I could not allow the sea a passage below deck.

***

'*Kay Ann*' rode the seas well broadside but the wind on the wheelhouse up forward turned her stern to the sea. A wave picked up the stern trawl door and breaking the lashings took it to a watery grave. The chain legs and trawl followed this and then with a bang, they were parted from the winch drum. The same wave washed me across the deck into the port scupper. The trawl had followed over the side, still with fish from the last haul in the cod end. The attached forward chain legs came up tight to the forward door and '*Kay Ann*' swung bows to the seas, steadied now with the aft door and trawl acting as a sea anchor. Breathless and wet I made the safety of the wheelhouse to hear the radio alive with calls for help down the Channel where the wind was coming from.

They were having it bad and soon I was to get it. Every time we took a wave the bow on '*Kay Ann*' was drowned in solid green water. I knew there was only so much we could take.

A monster lump of water came aboard, exiting over the port gunwale and the chain to the forward door parted, so losing our sea anchor. That was it, we had to ride it out, we could not go about in these seas. We lay nose up on the engine listening to the radio. It was not good.

They gave sixty knots gusting seventy and Dover had fifty to fifty-five in gusts. I was in the middle on my own and there was not a ship in sight. It was going to be useless to head for Rye harbour in this filthy weather. No way could you live in the seas of the red light at the entrance to the harbour at home in such shallow water.

I had no idea where I was now as the Decca Navigator had chucked its hand in owing to the buffeting it was getting. Everything in the cabin was either plastered on the walls or on the floor. The wheelhouse carpet was half an inch deep in water. I had to get a sea anchor away.

The first thing to come to hand was the rock hopper trawl in a tin bath lashed alongside the wheelhouse. This was a heavy trawl with a lot of chain in the ground rope. I managed to lash a new two-inch polypropylene rope around the net and through the two handles of the bath passing the end in and out of the net meshes. The brand new coil of rope stood in the wheelhouse between the seas running across the open deck. I hooked the gilson on, knocked the winch ends in gear and threw three turns of rope around the capstan head. Net and bath full of water slid away from its resting place alongside the wheelhouse, snapping the ropes that held it down and it swung up into the air. Then as we rolled to a sea, I whipped the end off the drum and the whole lot disappeared over the side. The tail end of the heaving halyard sang as it travelled up to the block on the masthead, then with a crack it was free of its prison.

\*\*\*

The rope snaked out of the inside of the new coil standing in the wheelhouse. A new rope of one hundred and twenty fathoms, it was rapidly vanishing like a big dipper at a fun fair. I had to slow it down and secure it to us. I slammed the sliding wheelhouse door shut to jam the orange snake in its travel. This slowed it down no end. Turning the coil on its side, I grabbed the end of the pile. Throwing the wheel house door open I dived for the winch and took some turns around any ironwork I could. It was just in time as the last of the coil vanished seawards. *'Kay Ann'* took the strain up and swung to her new saviour over three hundred yards long that now had the fast sinking trawl attached.

\*\*\*

I lay on the wheel and gazed out across the heaving mass of water and prayed she would ride the foaming waves. I turned the second bilge pump on just in case the first one could not cope with the water finding its way down below to the engine room via the ventilators, as at times they vanished beneath solid water racing across the deck.

My clothes steamed with the heat from the exhaust pipe that ran up through the wheelhouse. The compass did at least one complete somersault in its gyro nest. This was getting serious stuff. Around me, on the water in the same ocean, people were drowning and calling for help on the radio but I was helpless to do anything. *'Kay Ann'* was fighting for her life and mine. I could not find my Bible, everything was in a mess on the floor. I always had it alongside the books of navigation and charts. The light left the sky early that day, I prayed that dark angry night, for others, and myself all on the same sea.

\*\*\*

Once in the small hours I saw the lights of a large ship going down channel into the weather but he was well clear of me and I wondered had he seen my puny lights or picked me up on his radar? I doubted it for we were more under the sea than on top of the water. That was the only sign of life that night. The lighthouse of Dungeness was the first clue I had as to where we were.

***

Then as suddenly as it had come, the wind dropped. For sixteen long hours 'Kay Ann' had *'cuddled me in her bosom,'* never putting a foot wrong, so like her namesake on the dance floor. I hauled the sea anchor in on the winch to find the net and bath missing. Two hundred yards of rope had been enough to keep her head up to wind. Then we steadily jogged our way in to try and find shelter under what there was from the point. The Bay's water was still confused, the seas across the sullen looking water rolled in an endless mass.

The ocean had taken a real churning tonight. Here I found four ships sheltering from the storm, all weighing over a thousand tons. They had given up the fight to proceed down channel that I had endured in my little boat. I managed to put the anchor down and lay on the trawl warps of seventy fathoms.

***

That dawn *'Kay Ann'* was dancing around like a cork in a washing machine. I lay listening to the radio, it was four am before it went silent and I took my turn to call the coastguard up and report my position. They thanked me very much and that was it. I then called north foreland and tried to put a phone call through, but a familiar voice came up.

"Go to 8 'Kay Ann.'". It was Slipper, a boat from Rye. The owner had gone around to check his craft after the wind in the night and turned his radio on, for he had noticed that my berth was empty in front of him. He was flabbergasted to hear where I was and said he would phone home, as they must be worrying.

***

I lay down on the wet bunk in my wet clothes, not daring to close my eyes, as I was so tired. The wind had abated a lot but the sea was still rough. *'Kay Ann'* rode to the anchor wire like her namesake jumping hedges up on the farm on Napoleon and with a snatch she would rein herself up ready for the next. I was beat. No sleep for thirty hours and worn out. Just trying to keep myself upright in those seas had made my legs ache. I lay there and pondered, *"What am I doing here?"*

I wondered where my life had gone wrong. The girl I love was away somewhere and there had been no word, then Abigail had to go and leave. Kay was snatched by her parents and was powerless to stop them but Abby? She did it herself. Why was I so sad? Abby had gone, it was Kay I loved. Mum always said you must wait and don't get married until you are thirty. I always listened to her so maybe Kay was coming back later. I had no idea. Then it hit me! My mother ruled my life. My mother and father had always said that it was up to me to care for them, perhaps that is why my brothers had got out so fast. I was not allowed to think for myself, Mum did that and I knew now as the skipper of Slipper phoned, she would answer as she would not have slept last night. Nor would she until I had gone to her room and told her nearly everything of what I had done that night, where I had been and who with.

*"Did you have a good time then? There's a good boy. Now get to bed."* As if I was like a small child. This she would do today when I got home. *"Good boy?"*

After tonight, I was not a boy, I was now a man and was going to tell her so. For the last thirty hours I had been in *'Kay Ann's'* bosom and she had looked after me. I had nursed her far and she had not put a foot wrong. I was going to write to Abigail and tell her that no more was I telling mum anything. I was a man! My boat was my life at the moment and no more was mother going to guide me. *'Kay Ann'* had looked after me while others along the coast had died.

\*\*\*

As quickly as it had come, the wind had dropped to a gale, and then a stiff breeze and the sea had dropped to a big swell. I was going home trawl and fishless after thirty hours at sea, the winch clanked into action. The warp *'sissed'* up through the roller and then with a rattle and crash the hook was up. I slammed the winch out of gear and turning to the wheel pushed the throttle open, charging the swell. *'Kay Ann'* buried her nose then split the wave asunder. We were going home across a confused sea so like a dance floor, dodging all around us.

\*\*\*

As we rounded the point we picked up a bigger swell and the sea got a lot taller, but the water between the waves was as smooth as a millpond. We relished each and every wave. *'Kay Ann'* smelt blood and home. We rocked and rolled over and down the white horses. As we rounded the harbour arm and lined up the river only two people were out with their dog, they looked up as *'Kay Ann'* lay her starboard side into the sea, running her gunwale level with the water and showing her bottom off to the world like Kay had done those years before while doing the Tango with me.

Our decks were swept clear of anything moveable so nothing could slide off. No boxes or nets were left, all was lost in the previous night. Now only the winch stood proud. The anchor wedged up to the winch still attached to the warp. The swell across the bar to the river was massive but we knew our way. We came into the calm water of the river like a drunk rolling through sixty degrees. The two hundred and forty horsepower engine never missed a beat. It was our heart. We felt invincible. Why I had expected a crowd of folk to see us in, I don't know, but I felt disappointed that a brass band at least was not up there on the harbour arm to greet her and me safely home after the battle we had just fought together.

\*\*\*

A few of my mates came along as I tied up and coming aboard told me, *"You look knackered. We will make sure everything is turned off and give the stern tube grease. Go on home to bed."*

My old van started second time and I was off. It felt weird, no more tossing around, everything was solid.

Driving into the yard mum called out

*"Everything all right? that was so thoughtful of you to get a message to me. Moonbeam said you were safe."*

Moonbeam was a bloke I knew, a coastguard in our local station. He had been listening to my radio conversation with Dover all night and had phoned mum. I was too tired to say anything and clambered up the stairs, throwing my wet gear off as I fell exhausted into bed.

\*\*\*

I woke at ten that night after fourteen hours of solid sleep and had a bath. While I was soaking the salt out of my skin mum asked if I had had a good catch and where were the fish? She had been round the boat and it was so clean she hardly knew it, but the paintwork was rather shabby. Was I cleaning it to paint up? I did not bother to say anything. Poor old *'Kay Ann'* had been jet blasted. Any loose paint had been washed off. I dressed and left the house.

\*\*\*

It was now ten forty five at night. Where could I go to be alone? I knew where Kay and me used to hide out on the marsh away from everyone. I had a lot to think about, nothing made sense, but I was determined to shake off mother's grip on me. I was convinced that she was a big part of my problem. Later I drove home slowly, coming over the bridge by the moorings, I noticed that *'Kay Ann'* was alone again, the only boat not to have gone to sea. My heart hurt, I was alone again. When were we going to get our act together?

\*\*\*

Next day I returned to the boat and sorted the gear out. What a mess. Food and oil was on everything, including the ceiling. My Bible was under the clothes on the bunk and thankfully was dry. I lay on the bunk bed and dreamed the whole day away.

I slipped in the back door on tiptoe, ever so gently, it was two am by now, but not without mum hearing me.

"*Where have you been? You've missed the tide.*"

"Tide!" I said. "*I saw enough of that bloody tide yesterday night.*"

"*Now, now don't swear. You know I don't like it.*" I thought 'there she goes again, she doesn't like it. Tough!' "*Where have you been at this time of night?*"

"*I don't have to tell you do I?*"

"*What's the matter? Don't you feel well?*"

"*Yes, I'm fine, but I am not going to be quizzed by you every time I go out.*" It must have been the tone of my voice as I am never one to raise it usually that made her ask the next question.

"*Did you bang your head the other night in the storm?*" There she goes again, more of the same.

"Yes," I said and it has made me come to my senses. "*I'm not telling you any more of what I do?*"

"*Oh. Let me get up and look at you. Whatever is the matter?*"

"*Nothing I've had it up to here.*"

"*Don't speak like that, you'll make me ill.*" 'Here we go again,' I thought. 'I've had enough of this,' and slammed the door shut. I left in the car and drove to the sea wall. There I stood and stared out to the horizon. It was perfectly clear tonight with all my mates' lights twinkling on the edge of the sea where the sky touches. I looked at the lighthouse which I last saw in that gale and it reminded me of my Kay and the night four years ago when I asked her to be my girl and she said *'Yes, silly boy, I am your girl,'* and kissed me. I stood on that blessed sea wall for three hours that night, just dreaming of the times we had shared together before her fall.

***

Next day mother said nothing of the night but now took a new tack on trying to run my life. It was her health now. If things did not go her way, her heart would *'play up'* as she put it. I loved my mum and dad but he had little to say when mother was about. She ruled him as she was trying to rule me and fool that I am, I let her. People today, who knew her say.

"Didn't you know?"

"Well no. I never had a clue did I?" Growing up in those days you did as you are told. Today it is all so different. The kids watch telly and see it all going on, the parents have no hope of ruling them. It has become a sad, cruel world. Even today I am naïve about some things that I should know of.

***

Well the summer came and went, with the odd letter from Abigail. She was coming home at last as I had *'failed to go and get her,'* whatever that meant. I now planned to go by my small eighteen-foot fishing punt across the channel to Calais, enter the canal system of Europe and travel to the Rhine to pick her up. I had even got the Master Mariner's Certificate to navigate the waterways from the German Embassy in London, when another letter arrived that said, *'Don't bother,'* she would be home by then.

***

Days later I met her in the Mermaid pub. We spoke and it all started to come together again. Yes we were still friends, she was sorry. I said.

"Don't, it's nothing." She tried to tell me something, saying it was very personal, but I would not listen. It was private to her, I thought, not the sort of thing you talk about like the boys used to do in the pub. Of course I was wrong. You should talk of things that affect you and others but I had been brought up not to discuss with anyone the way you felt.

***

So Abby, along with Martin, Graham and me used to go to folk clubs. Dancing at all the halls had died out with the Twist and Beatles coming. We spent the whole winter together and I used to stay up Abby's until early morning each night and talk. Some days she came to sea with me. We were such good friends again. She gutted fish, she hauled on chains and she used to lay the trawl over the gunwale ready for next day. We had a whole summer together.

***

That following winter we again ventured to folk clubs with Martin and Graham. Other nights Abby and I talked and drank chocolate. The coffee was at last off the menu. I don't know why.

Then one night we ended up at my house. My mother and father were away, perhaps that is why, my diaries do not tell me anything. Somehow we did more than talk and she taught me a thing or two in the art of women and men.

From that day things went haywire. She was always busy. No she could not go out on Saturday to the club. I started to doubt myself. Was my mother right after all? All the time we were friends the girls loved my company. From that night on Abigail was so different, it did not make us closer to each other. You had crossed a bridge and there was no going back. I am afraid it put me off for many years and I decided *'never get close to a girl, it will always end in tears.'* Good mates. That was the way to love a girl, but do not touch. If only some of my mates had told me what to do. Why did Abigail, so wise in all ways, not say anything that night? Maybe my life would have been full of more joy.

***

We drifted apart and then I heard she was getting married. John was home from the air force for good. Abby got married but I did not go. I was too upset to see her wed. It meant I was now completely alone.

I never heard from Abby again. I turned to Martin and we played chess nearly every night for two years. Martin came to my house every night and set the chessboard up. Sitting on our own we played into the small hours. My mother was happy. Martin and I talked. What were we going to do?

All our mates were married and we spent hours at christenings of the married couples. I was asked five times to be the godfather of their offspring, but Martin and I had no girls. Still Kay would not leave my head. It got so bad in the end that one night he produced a paper with a load of adverts for partners in it. We discussed advertising in the lonely-hearts section for a girl. He had a go and on the day I wished him good luck. Later at eleven pm he was back at the chessboard.

*"What a let down that was, nothing like the photo,"* he said *"and old! At least fifty if she was a day!"* The picture of her she had sent him was twenty years out of date. She had cost him a fortune on grub. *"Never again,"* he said, so we dropped that idea and I resigned myself to becoming a grumpy and smelly old bachelor.

Then one night Martin failed to show up. I phoned his mum and she said he had gone out with a girl. Within six months he was married secretly. I tried going out with any girl who would accompany me for the night, but all told me the same. We were going nowhere all the time I loved Kay. Now I was ALONE.

## CHAPTER SIXTEEN

I left in sunshine to cross Romney Marsh to arrive at a wonderful old pub not far from her home. We were to meet at six thirty pm. I had given myself three hours to find the establishment and suss it out. This was to be the first time I had seen her for thirty-six years. She was now a widow and recovering from a life threatening operation. I felt I had to see her one last time. I had phoned a month earlier and left a message asking if she could meet me. Now I was feeling very privileged that she had phoned two days previously asking if we could meet. Such a lot of time had gone by. I was frightened that I may not recognise her. The girl who was my best mate in the sixties would surely have changed from the bouncy go easy lass I knew.

She was the only link I had with Kay. I had heard they were still friends and perhaps that is what drove me on to see her.

I had picked a big bunch of sweet peas to place on the table for her to see when she entered the pub so there would be no embarrassment for her if she had forgotten what I now looked like. I had no knowledge if she had ever seen me since she got married.

\*\*\*

The car purred as I left Rye and the sky darkened as a thunderstorm sailed over the cliffs at Fairlight, overtaking me out on the marsh. Sheep were running for any shelter there was and the wind increased to near gale force. The rain came down like hop poles and the road flooded. With all the lights on and front and back wipers going full blast, the visibility dropped to twenty yards.

I plodded my way, lost in thought of what to expect at the other side of this dark, highly excited sky. Traffic crawled along and across the marsh. This was supposed to be a happy occasion. I had set off with a promise of sunshine, now the whole world around me was fighting a glorious war. Was this a premonition of what lay in store? Was God trying to tell me something? I drove on in a dream.

As I neared my destination, the clouds lifted and as the thunderstorm passed on further into Kent, the tarmac started to steam. A summer's evening was in the offing. I found the pub, parked in the car park and entered.

\*\*\*

I sat in the main bar and ordered a coffee. A young lad called Jack behind the bar said it was all right for me to sit and wait two hours for the girl to appear. The diaries of mine, in which her name so often appeared, lay on the seat beside me. In them was her life with me. On the table I sat at lay the bunch of sweet peas. I waited in anticipation. What was I expecting? She was thirty-one years older and had two kids. Then a voice said,

"What are you doing here? You won't find any fish here?" I looked up and there stood Erne, a fellow I had not seen for twelve years and he knew me all dressed up in my best. Never had he seen me like this before. Always when we met, I was in my old dirty fishing garb miles out at sea. Had my appearance not changed in those years? Maybe my best friend's had not either. She said she never watched television so had never seen me on the telly or read about me in the papers or seen any of the books I had written.

*\*\*\**

As the last half hour ticked away I wondered would she come and would I know her? Now only thirty minutes separated our reunion, I was already into my fourth cup of coffee. The wind had dropped and the scent of the flower gardens out side filled the air. My heart was up in my throat. I was scared of the reaction I would show on her entry.

From where I sat I commanded a view of both entrances to the pub so as not to be surprised by her appearance. My body was shaking. *'Come on, it's only a meeting of an old friend for God's sake!'* I said to myself, as the large hand of the clock slowly, so slowly, fell to the right.

I changed seats to sit as far away from the bar and other people but still with a view of both doors. Fifteen minutes to go. Was she going to be late or would she even come? How did she feel? If anything like me, she could easily get cold feet. I had never felt like this. My mind flashed back to the time when I saw Kay naked for the first time. Maybe I had felt like this then. I could feel my heart beating and it was not good at my age to get in a state like this. I had to calm down or I'd have another stroke! I knew inside myself that she would not want that!

*\*\*\**

A young couple entered and sat opposite me. The poor girl kept yawning and looking at the top of the table. I had not seen them enter so I must stop writing this and take note. The girl of the sweet peas may enter and seeing me now, thirty six years down the line, decide that she could not go through with it, then flee.

I must stop scribbling but I wished to note my feelings, also her appearance, and the look on her face. I stirred my fifth cup of coffee and stopped. I was winding it up into froth! I lay my glasses on my writing pad alongside my pen. The young girl opposite lit a cigarette as I rolled a fag. Four minutes to go until six thirty, the first of July. Two minutes and my hands are shaking. My heart is thumping and there she is!

*\*\*\**

I rose to my feet and went to greet her. *"Hello"* was all she said. I gave her a kiss on the right side of her face, she stepped up to the bar and ordered a white wine with lemonade. She then opened her little purse to pay.

*"No Abigail I will buy that,"* and put my hand in my pocket. *"Come and sit with me and we can talk."*

*"I have not got long,"* was the first collective sentence she had spoken to me in all those years.

*"We have a lot to say to each other,"* I said.

*"I don't think so,"* she answered.

*"Yes we have, or I have. Those are for you,"* pointing to the flowers lying on the table. *"I picked them for you from the row in the garden."*

"I love sweet peas."

"I remember, you always did and these are yours," passing a bundle of letters to her tied up in blue ribbon. "I always gave the girls the letters they had sent me before they got married, but I never saw you after John came home, so here they are now."

"You have kept these since 1966?" She slipped the ribbon off and opened one from Germany. Her face took on a distinctly different expression as she started to read. Her eyes met mine and she spoke.

"Oh No!" she then tore them up one at a time, holding each one out in front of her to make a point. "Why did you keep them all?"

"Because that was our life for five years as real friends and to me it meant a lot. Now it is but a dream, a sweet dream."

\*\*\*

She had a lot to say but denied she knew or had heard from Kay, although I had heard that recently they had had lunch together. Why was she lying to me? What had happened? Did she know why Kay never wrote to either of us? Abby then started to cry. A woman of fifty-eight crying is not a pretty sight, I put my arm around her and she lay onto me.

"Sorry." She was 'so sorry' 'I did not know did I, after all this time?' "No-one has told you have they? It is not right." Someone surely had told me?

"What?" I said. "Whatever is it? Don't tell me Kay is dead, please."

"No, it's worse than that."

"What can be more terrible than that?" I said. And between sobs she went on to tell me that Kay had been in contact with her from the time she was moved from England. Then in 1964 she had heard from Kay with news that neither wished me to hear and that is the reason she had gone to Germany, she just did not have the heart to tell me.

\*\*\*

"You heard from Kay?"

"Yes, but I had fallen in love with you. You did not want to hear the news. I just could not tell you. She got pregnant and it was on her first and only date. She was distraught with guilt. It was with a nurse where she was staying, they only went out the once. She wanted me to tell you she was sorry and hoped you would forgive her. She said she would never come back and you would never see her again but she wrote to me often."

"How is Kay, can she walk."

"Yes she is fine. After she had the baby, which her parents made her give away, Kay decided that she had to come and see you and confess her true love for you. She came and stayed with me. She saw you at a party one night but her guilt got the better of her. She said you looked so happy without her, you were smiling. She knew of your ulcers and how unhappy she would make you, it was all her fault, you believed in not making love till you married and she had let you down.

She cried bitterly that night for you and my father went back one hour later to the party to bring you to her, but you were gone and the others there said you had *left soon after Kay showed so they all thought you were at last together. I was so unhappy for you Preacher. That is when I had to leave you, I realised I then had fallen in love with you.*

*\*\*\**

*"Then I came back from Germany and still you were alone. I tried to tell you as soon as I saw you but you would not listen to me. You do remember don't you? That night in the Mermaid."*

"Yes," I said. "You told me it was personal."

*"Do you remember those evenings we spent alone talking?"*

"Course I do Abby, and all that coffee."

*"I used to phone Kay afterwards and tell her you were still in love with her, but she said that what she had done was a sin in your eyes and you could never forgive her. Then one night she called me and told me she had met a man and was going to live with him in Australia. That is the night I took you to bed. I had to even the score for her didn't I? You were so green even then. It was not fair on you but I could not tell you of Kay. Can you ever forgive me, please? It has worried me for over thirty-six years. There, I have told you at last."*

"Kay?" I said. "Did she go to Australia?"

*"Oh yes, and had another kid, but life was not good to her. The years have taken their toll, unlike you and me. She has lost all her lovely looks and her man ran away from her, leaving her with the kid under seven months old. She never got married. She told one of her friends only last year that not marrying was the only honest thing she could do as she had promised to marry you.*

*There, Preacher, you have it all."* Abby looked at me and wiped her face. *"All I can say is sorry. Even I have not been fair with you. To think of all those times and everything we three did, and all that money you spent on us. And the places we went to. Do you know? I still have that laundry box with all those little things inside? To think once we were able to wear them. Do you remember the boot polish affair, and the girl up the wall? And look."* And she pulled her jumper down a little to show the round mark from the cigarette lighter, so long ago, still evident.

I was getting ready to cry.

*\*\*\**

I noticed the time, we had only been together for twenty-eight minutes and we had finished all there was to say. A tall rugged outdoor type of bloke wearing a pair of paint stained jeans and red checked shirt appeared from nowhere on cue, as if Abby had somehow signalled him. Abigail stood up and gave him a kiss on the lips, turning to smile at me she grabbed her handbag and flowers.

*"Stay a while Abigail. Look, you have two young men now to look after you."*

*"No, I must go,"* and he took her out on his arm through the door leaving half a glass of wine behind on the table. *"Goodbye,"* she said, half turning in the doorway to twiddle her left hand at me. I packed my diaries away, took a sip of her wine and left.

*\*\*\**

Driving back along the ridge of the North Downs, I stopped at a vantage point six minutes later to look west across a beautiful flat marsh that seemed to glow in the strange light, that you so often get after a storm.

The sea around Hythe Bay to Dungeness was picked out in its curve along the shoreline by white surf and fourteen miles away in the distance shone a ray of sun on Fairlight Hill that below lay the marsh and my home. Yes the storm going out did mean something. It was the end of a long, long dream with Abigail. Was Kay to come to mean the same thing, a dream I was never to have in real life. The sun beckoned me home to my marsh.

I had seen Abigail again, perhaps for the last time and she was happy. I thought nothing had changed other than the years. Still with the same hairstyle and figure and the walk, each step a little jump, but *'still a cold fish'* is the way one of my mates had called her and as I drove home I thought that was the best description for her. A sort of ease came over me, I had seen and spoken to her. I stopped on my way and climbed the steps to the top of the sea wall.

Standing there alone thinking over all that Abby had told me, I realised that the girl I had trusted and thought such a lot of had stabbed me in the back. The night at sea when I came to realise that my mother ruled my life was not the only reason my life had not progressed as I had wished. Losing contact with all my old mates as they had got married, it now dawned on me that the girl I had trusted and shared all my most private secrets with had been using them for her own use. Every time I got low, she was the one to tell me I had to have faith and patience, all along she had been praying it was her that I would choose. I was so dim of girls that I had never seen it.

Working on my own all my life, either on a tractor far out on the marsh, or at sea a long way from other human beings, I had had no one to talk to. Even up the pub in the evenings when I did go, my mates had long given up shouting at me so I could hear properly, choosing rather to huddle in close to each other and whisper the secrets of girls and others.

My misfortune was that at the age of nineteen to have fallen in love with the most beautiful girl of fifteen. She had been the first girl I had ever been out with. I should have had many girls before her to gain experience. Alas Abby had played on my naivety and when she left me, girls were still a mystery. Standing on the sea wall tonight it finally overflowed, for the last thirty years I had lived a lie. After Abby left to marry, I had buried myself in my work.

## CHAPTER SEVENTEEN.

The meeting that day with Abby opened my eyes. I longed for company, especially a woman who would hold me in her arms and tell me she loved me. Abby had confessed that Kay was still alive and I wondered how she had coped with her life. Mine was a shambles of deceit and lies.

In my box of keepsakes of the sixties, now moved from under my bed and sitting in my office, all the letters from Kay, I had not opened any of the letters for nigh on forty years having pushed them aside when removing Abby's old letters. Now I thought I would look at them tomorrow.

It was well past midnight when I eventually closed the back door behind me and crept to my empty bed.

\*\*\*

The following morning the summer's sun lit up the desk in my office as I took the blue ribbon off the bundle of old love letters that Kay had written to me before her accident all those years ago. How could anyone who had placed those loving words on paper not have meant what they conveyed? Each one of the words was penned and couched in a manner of conveying pure love, all addressed to me, a nineteen-year-old boy. I tied them back up and gave them a kiss as I placed them back into the bottom of the old pine box and shed a remorseful tear that ran down my cheek and splashed the top envelope. Too long ago, I thought. She was like Abby, a dream of a lost love, a delightful intrusion in my life all those years ago.

\*\*\*

Three days later a letter arrived addressed to me and marked in the top left hand corner of the envelope in large red letters *'Private.'* I shuffled it into the pile of post and took it to my office. Later, after breakfast, I turned it over and studied the white envelope. Something made me think that it was out of place in my humdrum life and I slit it open with my marmalade covered breakfast knife. The neatly folded white letter fell into my hand. Opening it out, it was the neatest handwriting and started, *'Dear Preacher.'*

It had been over thirty years since anyone had called me that, so I quickly read on. The letter was from Abby's daughter and she was upset that I had recently contacted and met her mother. The meeting had disturbed both her and her mother and could she now see me to find out a few things? I was invited to write to her at the university she attended and was asked not to tell her mother. Also, she said, she had news that she thought I would be interested in hearing. The tantalising way the letter was phrased, how could I not write back to the young girl?

\*\*\*

A week later I was to meet this twenty three year old girl in a pub of her own choice, alone. Leading up to the day, the days could not pass fast enough. I was wishing my life away to hear what information this girl had for me.

\*\*\*

The pub in Ashford was full of young people. I was conscious at my age of standing out as the odd one. The pot of coffee in front of me had long gone cold, it sat alongside my hat, which the girl had asked me to place on the table so that she could recognise me. A trio of young girls had been drinking at a table when I entered an hour before. Now, in an organised way, they got up and advanced on my table. The auburn haired one of the three asked me if I was the Preacher. I removed my glasses and could see the resemblance to her mother in her manners and face, and the way she smiled at me.

*"Are you Ann,"* I asked?

All three then drew the chairs out from the table and sat down. I was under instant scrutiny. Obviously stories of me had been told to them and they now wished to know if what they had heard were true.

The girl introduced herself as Ann and then her friends were made known to me. Ann told me that after the meeting with her mother the other day she could not stop talking of me. Seldom had my name been mentioned when her father was alive. The only time Ann could remember was when her father had caught her climbing in her bedroom window one night. Then her father had looked on in amazement as her mother burst into tears and neither of them could stop her. *"She said it reminded her of a time with a boy,"* and she gave me a lovely smiling look, *"you and her had got another girl into a bedroom window far off the ground. Was it true Preacher? Did you two stand on a dustbin that night?"*

*"Yes and afterwards she was crying and when I asked why, she said because no one would believe her and she wanted to tell her children one day, which she obviously has done."*

*"And why did you tear all her letters up, then keep them to give to her the other day?"*

That question really got my attention.

Torn up letters? She had ripped them up in front of me, and obviously after I left, she must have returned for them.

Ann wanted to know a lot of what her mother and I had done in the time she was waiting for her father to come home. I got the distinct impression that Ann and her mother were really close to each other and shared everything together. The other two girls were interested more in why I had wanted to meet Ann's mother after so many years. The torn up letters were common knowledge and Ann had even read them.

***

From the girls I learned that the relationship Abby had had with a younger man for six months had suddenly ended. The opinion among the three girls in the pub that night was that I had something to do with it and they wanted to know. In their opinion Abby had put up with a lot of sorrow and pain in the last four years and she needed a little happiness now in her life.

That idea I quickly knocked on the head, telling them that the reason to see Ann's mother was something entirely different to what they were all thinking. I needed a few answers as to the whereabouts of a certain woman we both knew years ago. Ann looked quite hurt as though she was hoping that I was trying to make a go of a lost love with her mother.

\*\*\*

Together we talked of what it was like to live in the nineteen sixties as teenagers, of how the world was changing and we were part of it, the music, clothes and cars, the size of transistor radios and no mobile phones. I am afraid I did most of the talking that evening and before I left, Ann gave me her mobile phone number and told me not to tell her mother, and could she call me any time again in case her mother got too depressed over seeing me, especially after the illness she had just gone through? I assured her that I would always be on call to do anything I could. At the same time Ann was writing her phone number down, I thought how the tables have turned. Once I needed her, now here was her daughter asking me to help her. Ann had said that she had gone through a lot of worry and suffering. Had I not also done an awful lot of mourning to the point of running away to sea on a trawler for most of my time? Now as I had got older the farm was my life *'Kay Ann'* had been sold and the new owner taken her away.

\*\*\*

I left the three girls talking to some other friends from university and drove home thinking over the events that had just taken place. Ann was Abby's girl all right, even down to the point of scheming. Surely tonight had not been her mother's idea? No, it was Ann's and she had help from the other two girls to try and get me going with Abby. The thought did cross my mind as to what Abby would say if I was to go and see her, but then I would be showing an interest and I had nothing to say to her after what she had done to me. Ann had no idea of Kay, that had become evident by the way the girls had talked. It was all about Abby and me. The way Abby had gone back to the pub and retrieved the torn up letters told me that there contents did still mean something to her and perhaps she had read more into our last meeting than she had let on. The young man that had taken her out on his arm was perhaps a smokescreen she had ready in case after all those years she could not find anything to arouse her feelings for me again.

Now it seemed possible that the way she thought of me thirty-eight years ago was once again coming to the fore. Suddenly for some reason I felt as though Abby could become a threat to my happiness. My mind was working overtime as to what I had said to Ann. She would more than likely tell her mother she had met me now if only to confirmed the story of the girl in the window.

The simple fact that we had met could stir Abby into thinking that perhaps I did wish to pick up from thirty-eight years ago.

\*\*\*

The ringing of the phone a couple of days later made me jump. Answering the instrument, a very familiar voice asked me to meet her in the same pub in which I had met her a while ago. This time she said she had more time to talk to me. Abby sounded an awful lot like the young girl I had known a long time ago. Her voice bubbled and sang with joy.

I was dubious about the fact that she wished to see me again, especially after the encounter with her daughter. She told me she had met an old friend of ours and I should really come to see her. My heart leapt, was she at last going to be honest and tell me of Kay. Surely that was who the old friend was?

\*\*\*

It was to be a lunchtime meeting this time, so all the afternoon lay before me. I left home at ten thirty to drive to the table I had reserved to dine at. A surprise for Abby I thought as I had told the lad my requirements on the phone.

\*\*\*

The trip out into Kent was done in good weather today, so unlike the last time I had arranged to see Abby. The lad behind the bar recognised me from my last visit and instantly turned to the machine to pore a cup of coffee.

Abby arrived driving a car, unlike last time, completely on her own and into the bargain ten minutes early. A peck on each cheek and she took the drink of white wine and lemonade I had bought her, thanking me with the remark,

"*You always did pay for us girls.*" The words, '*us girls,*' made me wonder if at any moment my Kay would suddenly emerge, but she had meant it as in the past tense, of long ago.

Lunch was paid for by me, as was the custom when with the girls.

It was a very hard time for her she said and seeing me pay brought so many memories flooding back. Why after all this time was I the one that picked the tab up? She told me that now she had money, in the sixties she had often gone out with me without a penny in her purse. She recounted the time we three had gone to London shopping in Carnaby Street and spent more than her father earned in a month. Abby placed her hand over mine resting on the table and gave my fingers a slight squeeze. Those spaniel eyes twinkled as they did those nights while dancing and I detected that wicked look she used to give me, but never realised the meaning of. Now I knew her charm. Kay was the stumbling block to her advances. The mention of her name made her face take on that pitiful look.

"*The other day, you will never guess who I saw?*" she said.

"*Go on,*" I said, praying for her to say those most wonderful letters that spelled Kay's name, but instead she led me on, telling me of a trip she had taken to Dover to do some shopping. There in a large shop she had bumped into Josephine.

"*You remember her don't you?*"

"*Of course I do. How is she?*"

"*Fine, she had been across the channel for the day. She now lives on the other side of London but the best thing is that she told me she sees your Kay at least once a month and has lunch with her. I told her you had made contact with me recently and she was delighted to know you were well. Also she told me she is hoping to come to the fete they hold in Iden each year. She has not been back since she got married and left the village.*"

This was more like the information I was daring to hope for! At last, a tangible thing to cling to if I ever wanted to see Kay again. Already I was thinking that if the feeling Abby had once felt was still there, was it possible Kay also had a glowing ember in her heart that with a little encouragement and a gentle fanning of love from me would once again flare into a passion. There had never been any love in my home, perhaps now there was a chance to move on. It was all thanks to Abby for telling me of Josephine. She even had her telephone number for me to use if I chose.

\*\*\*

The afternoon went quickly and Abby invited me back to her place as she had left the phone number of our old friend at home. I should have seen the warning earlier for there was no reason she could not have phoned me later to exchange it with me. Instead, in my eagerness to make contact with Kay, I followed her in my car to a delightful little bungalow just off the road out side a village near by. Abby did not wait for me to pull up, instead she was unlocking the front door by the time I got out of my car.

On entering, Abby called out for me to make myself at home. She was making a cup of coffee for me and would join me in a minute. The first door I opened held the gas boiler and on closing the door she called out from the kitchen,

*"Try the other one."*

Silly me. Why didn't I think of that! Abby was always the one to tell me what to do and always it was coffee. I took a keen interest in the room I entered, looking at the photos of her and her husband on her wedding day and recognised the church on the hill, which I saw every day. The way the trees and bushes in the photo were bent over and the confetti flying sideways made me realise that the wind was rather vicious that day, even though the sun had shone and I was at sea and forgotten the weather I had fought, just so I did not see or hear the wedding taking place. I must have had feelings for that girl then, even though I never realised, or why else would I have put up with such seas? But it was always Kay, and as that cup of steaming milky coffee came through the door, I was determined that it was Kay that I yearned for.

Sitting down on the sofa alongside me, Abby poured herself a glass of wine and soon made it clear as to where today was leading. She had the notion that the silver framed photos on the mantelpiece were not appropriate looking out at us and getting an ashtray for me, turned them face down on their glass. I knew then as she handed me the glass ashtray that tonight I could not just up and away. The way she leaned over to reveal her cleavage and noticed me looking said.

*"Yes it still shows,"* and instead of pulling the neck of the sweater down, she removed the whole garment she was wearing to reveal a lovely red bra and that burn mark from so many nights ago.

We had so much to talk of that the sun had set and I had drunk four cups of coffee along with her downing a whole bottle of white wine. The atmosphere was charged with romance. I was starved for female company and Abby sensed it, her arm around me never still. Eventually the long awaited embrace took place and my arms folded around her trim firm little body. From the moment our lips touched, there was no stopping as the old sofa, unlike the one we often shared back in her parents' home, became the place she took me again into Heaven. It was so long ago yet seemed like only yesterday. This time my eyes opened to reveal the beauty of her body then together we climbed the stairs to her double bed and did it all over again.

She was so easy to please, never since Kay had any woman ever told me that she wanted more than a kiss. Abby was enjoying every second.

Like a fledgling bird learns to fly, so I quickly found what pleased most. Together, locked in each other's arms, I had the best sleep that night for years.

\*\*\*

I awoke next morning to a gentle kiss to my face, then she sat on the bed beside me fully dressed and put her arms around me. We lay back on the crumpled bed, Abby looked into my eyes and kissed me, she was sorry for last night.

"Sorry?" I said. "It was marvellous," and gave her a hug.

"*It was only sex, please Preacher, don't read anything into it that is not there.*"

To be truthful, my mind was still sitting on the sofa downstairs. Things had moved so fast that I had not given today or tomorrow a second thought.

"I know," I lied, and she smiled at me.

"*I still love you but I don't want anything deep. We must remain friends. Don't lose touch again, please. You have my phone number. Ring me, we must do it again.*"

Even now Abby was acting cool. She wanted me only to satisfy her womanly needs. With her I was no closer to my Kay and if she knew of last night, would perhaps hate me.

\*\*\*

That morning I drove home with the telephone number for Josephine safely in my inside jacket pocket. Abby had even used that friend's meeting to get me to meet her, always plotting, even now after all those years.

That evening found me on the phone to the girl all three had known and liked. Getting married in the local village church, she had immediately left to live with her husband in Norfolk. Now, heavy into antiques, she was coming this summer to the fete that ran alongside the largest boot fair in the south. There she was hoping to pick up a bargain. While down in my part of the country she was staying with another of her old school friends who lived not far from my house and would love to see me again. This girl intrigued me, there had been many girls at school with Kay and I wondered who she was referring to, so asked which girl lives near me and do I know her?

"I don't know," she said. "*She was never one of the gang, I don't think she ever came out with us.*"

\*\*\*

I had a phone call from Abby about a week after I spent the night there but I made an excuse as to not going. Why should she use me? I remembered all that time she had known of the fate of Kay and would not tell me. I felt it was now my turn to hurt her lamentably. She had a boyfriend the first time I saw her, let another fool become her plaything.

***

That summer came and the day of the fete dawned fine. Josephine had also, like Abby, not changed a lot, only growing older but still the tennis crazy girl. Our hugs really meant something to me as she told me the news of my Kay and her life over the years. She had lunch with Kay, she told me, once a month when they all got together.

"Who is the all?" I asked, wondering what connection Kay and her had other than being old friends.

"We all belong to a reading group. There are now twelve of us. Each month we discuss the latest read and one of us nominates another book for all of us to read. It's fun, you'd love it. Some of the things our readers come up with on how the author got the idea for his story defy the imagination!"

"Why don't you read one of my books? Then later after you have all had your say you could introduce me as the author and we could see how close any of the readers got. Also if you don't tell them before, it could be a surprise. I bet you haven't had many writers talk to you about the book you have all just read and torn to pieces. Quite an interesting exercise for all of us I should imagine."

Josephine jumped at the idea immediately.

"What a scoop for me. None of the others has ever done a thing like that and it would give you a chance to meet Kay." Then after a few moments of thinking about it she said.

"Kay may not be very pleased being set up like that, I don't know if it's such a good idea after all." "We will certainly read one of your books and I will tell you what the members thought but to set an old friend up to meet you, I don't think so."

***

The sun shone on the day and I accompanied Josephine and her husband around all the stalls. The heat of midday beat down and so as to let her know I was not penniless, I had dressed up in a suit. The lightest one I had was cotton and charcoal grey yet even this was proving a handicap in the heat. Josephine's poor husband, twice had to visit the car parked as far as it could be, across a rough field to stash all the things his wife purchased.

That day I saw a side of the girl I once knew that I would never have thought possible. The way she could haggle over the price, it made me feel ashamed to be associated with her for I knew many of those she crossed swords with.

My neighbour's daughter had one such stall and the way Josephine drove her price down for a set of very old wicker measuring fruit baskets, made me cringe. Back home in the old barn I owned a hundred such half bushel cherry baskets. Now, forty years since they had seen the daylight, I was totting up how much Josephine would pay me for a bulk load.

At last one of the stall owners got the better of her, refusing to lower the price of a copper kettle and telling her the price was on the label attached and if she did not like it she could go away.

Eventually the heat beat us and with an ice cream each we found shade under the parkland's oak trees. There we planned to meet again later for dinner in the old pub we once used as our local.

*** 

The Bell Inn at Iden had changed from the days we knew it. For a start the old blue parrot that lived in his cage on the bar was long gone. The landlord had also moved on and a young couple now ran the establishment more as a restaurant than a village pub. The rooms had all been knocked into one bar and the toilets were no longer outside. A pool table now graced the area were we had once played darts. A large room after a bit of building work now formed a delightful dining area.

*** 

Josephine came in early to tender her husband's apologies. The sun and heat of the day had given him a terrible headache and he was sorry to miss a chance to hear of his wife's young days. So for the rest of the night I had Josephine on her own to talk to and find out about Kay. From what I had said over the phone and my meeting with Abby, she was well prepared for my questions but seemed on her guard. She saw no reason why I should want to meet Kay and was dubious about whether she wanted anything to do with it. I, she said, was on my own but she did warn me of Abby. The girls had fallen out with each other, she told me many years ago, but would not tell me what it had been over.

## CHAPTER EIGHTEEN

Josephine went back to Norfolk saying she would tell Kay she had seen me and had a lovely day and meal with me. I now had the exact location for Kay. She had not moved very far, living in Kent, only a one and half-hour drive from my home and worked as a part time dinner lady at the school her autistic grand son attended.

All the inspirations Kay's parents had held for her had never been realised. I felt so sorry for her especially as her education had been a large part of that court order. It was as much a part as my older age had been that her schoolwork was suffering. Was I in any way the reason she was now a dinner lady?

\*\*\*

My mind worked overtime trying to think a way up of accidentally bumping into her but the environment of her job gave little scope for an old man like me to cross paths. Surely at my age I would stand out amid school children?

Josephine phoned about the old baskets I owned and asked if she and her business partner could visit to see them and at the same time look at all the other old junk I had told her I owned over dinner.

\*\*\*

The new transit van parked up on time on the day specified. Josephine was keen to see the inside of the old barn. Her husband climbed out as he had decided he too would like to see the place along with another chap whom they introduced as their partner. From the very start I did not get on with the so-called partner. He had to moan about all the mud in the yard and I did not feel inclined to tell him it was not good old Sussex mud as Josephine described it, but the leftovers from the herd of dairy cows that had spent an hour feeding from the silage troughs where they were fed at milking time.

As Josephine clambered over a pile of bushel apple boxes to look at the baskets in the back of the barn she gave a squeal of delight. Hidden between the one and half bushel wicker baskets were a few quarters. Precious relics of the cherry orchards of Kent, she told all of us.

*"Now gently remove all those blessed wooden boxes,"* she told her partner and *"don't let any of them stacked at the back fall onto the tinder dry wicker baskets, as the woodworm holding each other's hand, was probably the only thing holding them together."*

Josephine, who looked like the boss of the whole outfit, gave the orders. The partner looked none too pleased to be told what to do as she stood watching and talking to me.

*"You know,"* I said to Josephine, *"Kay loved those wicker baskets so much that I gave her a couple and she had them in her bedroom. She kept all her old childhood dolls in one and the other she painted the top rim red and used it as a paper basket under her dressing table."*

She was so proud of them especially as they have the name of our farm in Kent stencilled on the side. The partner who was partly hidden in a cloud of chocking dust was showing a lot of interest in our conversation and had to tell us that the bloody things even then had terrible woodworm and he had made her burn them. This took me completely by surprise.

"How did he know?" I asked.

Josephine took me aside to tell me that he had once been Kay's boyfriend.

I instantly had the suspicion of was that the reason I disliked him the first minute I had clapped eyes on him.

"Now he is only the man with all the money but don't say anything," she whispered, "*Things are not good between him and us. I tried my hardest to get Kay to come with us, instead of him, but he insisted, I did not say anything to her of how you still loved her. I saw her the other day and she was so interested in our meeting at the fete. She wanted to know everything you have done in your life, but you did all the talking and I never got the chance to ask you anything of yourself. I don't know anything of you other than what we did when I lived in Iden.*"

\*\*\*

"*My life has gone on as usual farming and fishing, with my bees thrown in along the way. I lived at home with my parents until they died, then took over. I still live in that big old rambling house,*" pointing at the old low red tiled house standing in the corner of the rambling farmyard.

"That's a huge house for one to live in, do you live alone."

"Off course but only use three of the rooms."

"You never got married then?"

"Of course not, I was waiting for Kay, and then it was too late. Who wants an old bachelor like me?"

"You're not that old for goodness sake! You're only a year older than me."

Josephine was all this time looking into everything. "*That,*" she would say to her husband or Paul, the partner, who had now exposed the piles of baskets ready to load upon the van. Then in a last desperate effort to fill the van say, "*I must have that,*" referring to a large flat brown sink that mother had used for years until she had got dad to fit a new white one in her kitchen. The back of the barn was full of old furniture, some put there by my grandparents and very old.

"*All those please Preacher, please you don't want them do you and how much for that old brass bedstead?*

"Twenty pounds, how's that? You want to buy the barn as well?" I sarcastically asked and the partner hearing, piped up.

"*You selling it? I could be interested in this place if you were? The old beams and tiles alone could fetch a fortune!*"

"No I'm not, anyway load that sink up and don't chip it any more, it's had a hard life as it is." Josephine's husband said nothing for the whole two hours all three were with me.

\*\*\*

I waved the van off and shut the gate. Josephine had nearly cleaned me out of the whole barn full. More than pleased to see Josephine, I was happy with the three grand wad of notes, which she had paid me. I put the kettle on in my kitchen come office and gently lifted the old clock on the mantle piece and slipped the money beneath out of sight, ready to take to the bank the next day.

The kettle sang at the same time the phone rang and a familiar voice asked me if I could do her a huge favour, but she could not ask it over the phone. It was urgent and could I see her this evening? Abby seemed to be nearly in tears to the point I asked if everything was all right.

"*Yes, but please come tonight.*" She was desperate to have a favour of me and "*no it did not involve her soft warm bed.*"

Abby wanting a favour sounded like the old Abby I knew and if I was right, it would involve me shelling out a penny or two. A glance at the clock and thinking of the stash beneath told me I had had a good day, so why not visit Abby, if only to find out what the matter was. I told her to expect me at seven thirty and she said she would cook dinner for the two of us.

***

Drawing up in her drive, she came out to greet me.

"*Darling so glad to see you.*"

Always she had called me darling, it seemed to be her pet name for me, and I thought nothing of it. Not until I had taken off my coat and gone into the sitting room did the significance of it hit me. The pair of tall tapering red candles stood ready to light the table, laid with two places. The room was lit by two standard lamps, one each end of the sofa and the curtains were closed even though it was still daylight outside. Abby had vanished into the kitchen and I went to find her.

"Sorry," she said, and put her arms around me, giving me a kiss on the lips. "*I had to hurry back as you came, I have a lovely soufflé in the oven and it's ready now.*"

Over dinner Abby would tell me nothing of the huge favour she wished to ask, she said that I would not think it too huge a price, especially after tonight with her and what she had planned for the two of us. My presumption was right Abby was going to cost money and it did involve the bed.

Abby was not only clever, as I knew too well, but very persuasive. My feeble pleas of, "*I must go home,*" went unheard.

"*Kay*," she said, "*would not approve if I left her in her hour of need.*"

Kay I thought would not approve of what she was suggesting either, but was I ever going to see my love again and now here was a woman that I had once felt a lot for and I a man craving a little love, I could not see her need but Abby had her way and we spent the night between her sheets.

***

Her laying over me with that lovely smile and those large spaniel eyes awaked me, asking if last night had ever been as good. Her naked body slid from the bed as she said she would put the kettle on and bring me a cup of tea. At last I thought. She knows what tea is! She came into the bedroom with two cups and a letter in her hands, still with no clothes on her trim and shapely body. Slipping back between the sheets, she took the letter out from the envelope and opened it out. She then started to cry.

"This could be the last time you come here," she said between sobs. "Look. I can't pay. Since my husband died and paying out for my daughter to go to university, all the money has gone."

The way she touched me with her soft hands, playing with the hair on my chest. I looked at the paper before me. A final demand from the council for three years' rates stared back from the paper at me and I gulped.

"Abby," "there is three years here! Have you not paid anything or spoken to them, for they are now taking you to court next week."

"I know," "she said, and buried her head in my lap. I was praying you could do something."

"Like what?" I said. "Pay the bill."

"Oh will you, please? I will show you how grateful I am," and she put her leg over mine and kissed me at the same time. I lifted her head from mine and said,

"Abby, we must talk."

"No," she said. "Let's pow wow," and she gave a sigh. "Now you like that don't you?"

\*\*\*

I left that house which I now thought I had a share in, to Abby standing on the front step waving my cheque that was made out for more than the notes under the clock to cover back home in the kitchen. Abby had got her way again and at no time had she told me a thing about Kay, only mentioning her name once. I thought the crafty woman had satisfied her womanly cravings and I had paid the bill. What did that make me, or more to the point, her? This, I swore to myself, had got to stop. Twice now she had lured me into her bed although she knew my longing for her best friend.

\*\*\*

Somehow I had to find a way of seeing Kay. I felt that I could not just walk up to her and say *'remember me.'* The old brain had got to get to work. It also worried me that Abby had used her body to pay the bill. Did she make a habit of getting men, for I knew she had not worked since her operation? The first time I had seen her she had a young man. What had happened to him or was he another customer? Also, did Josephine know of Abby's habit and was that the reason the girls had fallen out? It all seemed to make sense now. I remembered the time she told me why she had been expelled along with Kay from school. Then she had said it was *'only a bit of fun.'* I wondered how she was hoping to pay this year's rates. The idea came to me to pry into her life by ringing her daughter to tell her of my concerns for her mother. Of course, I would never tell her of our involvement together.

\*\*\*

Four nights later I met Ann and her friends in the same pub as last time. The girls wanted to know how my search for my lost love was going.

"Not very well," I told them.

"You want us on your case?" one of them said, and they drew their chairs closer to me.

"First I need to talk to Ann alone," I said, and the two girls gave each other a look and giggled.

"Five minutes," they said and left together for the ladies.

***

"Ann, I am concerned over your mother. How does she live in that lovely house on her own? Did your father leave her comfortably off with a good insurance?"

"You know," she said. "You were there the other night," and I gave a gulp at the same time fixing her with my eye and drawing my head back.

"Me there?"

"Yes, you must have been for you left that lovely cheque on the kitchen table." Silly Abby had only put it down where she could see it when she came home hadn't she?

"Oh that? Yes." There was no good denying it for she knew, but how much I was not prepared to say, and Ann said,

"Mother deservers a little happiness."

Ann told me she did not have a man friend other than me to look after her. With that I felt privileged to think that not only did Ann know but also that she didn't' disapprove. Her sly wink, so like her mum's, told me enough.

The other two girls arrived back and sat down close to us.

"Together," Ann said, "we must have what her mother always said was a pow wow."

***

Two hours later and with me buying all the drinks for the girls, just like old times, we were no closer to solving my problem. The girls suggested that we meet in a week's time and meanwhile they would all have a think. I told them I could not make that night, as I had to be in Sheffield to attend my book signing ceremony. They opened their mouths and stared at me.

"You have a book coming out?"

"Yes, that's right."

"How exciting knowing a writer. What's it about?"

"A novel, rather special," I told them.

"Is it your first book?"

"No, it's my sixth actually," I said. The girls nearly stood up and bowed to me.

"Sixth! You are famous!"

"Not, not at all."

"I have never seen or heard of you. Do you use your own name?"

"No, never, and I'm not telling you what it is!"

"Go on! I won't tell and mother will be so thrilled!" said Ann.

"Your mother has one of them," I said. "I saw it in the bookcase the other morning."

"Mother told me you gave her that money the other evening. Did you stay all night with mum?"

I sensed Ann was putting the two together, and she leaned over the table and gave me a kiss on the cheeks.

*"Thank you,"* she said, *"I'm glad it's you, mums got loads of books which one is yours, go on tell me please."*

"Never," I said you will have to work it out."

With that we set a date for the three girls to meet me on Friday.

***

Next morning I had a lovely letter from Abby thanking me again for the money and telling me the court proceedings had been dropped. She said that she hoped to see me again soon, it would be just as nice and wouldn't cost me a penny.

***

On Friday I was late, which the girls took pleasure in telling me was not polite. I was sorry I told them, I'd had to talk to some school children at a school to gather information for a new book I hoped to write off, *'a day's life in school nowadays'* to compare with when I attended one of the establishments. One of the girls slapped her hands on the tabletop.

*"That's it, the perfect way to meet Kay!"* Could we not approach the school where Kay worked and explain that they had been chosen by me to spend a day with a class of autistic children, to get an insight into their every day life at school? That way I could have my midday meal with them and with luck meet Kay.

One of the girls said that such a thing was possible, people were coming to university all the time doing time and management surveys. The only trouble they saw with the plan was that a distinguished author, who they all now thought I was, would surely be announced to the assembled school, asking them to be on their best behaviour as I was going to write about them.

Then Kay would know I was coming and could hide away. No, that idea was a non-starter. That was until one of the girls suggested I used my pen name and Ann said,

*"I know what that is I looked at our books at home and one has the photo of you Preacher on the books back cover. Even mother had not realised the fact, and it is one of her favourite ones."*

***

I left the three girls that night with a mild sense of satisfaction that at last I was hopefully going to see Kay again. One of the girls' fathers was a teacher and she said he would be only too willing to write to the school suggesting that they took up the offer of me visiting them. Ann said her mother knew of the school. I begged Ann not to tell her that it had anything to do with me and she had assured me that she would not even let her know. The address she said was in the phone book beside the phone at home. She could copy it without her knowing.

***

The phone call a week later from Ann was encouraging. She asked if I could meet them this Friday, usual place, at seven thirty.

Tonight, as I entered the pub early, not three but five lovely young girls sat there to greet me. Never had I had so much female attention showered on me. Ann had got her mother to tell her where she had bought the book and they were delighted to find it on all the bookshop's shelves in town. Tonight each of the girls had a copy for me to sign.

The private signing session took half an hour, as each wanted a dedication to them personally. Each copy had by the end of the evening a short story added inside the flyleaf. The girl, whose father was a teacher, had received a reply from his tentative enquiry and they would be delighted to have me for the day. The chatter went on and on. What was I going to wear and what age group was I hoping to be with all day?

Then, what was I going to say to Kay when, as I sat at the long table with the children at dinnertime, she leaned over my shoulder to serve me my food? The girls had even thought up the length of table in their minds and I would not have been surprised if they had not drawn up a seating plan of the whole affair! There was one thing none of the girls knew, which I did, and that was that Kay belonged to a reading and writing group that met once a month. It was surely only a coincidence that she read?

She could not know that I wrote books, even though I still had a love letter from her dated nineteen sixty two, asking me not to write a book of our time together as she stated it would offend her parents and they would not like that. Surely Kay had never read any of my novels or realised if she had, that the theme of all of them was her and my love for her. That fact I kept to myself, swearing never to tell anyone of my passion and anxiety for the girl. Two of the girls had hit on the nerve when they asked me how I thought the ideas up. *"All in the mind"* I said, I always told people who asked that same question, so saw no reason to tell them any different.

\*\*\*

The letter came to me the following week telling me that the school would be thrilled to have me and asking for a date when I wished to come. They had the perfect class of fifteen year olds for me to accompany for the day. They were all interested in the English language and art. If I would tell them the day, they would love to send me the menu for the dinner so I could choose my preference. They wished me to eat with the teachers. I saw no problem with that, surely the dinner lady served them also? And the time when Kay and I met again would be better with adults present instead of little kids.

I immediately wrote away to them with a date. The menu duly arrived and I phoned them and had a chat. The headmaster I spoke to was delighted with my choice of food and the fact that they had been singled out to host me. Who the poor man thought I was did not thankfully come up!

\*\*\*

In my excitement of meeting Kay, I prepared myself the best I could. The morning I set out to drive to Kent the weather was foul. Rain lashed the windscreen making the visibility hazardous. My mind was not on the road. The thought that today I was to meet my love made my chest ache. All the planning for the forthcoming event left my head. Nothing of what I would say to her made sense. There was so much to ask that it would take years to remind her of the past. Yet I wanted to ask and tell her all in one sentence, nothing was going to plan. The meeting I was sure would not be of a hugging and kissing sort, but in all reality, the whole thing could embarrass her. I must stay calm. The hurt in my body as I thought of the possibility that maybe she would resent me just being there. I had to forget it and concentrate on the road first or an accident would rob me of ever seeing her again. Too quickly the town came up on the roadside boards and I had to find the school that was expecting me.

\*\*\*

The head teacher greeted me with a firm handshake and as I was twenty minutes late, escorted me to the classroom to introduce me to my fellow pupils for the day. Twenty-six excited kids started to bombard me with questions that I tried my hardest to answer truthfully.

\*\*\*

The morning passed quickly and I had forgotten my reason for being there. Seven of the kids showed a large interest in the way I wrote and along with the others, said they could not imagine where to start writing a novel. I told them, "Start like you would talk to anyone you did not know. Imagine you had never seen the person before and they said they looked after old people in a nursing home and you suddenly remember a funny thing that once happened to you when you visited an old relation in such a place. Well, just start to tell your story and take it from there. Then later you can edit all the words out that are not needed. You will find after time that it comes easily to you."

\*\*\*

Noticing the time, I told them that after lunch we would write a story each of two hundred and fifty words using as many different ones as we could. The head teacher had come into the room as I was talking, to escort me to lunch. The bell sounded and the class filed out in a smart order. The head looked at me.

*"Getting a good feel for the class I hope, all the children are like this,"* trying to make out that there was never any shouting or pushing. I knew how kids acted but said nothing, letting him think that I was getting plenty of material to write about. I was more interested to know where he was now leading me.

All the kids had gone the other way! We were walking in the completely opposite direction to enter through a door marked *'Staff Room.'* A gentleman instantly latched onto me, asking a lot of questions and I thought *'he must be the English teacher,'* but turned out to be the maths principal. Taking our places, my heart was up in my throat, my appetite completely absent.

The door opened and a trolley of plates containing our food rattled into the room. My disappointment obviously showed as the person sitting beside me enlightened me to the fact that it was a privilege given to the best behaved each week to bring the food and serve it to the staff.

My plan to meet the women cooks and dinner lady had been thwarted. Why had I presumed it would be so easy to meet Kay again? The only good thing was that no one knew my real name. To all of them I was just a published author and had used my pen name, the general public still unaware of who I was. I was so close, yet no nearer.

*** 

On the wall of the staff room I had noticed a sheet of paper pinned to the notice board showing when all the staff wished to take their time off. Among the names under the kitchen staff was the name K Drew. My girl of so long ago was still using her maiden name. Abby had told me the lass had never wed and I thought of Paul the partner with all the money of Josephine's antique firm that had once been her boyfriend. Then surely they had lived together for he had told us he made her throw the wicker baskets away.

***

The class was writing when I arrived back at the room. Many of the pupils were already well into their story. I told them they had one hour and suggested a story line like, how the dinner they had just partaken was to their liking and what they thought of the staff serving it to them. E.g., did they willingly give second helpings like in my day? The class looked stunned. Many of the girls had hoped to write steamy love stories and the boys a day playing football. The ones that had started to write, I told to somehow switch to include the same topic. Not one of the class realised I had asked for stories on this lunchtime, hoping that at least one would mention Miss K Drew.

***

The head teacher looked in at three and was impressed. He stated he was drawn to the classroom as soon as he entered the corridor. All was peace, not a sound disturbed the air. What were the children doing?

A few moments before, I had walked around the room and noticed that one of the girls seemed to show a flare for writing, so called the class to attention, saying that they could stop now and would that girl, pointing her out with my finger, please come to the front and bring her work with her. I could tell by her work that she loved the English language and enjoyed writing and would not be afraid to read it to us.

The head knew the girl and said she was very bright. The young girl read her essay out aloud and clearly to the room. I noticed a couple of the others push their work aside and fold their arms as if to say, *'trust her to do it right.'*

The applause after she had finished reading was cut short as I asked the most disappointed looking lad, to come forward and read his effort at describing lunchtime. The poor lad would have refused my order I think, if it had not been for the headmaster standing beside me. He reluctantly read the two hundred words he had managed to write out.

*"That is the typical first try at writing,"* I said, *"like I did,"* and the class clapped his efforts. Then I told them that in my opinion he had done the best essay out of the two. The talented girl had hurried hers to finish in the time given. *"In my opinion,"* I told them, *"no story should ever be curtailed by words or time. A good tale took as long as it was necessary to tell, no longer, no shorter.*

*To condense it too much ruined the full flavour and to drag it out was using too much padding."*

The boy told us what time he went to lunch, what the food was like, his likes and dislikes, how warm the food was and how he enjoyed it. The shepherd's pie was his favourite, followed by apple crumble and lots of custard like Miss Drew made. She always gave him extra and he loved her.

This was more like the stuff I had been looking for. He went on. The cook's hands were always clean and the women never shout at me, even when I spill things, which I do often, but I can't help it. My hands shake so much at times but I have pills from the doctor to stop me shaking. He loved dinner times with all the chatter and noise of plates and forks rattling. It was always warm in the dining room and he always sat next to his best friend, Susan, because she understood him.

In a way I felt for that boy and all the other young children in the school.

The class was spellbound as to the detail the lad had woven into the few sentences he had written. I told them that I would take all their compositions home with me and read them. The class clapped me and thanked me for a very interesting day.

## CHAPTER NINETEEN.

Next day as I worked away in my office, I could not concentrate on the article I was writing and hoping to finish that day. How I had been so close to Kay yet not seen her. If only I had said something. I was supposed to be at the school with the sole purpose of studying a day in the life of the modern day school kid. Why had I not asked to see the difference of the kitchens nowadays to see how they had changed? Looking through that window yesterday, I had noticed a large microwave oven and an electric kettle, nothing like the large aluminium ones that our dinner ladies had used on top of the gas rings. Then they sat there hissing, full of boiling water, for hours. Taking a notepad up, I started to make notes of questions to ask next time. Tonight I had an engagement with three girls in a pub.

\*\*\*

I was seated long before they come in talking to each other, then on seeing me rushed up to me in there excitement all talking at once.

"How did it go? Did you see her, did she remember you?" And Ann's daughter the one thing they all wanted to know?

"Where is she?"

"Don't be silly! She's not here," one of the girls said, and sat down beside me and put her arm around me to comfort me. "Get the drinks in Ann and let's hear how his day went."

"Ok."

Putting the drinks on the table and sitting down, Ann said.

"Let's hear it, you did go didn't you?"

"Yes and I had a wonderful day. The trouble came when we had lunch. I ate with all the teachers in the staff room and the food was brought up from the canteen and served by the top pupils. Later all the cookhouse staff had gone home but I am invited back next week, then I intend to ask to see the kitchens."

"Good. Go for it John! You have nothing to lose. What was the name of the school again?" I told them but one of the girls said she had never heard of it.

"Neither have I," another said. "What is the size of the school?"

"Large," I said. "Bloody huge one could easily get lost in it all day."

"Let's meet up here again next week and hope for better news John. Now how's this latest novel of yours going? Have you solved how they escape?"

For the next two hours we four sat plotting and planning how my latest book would end.

\*\*\*

It was midnight before I got home to bed and for the next two days I was busy writing. The phone rang and it was Abby. She wanted to see me immediately, it was important and something to do with Kay. Putting the phone down I thought did I really hear straight? Abby wanted to talk to me about Kay.

\*\*\*

My knock on her door got a swift acknowledgement. Abigail opened it for me to enter.

"*Preacher, I knew you would come!*" Of course she did, I thought. She had mentioned Kay and knew I could not resist that subject! She put her arms around me and kissed me on the lips.

"Kay," I said. Gently pushing her away from me, "*you said you wanted to talk of Kay.*"

"*Come into the sitting room and sit down.*"

Together we sat on the sofa and she cuddled up to me.

"*Preacher, you have been seeing my daughter. She told me you have been trying to meet Kay. You are acting like a fool, forget her. Going to the school where she works and pretending to be interested in the pupils, you will get arrested. Can't you be satisfied with me?*" And she pulled me onto her and kissed me.

So that's what it was all about today. She had found out about my meetings with the girls and the school. She was jealous. After all this Abby was still in love with me as she had told me she had been long ago. Why was I surprised? I was still in love with Kay. Perhaps you never forget the feelings for a loved one even if you have had another love like Abby had. She had married and had children, now all that was behind her and I had come along. Did she see a last chance of future happiness loom over her horizon when I had contacted her? Abby was most adamant that it had got to stop. She would not stand for her girl having anything to do with Kay and me getting together.

That night I left Abby in tears and in an angry mood. I had my own ideas what I wanted to do.

\*\*\*

The school phoned me a couple of days later to tell me they had no idea that I lived so far away and that the coming week was not satisfactory to visit. They would contact me to arrange another day. They were sorry and thanked me again for the last visit. I was never to hear from them again, but did meet the girls with Ann on Friday night as planned. Ann told me that she had spoken of my trip to the school and my hopes of meeting Kay, thinking her mother would be interested as once they were all such good friends. Tonight she was furious with her mother interfering as she had done. We all thought the call from the school had resulted from Abby "*sticking the poison in.*" To us all it now became clear that that road to seeing Kay was closed. Another way had to be found. Ann promised never to tell her mother anything about me again and hoped she "*rotted in hell!*"

The escape scene for my next book was sorted out to everyone's satisfaction and I left the girls to it, not making a date to meet again. To me, Ann and her friends were history. Ann had been the cause of her mother's interference. In a mood I slammed the back door shut and went to bed muttering Abby, she was the cause of Kay being so far away for so long. Now, at the first chance of reconciliation, she had done it again.

\*\*\*

Abby phoned the following day to say sorry that she had hurt me again and could we ever be friends again? She said she would do anything to see me happy so I told her to keep away and out of my life.

\*\*\*

The phone rang that night as I was preparing to go to bed and have an early night. Josephine enquired as to the other rubbish, as I called the old furniture, and farm equipment out in the barn and other sheds dotted around the yard, wondering if I would be interested in selling it to her. All the old pottery flowerpots she said were most interesting. Then she got onto the real reason she had phoned so late. She told me she had only just managed to get off the phone from Abigail. For over an hour she had been bending her ear as to what I was up to. Josephine said she was most alarmed to hear that I had pretended to be a famous author. I told her that I had never told anyone that.

*"Well Abby thinks you are. Anyway, what were you thinking, going to the school where she works? That my dear is the last place Kay would want to meet you. So embarrassing you really don't have any idea do you?"*

*"Now, those old flowerpots, will you sell them to me and if so I will collect and we can talk about a way to meet Kay if you are really serious, but I must tell you she has aged and not for the best, but don't ever tell her that."*

Josephine hung up and I went to bed to ponder on what Abby was up to ringing Josephine and telling her all that I had been up to. She had no business. What else had she told her?

\*\*\*

All next day I spent out in the barn sorting the hundreds of old flowerpots out into sizes and types. Some were square and a lot of the round ones not as circular as they should have been, telling me that they were very old, thrown on a potter's wheel, unlike the kind today, all perfect from a machine. Father and his dad had never thrown a thing away and under a pile of Victorian beehives, I discovered a pile of old shoes and boots. Like the heap of old horse harnesses I had unearthed in another corner hidden behind an assortment of old chairs, including a very fine rocking chair that I decided I liked the look of and would keep. I sat in the old chair and it felt comfortable, for over an hour I dreamed of meeting Kay now that Josephine was at last willing to help.

The fact that Abby had phoned Josephine worried me, I decided to call Ann and see if she knew what her mother was up to. The sheer fact that Abby was jealous of me wanting to meet Kay made me realise that she could and probably would, do anything to jeopardise any plans I had in the future. I had been a silly old fool to go to bed with her after all this time. That girl was trouble. I knew that she had done everything she could to keep us apart forty years ago, now she would do anything she could to do it again.

\*\*\*

Ann was most surprised to hear the news.

*"Just like mum,"* she said and by the tone of her voice I got the impression that she had made up her differences with her mother and they were speaking

again, even after what she had said about her. Caution on my part was called for. Ann knew I had spent the odd night in her mother's bed, now if I stirred too much the two of them together would ruin any chance I ever had of reconciliation with Kay.

Making my apologies for troubling her, I rang off to await the visit from Josephine and her partner with the van. It was scheduled to take place in a week's time. Plenty of time I thought, for Abby to do anything else she had planned.

***

The Luton van pulled into my farmyard at nine thirty, driven by Josephine and this time alone, at last I reasoned we could talk all the time as we loaded all those pots up. The absence of Richard, who was always trying to hear what we were saying, made the day rather enjoyable. Kay, Josephine told me, had said nothing about someone trying to see her at school but she was disappointed not to have seen the man and had got two of his books out of the library. She told her that she could tell a lot about the person that had written them by the way he wrote. In her opinion the man was a kind, loving man. Josephine said she nearly laughed at the first mention of that, as Kay had no idea of my identity. Josephine said she had a hard job not to tell her but valued her friendship. If Kay knew that she knew and had seen me she realised she might not take too kindly to it. They had never, as far as she knew, had a secret between them.

With the pots loaded she took a look around the place. The beehives she *"had to have,"* as a feature she said. Painted white, they would look ideal, people bought them to place in their gardens. Attention now turned to the pile of old shoes. Those she was ecstatic over. Some dated back over a hundred years and looked like new. She said,

*"Never mind, the odd little button missing. That could be replaced."* The harness she was not so sure of but told me to keep it dry and safe and she would see what she could do with it. Pubs, she said, liked that sort of thing to hang on their walls.

With the work done I invited her into the house for something to eat and drink before returning home. Now I hoped to hear more of what Kay got up to in her life. Alas as soon as she entered the door her eyes saw the antique clock above the fireplace on the dusty mantelpiece.

*"Does it still go?"* She asked comparing the time it showed to her wristwatch.

*"Yes,"* I said, *"always keeps excellent time."*

*"It should, it's by a famous French maker."*

Then she saw the old rocking chair. *"My God! You don't polish that very often, do you?"* She was looking at the relic I had retrieved from the barn.

*"How much?"* I said.

*"Fifty pounds,"* Josephine said and she was off. *"What else you got hidden in the house?"* So I took her upstairs to my grandmother's old bedroom that I had never bothered to go into for over twenty years.

The wardrobe was full of the old clothes she had long ago stopped wearing before I was born, but the surprise came as she lifted the lid to a long wooden chest. There was my grandmother's wedding dress neatly folded in thin tissue paper. Under this was a small dress of white lace. Josephine immediately recognised it as a christening gown, over one hundred years old.

The old hats covered in dust on the top shelf of a wardrobe brought gasps from her.

"*Look at these!*" she said, taking one carefully in her hands. "*Imagine a hot day in summer walking out one afternoon after church in this!*" The huge brim hat covered in painted clay fruit looked monstrous. "*I really can't value these things for you Preacher. They are for a specialist. I wish I had brought one of the other two with me, that's their line. Look after them please.*"

I never thought of asking who the other two were. We then shut the room up and answered the whistle from the kettle that sat bubbling on the stove down in the kitchen.

"*How many rooms do you have in this mansion of yours?*" she asked

"*Twelve,*" I believe "*Never bothered to count them. Only live in three of them, the rest are all shut up. Have been since dad died twenty years ago and he never went in them after mother died.*"

"*That was forty years ago they must be full of cobwebs now. Would you mind if I came back another day with Richard? That is if you wish to sell the odd thing or two.*"

"*Of course not have whatever you like that I don't use.*"

Josephine left me that day with the promise that she would do anything she could to help me meet Kay but did not want to do anything to upset her relationships with her. I was an item a long time ago, she said.

After she left I counted the money again. Six hundred pounds for a load of old rubbish I thought and she had willingly paid me in cash. I tucked the money under the old clock out of sight.

*\*\*\**

The summer was past its best when I had another call from Josephine. Was I looking after the items in the house? She was sorry that she had not contacted me before but she had been to America selling antiques. The news she wished to tell me nearly made me fall over. She and her husband were coming to the old school reunion later in the autumn and guess who they had coming with them? Kay! Was it possible for me to book a room for them in some guesthouse, as they did not relish the drive home afterwards? I assured her I would do it tomorrow and let her know.

My mind was working overtime. Kay was coming to my town and would be stopping the night after the old scholar's reunion. Perhaps I could dance with her then while she was in my arms ask how she felt about me after all this time. Josephine had remarked that she liked the way I wrote. With luck I could have the book I had written years ago that she had forbidden me to write of our romance printed and present her with a copy. There was not a lot of time to do it but it had lain in the drawer of the filing cabinet ready to publish for years. A publisher could not be found in time, it took at least a year to get a book in print, but I could find a printing firm to make a few copies quickly but would have to pay to have it printed. Then presenting it to her would be a golden opportunity to talk and hopefully spend the rest of the evening with her.

\*\*\*

Next morning found me up the most prestigious hotel in town. The Mermaid was owned by a couple of people I knew. The lad had gone to school with me and his wife was the owner. On asking at the reception desk by name for him, the girl in charge rang through to his office, then told me to enter that door, pointing to a door opposite me. Malcolm was overjoyed to see me. I told him my plan to put my friend and her husband up in one of his rooms for the night. I was paying. I also wished for another room, *"the best in the place,"* I said.

"That, Preacher is the honeymoon suite, with a four-poster bed, the lot," he told me.

"Please," I said, *"It's not booked is it?"* He made a phone call to the front desk.

"It is now," he said, *"all yours for the night, who is she?"* giving me a sly wink. *"A bottle of champagne on ice will be waiting in the room with two glasses, compliment of the house. Now do I know her?"*

"Well you may remember her. She was my dancing partner for two years a long time ago."

"Not Kay Drew?" "that was the only girl you ever talked about and I wager the only girl you have ever known."

"Keep it quiet for Heaven's sake," I said "Don't tell anyone, she may not even want to know me after such a long time"

"She will be a silly girl if she doesn't," he said. "Good luck."

\*\*\*

On arriving home I told Josephine on the phone that two rooms had been booked and paid for. I refused to tell her where, only that it was in the town. She tried to insist on sending me the money but I told her I would not hear of it. The owner, I told her, was a friend and as it was out of season he was more than happy to have two rooms occupied for the night. Breakfast, I told her, was included. Josephine again wanted to know where, she said Kay did not want to rough it and she was not sure that the rooms would be good enough, more like a doss house knowing me, she said which I thought was rather rude of her! I knew my home was full of dust and none of the furniture was ever polished but me and my dog didn't mind that' at least the bathroom, kitchen and our clothes were regularly cleaned.

\*\*\*

Looking through the Yellow Pages, I rang a few printers to ascertain a price for printing and binding a book. The cheapest one could not undertake any work for a couple of months so he was no help. Another firm said that they would complete the printing job in a week so I paid them a visit and much to my delight, the deal was agreed upon. I paid a deposit of half the cost, the rest of the money to be paid on completion in ten days time.

I had a friend who was a bookbinder by trade and he told me that as soon as I had the book in my hands, to take it to him, he would bind it in leather and emboss the spine and any title I liked in gold leaf. He assured me that the finished article would make any girl proud, especially as she was the main character in the pages. A lovely red with gold trimmings, I said, would be excellent.

\*\*\*

I could not concentrate for the rest of the day and that night I tossed and turned. Kay in Rye and I had booked the hotel for her! I wondered as I walked the fields next day whether the crops would be ripe and the harvest finished by the time she came to the reunion. I remembered how she loved this time of year, the smells and colours of autumn were her favourite. As I walked a large field of winter wheat that was just ripping into ear, I noticed a large white Luton van pull into the farmyard. The sight of Josephine stepping out of the driver's door and a man, who I recognised as Richard, made me half run to the house. Luckily my shouts were heard as they, after knocking with no answer, were preparing to leave.

"Preacher! Thought you were out. Just called in on the off chance, had to come down south to drop an item of furniture off for Richard. He was so interested in what I told him about your lot. He wondered could he see in the rooms today." I showed Richard the way and suggested we leave him to it while Josephine and I talked. He would hardly nick anything without us seeing, I said. "He," she said, "I believe is completely trustworthy when it comes to that, it's the loading that we have to watch with him."

I took Josephine into the dimly lit front room. She was bursting to know where I had booked them into for the coming night. I detected that that was the main reason she had shown up today. Richard and all the furniture was an excuse. She promised not to tell Kay if I told her as after I had phoned she had called Kay and told her it was all laid on. Kay was delighted to think that it would be daylight before they left the next day and had suggested that as it would be a Sunday, they three could walk around the town. It was such a long time ago that she had seen it and the place held many fond memories for her.

"Memories," I said, "of me and her I hope."

"Most likely," she said. "She did not have another boyfriend and she goes on the whole time about the old times and she did mention your name."

My heart leapt.

"She occasionally talks of me?" I said.

"Not in those sorts of terms, no, only how happy she was with you and Abby."

"Do you see Abby often?"

"Never, not since she married, funny girl, that Abby. We all fell out with her, you know the things she said and did. Then I saw her in Dover and she was so pushy as if nothing had ever happened."

"What did happen?" I asked. She leant over across the space between us.

"She and Richard had an affair while he was living with Kay. You do know they lived together don't you?" and she put her hand on mine "Abby got real nasty, accusing Kay of all sorts of things. None of them were true. Kay threw him out and so did Abby. He was real nasty over the split and accused Kay. Still does really, won't talk to her with a civil tongue. I do believe Kay still carries a light for you. She never would marry Richard."

That little glimmer of hope made me tell Josephine that along with the room at the Mermaid Hotel for her and her husband, I had also paid for the honeymoon suite for Kay and my wish that Kay and I could pick up from where we had been made to part. *"Josephine told me not to rush anything and anyway, what had made us part?"* I told her.

"The court order of course." She looked up into my face.

"What court order?" It was the first she had heard of it. I explained it had come in the post and I had gone up to Kay's house to talk to her parents, they had a real go at me. Then that afternoon the police had paid a visit to this house, sat where she was now and told my mother, father and I never to go near the place or try to communicate with Kay again or I would go to prison.

*"It was a different world then,"* she said. *"We all did what we were told didn't we? Think of trying to tell your teenage child what to do today!"* And she laughed. *"Now Preacher. Have you really booked the honeymoon room for Kay? Such a romantic gesture! I hope it all goes well but as I told you I mustn't get involved. If she finds out that I have been plotting and helping you to meet her, she would go spare!"*

\*\*\*

Richard entered the room as we finished the second cup of tea.

*"What a treasure house this is,"* he said. *"Look at the items I have noted down on this jotter I picked up on the hall table. I hope you don't mind. I never thought to bring a notebook with me. Don't usually find that amount in one house."*

The notepad he had in his hand was the one I kept beside the phone and on the top page written in large capital letters was ABIGAIL, followed by her phone number. There was no way a man astute as him could have missed it. The only thing was would he make the connection? I snatched the pad from his hand. He had written down each piece of furniture that he was interested in and alongside it placed a price he would pay. I looked him in the eyes. Standing up over me sitting there I got the same impression that I had first had of him, and that was *'I don't like you.'* His manner as he handed the pad over to my snatch had been such as *'not in so much hurry my friend.'* My notepad and he never asked, then to try and stop me looking at what he had written did nothing to please me. Josephine stood up and told Richard,

*"Right, let's leave Mr Tiltman to look over what you have selected. You will contact me Preacher, won't you?"* and gave me a wink. *"Let me know what you decide to do."*

You could tell by the way he moved that he wished to close the deal now and load the stuff up.

*"Let's take something surely,"* he said. *"You don't use it now and it's a pity to

*keep it locked away."* Josephine leapt to my defence.

"Leave it Richard, Preacher is a friend of mine, leave it."

***

That night she phoned me to apologise, saying that she should never have told him of my heirlooms.

"All the way home," she said, *"he talked of you, wanted to know everything about you, how we know each other, how long ago, and did I ever know of Abby?"* The hair on the back of my neck rose.

"Abby! What did he say of her?" I asked.

"Only did you know her and was it the same Abigail on the paper he knew and had all the trouble over."

"What did you tell him?"

"The truth of course, that we were all good friends but that was a long time ago. Preacher. What's the matter? You sound alarmed."

"You bet I am. That notepad he picked up from the hall table to price everything on only had Abby's phone number on top of it didn't it? He must have seen it and was getting you to confirm it was the same person."

"My God!" she said. "Well good luck to him. She's welcome to him, they are a real good pair the two of them. You don't mind do you? And anyway why did you have her number in the first place?" Thinking on my feet, I said

"She phoned a long time ago and told me you had met at the port."

"Preacher. Don't sell anything from your house, please. Richard told me that he had found a couple of pieces that were priceless and had only offered you a fraction of their worth. Let me get a real expert to assess the stuff. Don't sell to him. To do that to a friend of mine is unforgivable." Promise not to do anything until I see you again in two weeks time at the school reunion.

***

After the visit to the hairdressers, my next port of call was a little shop that specialised in manicures. My hand and nails were scrupulously washed and made smooth, the dirt from beneath the nails removed and polished. Leaving there, the tailors welcomed me with open arms. A new suit, shirt and tie and I was ready for another bath and a close shave. A good lot of Brut aftershave and I was ready three hours before the school opened its doors for the night. A visit earlier to the hotel asking them to place the book that I had received the day before from my mate and a bunch of flowers to accompany the bottle of champagne in her room and I was prepared for anything. My wallet was well padded with notes as I remember she always said I was a millionaire and could never resist a peep into its interior. Tonight I was to win or lose my love forever. Never would a chance like this come along again. My heart had been beating fast all day. Now as the hour drew close, I checked everything. My wristwatch I thought could have been of a better make but I hoped that we would have more to say than discuss the time of day!

***

Arriving at the old school early I was amazed at the number of cars in the playground but had no trouble parking. The large blue doors were open and I casually walked in looking around to see if anyone I knew was present. By the look of things half the town was there and I was unfortunately well known. There was no way I was going to be able to just show up and say *'fancy meeting you here.'* There must have been the whole school of sixty-two assembled. I was glad in a way that they had all lived as long as I had, though many of my friends had long since died. I felt an impostor as none of them were from the fifties when I had attended and the idea hit me that perhaps the next ten years for them could be their last, a morbid thought to have tonight when I was praying for a long life with Kay! The chap that farmed next to me came up and spoke.]

"*I didn't know you went here to school, can't remember you. Whose class were you in?*"

Looking at him I told him I had left before he started but was hoping to see someone who I hadn't seen for years. "A girl I bet," he said. "*What's her name?*" I saw no reason not to tell him for soon I hoped everyone would know. "*Come on,*" he said. Who is she?"

"Kay Drew."

"*Kay Drew? By God! I thought you lost her to someone else years ago. I remember all us lads eyed her up. The best-looking girl in the school she wouldn't have anything to do with another boy. She always said you and her were getting married when she was old enough and then she vanished. You never did marry did you?*" Then he started talking about farming. I made my excuses and left. I had a quest tonight and farming was far from my mind!

***

The hall quickly filled up and the speeches were made. I stood in the corner at the back trying to spot Josephine and Kay. Scanning the sea of backs of heads, neither was to be seen and I had that sad feeling that perhaps they had somehow met a difficulty and were not coming after all. The music started to play. I was miles away wondering what could have happened to them. Surely Josephine would have phoned? She knew I had booked the hotel room. Then my heart missed a beat. A table in the middle of the hall had six people sitting at it and the one getting to her feet was Josephine, looking completely different in a frock instead of an old jumper and jeans like other times when at work. I could not see the face of the auburn haired woman sitting with her back to me but I did recognise the woman she was getting to her feet to speak to, a shiver ran down my back. Abby! What was she doing here? The body language of Josephine told me that something was wrong. As she stood facing Abby, she gave her a push as if telling her to go away. Josephine's husband now stood up and started to remonstrate with the two women. The woman whose face I could not see now turned to look away and face me. Kay was staring right at me but did not recognise me in the shadows. Her face was as radiant as I had always known it to be. Abby, Josephine and her husband were making their way to the door as I showed myself. Josephine saw me move and hastened me over.

"Preacher! Outside, quick! Abby's drunk and mad!"

Why she wanted me outside with Kay so close and not knowing I was there made no sense. A glance towards Kay showed me that she had her head in her hands and was staring at her lap. *"Preacher! Outside,"* made me move as Josephine gave me a shove to hurry me up. Outside Abby ranted and raved on. She knew of my plan to meet Kay and was having none of it. She shouted at me did they know I had been sleeping with her? And she beat her chest with her hands.

*"You never needed her before now so leave her alone. She is a wizened old maid. I would be better for you, you know that. I know of your plans for the night."*

Josephine's husband told his wife to go inside and comfort Kay. Him and I could sort Abby out. Abby quietened down as Josephine left. She said she was not going home and knew of the Mermaid. She was not going to let it go. Kay had a right to know the truth she and I were planning to live together, and with that she produced a piece of paper from her bag. *"Look. I have proof,"* thrusting the letter of receipt for her rates from the council office with my name on it acknowledging my cheque.

*"This right?"* he said. *"You pay her rates?"*

*"Only the once last month."*

*"If this is correct,"* he said, *"What's going on?"* Abby was rapid with the answer.

*"Can't you see? He lives with me and I'm not prepared to share him with her in there."*

*"Look. I don't know what's been going on and I don't want to. Stay here Preacher and you Abby, go home."* He disappeared in through the doors, to leave Abby and me looking at each other.

*"Don't have anything to do with her, please darling. Come with me. If you see her I will never leave you alone."*

*"Look Abby. You and me were a mistake. All my life you have tried to come between Kay and me, now go home and forget me, please."*

*"I will see you up the Mermaid later,"* she said. And turned round and left. Josephine arrived at my side as she vanished out of the playground gate.

*"What's going on? Kay is in tears in there. The things Abigail had to say really upset her. What's this about you paying her rates?"*

*"I only met her the other month and she was in financial difficulties and likely to lose her house. Her husband had been a real pal to me when we were younger and I couldn't see her made homeless."*

*"Then you slept with her didn't you?"*

*"Abby was so persuasive. I don't know what came over me."* And as I started to cry she put her arms around me.

*"You were lucky. I understand Abby is a bitch. She used you. Now she knows of the Mermaid and intends to cause trouble. Kay is upset and I don't think it's a good idea for you to suddenly turn up tonight like planned. It's too soon after that exhibition of Abby's. Leave it please Preacher. I will phone you soon, please."*

***

It was only eight thirty and tonight had been a disaster. What had Abby said? How was Kay taking it? I left, and knowing Josephine or her husband would say nothing about me being there. As it was early, I walked up the streets and climbed the cobblestones to the Mermaid to look in the window and dream again like last time I came close to Kay at the school. There, large as life, sat Abby at a table with her daughter. Neither she nor Ann saw me as I ducked out of sight. Christ! She was waiting to ambush us when we entered later. That did it. Josephine was right, not tonight. Kay needed time alone to think.

***

Disappointed I retraced my steps to the car and returned to the old lonely house. Drawing up in the yard, an old barn owl watched me park and walk to the door and I mused, *'are you as wise as they say you are? If so, let me into your secret for tonight things had gone terribly wrong.'* I lit the fire and sat in the dog hair covered armchair still in my new suit, drinking a cup of tea and gazed into the flames as they flickered towards the chimney. Was it that difficult to meet the only girl you had always loved? The old clock ticked the hours away and as it chimed midnight I thought how different tonight had turned out. Instead of waltzing into the hotel with Kay on my arm, here was I looking at a fire that had nearly died. Her, now having to run the gauntlet of Abby waiting for her to go to her room alone, to be greeted by a book of our love for each other so long ago, bouquet of flowers and a bottle of champagne. No doubt the drink would have a little note saying, *'Compliments of the hotel,'* but the flowers that I had asked for would have the card saying, *'With all my love, Preacher,'* attached. Would she now think I had sent them knowing she would be there as a way of saying, *'Sorry I'm with Abby?'* I prayed that Josephine would find a way of telling her that I had hoped to meet her but after the kafuffle with Abby, I had left her alone at the school.

***

The dog on my lap licking my face woke me to the daylight flooding into the room. I had fallen asleep in the chair and my new suit was crumpled and covered in dog hair. A glance at the clock told its own story. Eight hours of sleep had fortified my body to stir again to life. Letting the dog out of the house, I started to think of Kay and how had things gone on their arrival at the hotel last night. I could hardly phone to find out. I must wait until Josephine was alone back at home, then I could discuss with her the outcome of last night. Knowing that they had hoped to look around the town today after breakfast, I left it until nine o clock that night before I phoned Josephine.

Her husband answered and told me to hold on. She came on the other end bubbling over with the news that Kay had enjoyed today and they had driven by my farm and had remarked how the old house looked so beautiful and she had longed to live in one like that. Josephine said that Kay had not believed half of what Abby had said and paying the bill was the sort of thing I would have done for any of them, but she was shy to visit me as I had sent her flowers last night for her room, and she had not read the book yet. She said even if there was some truth in Abby's claim, it showed I still felt something for her.

"*I nearly told her the truth about you paying for the room and how you were there last night but then thought better of it in case she wondered why you did not appear to declare your love for her and stop Abby's vicious tongue. As a friend I could not tell her it was me that told you to go away last night. Then she would think I was no better than Abby, trying to keep you two apart. I really believe she still loves you Preacher.*"

I told her to tell Kay she had heard from me, to tell her that I loved her and give her my phone number. Josephine promised tomorrow she would and we both hung up.

*\*\*\**

The old blue van drove into the yard as I was feeding the pigs. Richard stepped out of the driver's side, his mate was a real bruiser of a type and followed him across the yard.

"Good morning. We were in the area empty and I thought I might be able to take a couple of pieces of that furniture. This is Bob, he's a real expert in the sort you have and can give a better price than me."

As he had walked across the yard I had already made up my mind that no way was I doing business with the likes of him.

"I don't think so," I said.

"Let Bob have a look. He will know the going rate and we do have cash. Just a couple of bits, that's all."

Bob said nothing but Richard was insistent that they had to have something.

"Good morning," I said, and on entering the house, slammed the door shut. Half an hour later they slowly drove away. I phoned Josephine but the voice that answered told me the shop was shut today and *'please leave a message and they would get back to me.'* Following the beep I said,

"Phone Preacher, it's urgent!" I put the phone down and went back to work.

# CHAPTER TWENTY.

Lunchtime found me up in the top meadow out of sight of the house. How they found me I have no idea. They must have been lucky to have gone to the sixteen acres and seen me. The two women and a lad appeared at the gate before I recognised Josephine. Then my gaze of disbelief as they walked across the field made my body turn to a run as my feet took hold of the turf. Kay was leading the pack of three, striding straight at me! As I ran at her she stopped. Josephine stood slightly to one side as my arms wrapped themselves around Kay. The impact nearly knocked her over! It was so sudden, she had no time to object. I swept her off her feet and half turned her around, at the same time finding her lips with mine.

"Kay! Where have you been? I have waited so long for this moment."

"Steady on Preacher, not in front of my grandson please!"

Those words! The first I had heard from her in thirty-nine years were enough to stop me in my frantic desire to carry her off forever.

"Your grandson?" And as my eyes peered over her shoulder, the young lad grinned.

"She your grandmother" I asked. He did not answer, instead Josephine spoke.

"Peter is Kay's daughter's son." I looked at the woman in my arms, now aged like me, and no longer a shy little girl. This lad was the child from the baby Abby told me she'd had out in Australia. Kay was now a fine looking grandmother. By the way she had held me and had been striding across the field towards me, she was also a very fit lady.

Before me, here in this field, was not only the woman I loved, but also the boy I had met at the school in the spring and who I had picked out to read his composition to the class. Why had I not asked the children to add their surnames at the head of their papers? Then perhaps I would have got a clue that I was so near to this very attractive woman any man would kill for.

"You the writer man who came to school?" he asked.

"That's right Peter. You never told me who your grandmother was, did you?"

"No, and you never came back."

Kay was taking a lot of interest in our conversation.

"It was you that came to his school to talk to them. Peter went on and on about the lovely man. I'm sorry I missed you. Josephine, did you know?"

"No of course not."

A peculiar calm came over the few of us as we all looked at each other then I held my hand out to greet the lad.

"Peter. How nice to meet you."

"You the Preacher?" he stammered.

"That's right."

"Gran talks a lot about you," he stammered, "can I stroke one of your pig's mister?" I felt sorry for Kay and the boy.

"Of course, come on and shall we bring gran along with us?"

"And Aunt Jo?" He took my hand and together the four of us walked back across the fields to the house. Kay slipped her arm around me and smiled looking across me at my hand holding the lad's so meaningfully. After all this time neither of us needed words. Josephine was the only one to speak. My heart was up in my throat and I could hardly believe what was happening. I think words would have choked me.

Reaching the yard I got a bucket of pig nuts and Kay and I stood aside as Aunt Jo and Peter petted a few of the old sows. Kay and I stood looking at each other. She noticed the tears forming in my eyes.

"You have not changed a bit. Still crying and needing a good shave."

"You remember then?" I said, "That first time all those years ago." She smiled.

"How could I forget?" Those brown eyes of hers said the same as forty years ago and we kissed like teenagers, to the embarrassment of Josephine.

"All right you two, leave it out. There's plenty of time later for that!" Every word I had heard today since they arrived had lifted my spirits that today was only the beginning of my life.

The four of us went to the house as Peter soon tired of feeding pigs. He had heard about the old house, full of empty rooms and cobwebs and wanted now to explore the *'ghostly house.'* I led the way holding Kay's hand like a love struck youth daring to breathe unless I awoke from the dream.

I had entered this house for the last sixty years and never banged my head on the doorframe, until now. The thud as my skull came into contact made me realise this was no dream. The other two ducked their heads as one should and I said, *"Welcome to my home Kay."* Kay was much too interested in looking around that she did not even acknowledge the greeting. Josephine told Peter not to touch anything as he tried to swing from the mantelpiece.

*"Mind that clock,"* his grandmother said. *"That's very old,"* and she moved to grab him.

*"This furniture you have,"* said Josephine. *"Well Kay is the expert I told you about. She will tell you the truth as to its real value."* I turned to see her holding Peter's hand, smiling at me.

"Honest Preacher. She told me of this house full of antiques but never told me whose they were, I promise."

"Come on," I said. "Let me show you. I wouldn't let Richard in." I got no further, Jo pulled me around by my shoulder.

"What do you mean, wouldn't let him in? Has he been here lately?"

"He came with a rough looking bloke in an old battered blue van, wanted to take a couple of pieces back with him."

"Don't have anything to do with him," said Kay. "He's a crook. What did he want?"

"A couple of pieces he said."

"Which ones" Jo said urgently. *"He will clean the whole place out, we don't have anything to do with him now if we can help it, but the other month he helped us out with the van and he was coming this way. Now come on Kay, I bet you can find out what he was after."*

"Here's the list he made out when he was here," I said going to the sideboard and rummaging through a pile of paper that was mostly bills, *"with the prices he reckoned they were worth."*

Kay took the paper and I took Peter's hand. As we climbed the stairs he looked up at me.

*"You going to be my granddad?"*

I kept quiet. Obviously having heard Kay and Jo talking, I thought. My grandmother's bedroom was the first we entered. The old four-poster bed looked forlorn. The curtains surrounding it old and dirty, cobwebs knitted a pattern across the void over all the bedclothes and feather cover, Mother's dressing table she always said was her wedding present from her mother stood against the wall. The silver at the back of the mirrors tarnished around the edges trying hard to reflect the odd bottles and things that stood on it. Kay stood and stared.

*"Preacher. When did you last clean this place?"* Her expression on her face made me think that she was shocked at all the filth.

*"I never come up here."*

*"I can see that! It's a time warp!"* That, pointing her finger over to the third ornate dressing table in the room, *"is priceless much too expensive for me to buy. How much did Richard say it was worth?"* And she nervously fumbled the sheet of paper to read the column of items. *"The bastard!"* she exclaimed. *"Look Jo! Five hundred pounds! It's worth that in thousands and ten more. No wonder he wanted a couple of pieces if the other stuff is as old as this. The bed alone is worth what he put that table at. I can't buy this Preacher, let me look at the other rooms. It says here that there are three more. It is a large old house isn't it? I love the way nothing is level or square. It's got real character."*

The light from the windows caught her auburn hair and I could see the young girl I had fallen in love with so long ago. She smiled at me still holding Peter's hand. *"You two are really getting on with each other. So many people haven't got the time for him,"* and he looked at her.

*"He's my granddad,"* he said.

*"Could have been,"* Kay said and the sorrow showed as she spoke to him and stroked his head. Josephine looked at us as I took Kay's hand in mine.

*"Still could be,"* I said and all this could be yours, sweeping my left arm around to gesture to the room.

*"You don't' mean that Preacher! You hardly know me. You may think you do but that was a long time ago."*

*"I'm ready to find out now all there is,"* I said, and placed my left hand on her other hand, squeezing it tightly. Peter ducked out from under our hands and stood looking along with Jo at us staring into each other's eyes.

*"Come along Peter, let's leave them alone. They have a lot to talk over together."*

***

It was half an hour later that we made our way down to the kitchen like naughty little school kids ashamed at what we had done, to enter the room to find Josephine and Peter drawing pictures of the pigs. Josephine hoped I did not mind them using all the paper on the jotter she had found beside the coffee pot.

"Well?" said Josephine, grinning at the two of us with our arms around each other. *"Are you Preacher going to find out about her or have you done that already and stirred the dust up on that old bed?"* The expression on Kay's face made Josephine sense she had said enough and I felt Kay's' arm tighten around my waist.

*"Preacher and I have talked, that's all. He's not changed, he's still a gentleman,"* and she gave me a knowing look. *"A bit wiser and not as green but he knows how to treat a lady,"* and she brushed her hands down her sides as if trying to wipe the imaginary dust off.

*"Don't try to explain. The look in your eyes tells me that I don't think it is a good idea to buy anything today from Preacher. Think it could be all yours soon anyway. You don't want to sour your friendship now with him by insulting him by buying his home."* Peter had got to his feet from the chair and was tugging my arm trying to show me the drawing he had done of the old sow with her litter of young. I think the fact that I let go of Kay and took an interest in Peter's scribbling did more that day for Kay and what she thought of me, than anything I had ever said, or was ever to do. She took the two of us in her arms and squeezed us tight.

*"We have to talk Preacher,"* she said, *"only not now."*

*"We need time alone,"* I said and with Peter telling me *"I want to come again, lots,"* the notion came to me. *"Why don't you two come for a holiday with your daughter? There's plenty of room."*

*"That's the solution,"* said Josephine who had been standing trying not to notice our embraces.

*"That's settled,"* I said. *"A week in the country for you my boy,"* and he let the two us go and ran to Aunt Jo.

*"I'm going to live here!"*

*"Only for a week,"* she said, cementing the proposal I had offered Kay. No way could she disappoint the lad. Kay looked at me.

*"We must speak of this, I will phone you. Now we must go. Preacher, you be careful won't you, and don't let Richard in the house, that is if he has the nerve to return and my bet is he will."*

\*\*\*

I waved the there of them off up the lane and wondered where today had gone. The rooks were all flying over the house, heading for the wood to spend the night, high up in the tallest trees. My dream had very nearly come true, I thought as I made my supper. Kay was coming to stay and sleep in my house!

Up in the bedroom she had told me she still felt an attraction to me but needed time, things were going too fast, and she had told me not to get any ideas at the moment.

\*\*\*

The following week flew by. The next morning I had gone into the town nearby and enlisted the services of a firm of industrial cleaners, telling them that I needed my old house spring cleaned or more to the point, 'dug out! The last remark had made the girl receptionist smile.

The owner had arrived that afternoon and priced up the job in hand, and we had agreed the sum to complete the work in that week. I had awoken the following morning to a fleet of cars in the yard and a battalion of women cleaners with brooms, mops and hoovers. One of the older women even offered to cook my breakfast and I suspected she wanted me out of the house sooner rather than later!

***

On the Friday one could have been forgiven for not recognising the interior. All the cobwebs had gone and the light actually managed to enter each room through the glass. The carpets no longer gave off little clouds of dust as one walked the rooms. Even the dog's cushion and rug had seen the washing machine. The furniture had taken on a new look, no longer were you able to write your name on the accumulation of grime. The lady who had cooked my breakfast turned out to be the boss's wife. She had heard from her husband of the odd offer to clean a house. They usually did shops and factories. He had told her the price and given her the opportunity to enlist some of her friends to undertake the work. As I lived all alone she had suggested I employed a cleaner for one day a week to keep on top of all the dirt I walked into the house. So from that day I employed one of the women to clean each week.

***

Kay had phoned in the week and we had talked for three hours on the phone. Peter had done nothing but talk of the farm and me but mostly of me, she said. Her daughter thought it a marvellous idea, she and her husband had never been alone in fifteen years since his birth. It would be such a lovely gesture for her daughter and her husband to stay the whole week. She and I could look after Peter and give them a little time to be on their own.

I told her that I had had a tidy up and she told me not to do too much as she loved the place as it was. My heart sank as she spoke those words. My image looked back at me from the items in the room. There was not a stick of wood that did not gleam with the polish the woman had lovingly and laboriously rubbed into it.

Next day I had told them not to do too much but I think they saw that as a way of trying harder to get a shine on everything!

That weekend I had visitors. Kay and her daughter pulled into the yard as I climbed down from the tractor. I had to admit that Kay had changed over the last thirty odd years but her daughter was the image of her at eighteen. Kay saw me staring in disbelief and the expression on my face told her my thoughts were back in time.

"*Preacher. Meet my daughter, Christine.*" My hand fell on her shoulders and I had a job kissing her on the cheek and not fully on the lips like I had so often done her mother.

"I've heard a lot of you over the years," she said. "Mother is so lucky to have found you again. She tells me you are so good with my boy and he loves you. I hope you don't mind us coming down here today but he has not settled since his last visit. His father has taken the shop over today. I had to come and see the place for myself and mother showed me the way."

The sun shone in her hair and I remembered a certain day her mother and I had first met. She was only fifteen and with a friend and had stolen my hat as a dare before running away across the field with it. The sun that day had lit her hair up as she threw my old cap up into a thorn bush and giggling, ran off.

"Come in, have a cup of tea," and I opened the door. Kay grabbed me by the arm.

"What have you done?" She said, hardly recognising the old kitchen on entering the door. Then she let go of my arm, ran into the hall and we heard her ascending the stairs in haste. *"Preacher!"* Her voice made Christine and I run up the stairs to find out what all the shouting was about. Kay stood in the middle of my grandmother's bedroom crying. The old curtains now looked like new with the wash they had had and the sun was shining on the embroidered patterns of the bed covers. The polished dressing table reflected the rays of light back at you. Christine stood admiring the room.

"Such elegance," she said. *"Is this the honeymoon suite?"* Her mother gave her a look of disapproval.

"No. It's his grandmother's room."

"I thought you said she was dead."

"She is."

"But it is so clean, it's had a woman's touch. Mother, are you sure he lives on his own?"

Kay looked at me and smiled.

"I have a woman come in every Monday," I said and Christine relaxed.

"I hope the cleaner has not ruined any of the old things. Nothing was thrown out was it Preacher?"

"Of course not, you loved it so much that even Josephine won't touch any of it. That is for you to decide if you take me on," and she tried to hide her face from us.

"Are you proposing to my mother?" Christine said.

"No, certainly not," said Kay, then I realised that perhaps I had hoped she would have responded differently but I was dreaming. Kay was embarrassed.

"What are the other rooms like?" Christine asked.

"I don't know," Kay said. "I only ever saw this one and that was too much. The place then had not seen a woman for years."

"Come on Kay. Look at the other part of the house please." We left out my bedroom on the ground floor, as it was still a tip. Books, magazines and dirty clothes lay everywhere. The women followed me down the stairs to the door of the old living room. Opening it, I bowed and said,

"Welcome to my home." Kay only took one step inside before she turned to look at me.

"Preacher. Please tell me you don't come in here very often," and my gaze followed her eyes around the room. *"A time capsule if ever I saw one,"* she said. *"Do you know what that is?"* stepping across the floor to run her hand with a gentle touch over the polished table in the centre of the room. *"This is an oak refectory dining table and those are a set of Joint Stools and those chairs at each end are Wainscot. That Welsh oak cupboard with all those old pewter chargers on it is a Tridarn."* Christine stood smiling at me.

"Mother knows her old furniture." This room has not been touched for years. "Preacher did your mother ever use it?"

"No. She hated it. The fireplace alone took nearly all morning to clean," and we looked at the huge inglenook with the massive smoke blackened oak beam spanning the full width on which stood a pair of battered slanting candlesticks alongside an impressive oil lamp.

*"You know what you're talking about don't you?"* I said putting my hand out to hold hers.

*"I love it but not as much as that old seventeenth century Jacobean panelled tester bed upstairs. That's really old!"*

"You know a lot," I said and her daughter said,

*"I would hope so, that's what we do for a living and some of the prices she charges makes me shudder when the customers ask the cost of something and I have to tell them. You've never been to our shop have you Preacher? You must come up town and look at it."*

"Love to. Where is your shop?" and she produced a little card from her pocket.

"Let's look around the farm now shall we? That's what we really came to do. Peter keeps on about it."

***

The sun hit the body with its heat.

"The house is so cool," Kay said. *"Is it cold in the winter?"*

"No, that's the funny thing about it. It stays constantly the same temperature all year around."

Christine poked her nose into every shed around all the straw stacks in the yard as if looking for something.

*"Checking Preacher, don't mind her. She is making sure it's safe for Peter to come and stay. We can still come can't we?"*

"You all can, especially you for the rest of your life." My eyes were pleading with her and she saw. Her arms took me and gently we kissed out in the middle of the cow yard, standing in half an inch of cow dung! Kay saw the funny side of it as she followed my eyes down to the ground.

*"So romantic!"* she said. *"My father always said it was good stuff. I will have to give it a lot of thought before I can live here,"* she said. *"There is such a lot of sorting out to do. Give me time please Preacher"* and her voice took on a different chord.

"Kay. I don't want you to just come and live with me. Let me court and romance you for a while like old times, then maybe if you feel right you would do me the honour of becoming my wife." The tears rolled down her cheeks. "Kay, don't cry. We are adult now, none of that slushy stuff."

"You can talk"! She said. "Always crying!" Christine coughed as she approached us from the back of the barn but we had seen her coming. The three of us decided that as the farm looked safe for her son to come and roam in, it was time now for lunch and we all left the farm for the local pub for lunch.

\*\*\*

Late that afternoon the girls left with the promise that I would visit their showroom the coming Monday. That night I lay in bed and dreamed of the sun forever shining like it had today on the farm, and of Kay and I strolling around the place that would one day be all hers.

\*\*\*

That Sunday I went to Morning Service, thinking I had better show my face before Kay and I had to ask him if he would marry us. I didn't want him to have to ask me if I lived in the Parish in front of Kay.

\*\*\*

Monday saw me all dressed up heading for Maidstone. Leaving at eight, I found myself in the old city at nine thirty. Only ninety minutes away yet she had lived here for so long away from me and could have been anywhere in the world. After asking a few people where I could find the street, I walked along the pavement, to be confronted by a large shop inside which stood a collection of pricey antiques. Looking up at the front I read along the top of the shop, *'Forever old, but loved by all.'* I had arrived.

The brass door handle turned with ease and a little bell on the inside announced my arrival. Kay came out of a little door at the back and embraced me.

"*Welcome to my home,*" she said. "*I've seen yours, now see mine. Christine will be here later.*" I ran my fingers across a tabletop beside me wondering what history it could tell. If only it could talk! A quick look at the stock in the shop and I followed Kay up the stairs to the large flat above, for a coffee.

"Who owns the shop? The rent must be astronomical!" I said.

"I own it," she said. "Richard and I bought it together years ago before property rose to the price it is today. I paid the mortgage then when he left me." She saw that talking of her and him was causing me pain. "I'm sorry Preacher but it was a long time ago. You have had girlfriends haven't you?" The tears in my eyes I believe told her before I gave my answer.

"No, never, I always hoped you would be mine one day." She hugged me.

"Perhaps I will be, there are a few things to sort out though. First, you must meet my son in law. He is coming with Christine at eleven. I hope you like him."

The little bell rang and Kay rose from my lap.

"I bet that's them now." I had hardly got my cup of tea stirred and Bob came bounding up the stairs, his hand outstretched ready to meet me.

*"Preacher. How nice to meet you! You're to be my father in law, I understand?"*

Kay looked at me and smiled. *"It looks as if we are getting married after all, no matter what we say!"*

She drew herself up to me and cuddled into my shaking body. Kay had just said yes and I had for the last forty odd years dreamed of the time I got to my knees and asked her, now all that belonged to yesterday. Obviously I had been discussed in their house. The decision had been taken out of my hands! The smile on my face greeted Christine and Peter as they entered the room. He was overjoyed to see me and wanted to know if I had come to take him to the farm.

*"Next week, I promise,"* Kay said. *"Meanwhile Preacher has some things to do."* I looked at her. She squeezed my hand. *"That old bed needs a lot of airing before we put it to use."* I was high in the clouds at that remark. Kay was a girl of the sixties when I had last known her. Never would she have spoken like that. Even I never would have put it so bluntly, even today, but she had lived while I had stayed at home on my own and had never gone out looking or socialising with others. The thought of Kay in that old bed with her daughter's knowledge seemed rather embarrassing but I suspect that one's children must realise the fact at some time in their life that mum and dad sleep with each other.

\*\*\*

That night I left the shop which Kay was going to be a sleeping partner only in, letting her daughter run the business. Kay said the home she was going to was not that far away that she could not commute one day a week if needed. Her daughter told her she deserved some happiness and that they would be fine on their own.

I left to drive home to air the bed, all the time thinking that all my life I had been living so close to my love. It was like spending your whole life next door.

\*\*\*

The shop in town had to order my request for new sheets of cotton the size I needed to replace which my grandmother had used fifty years ago. The feather cover, the dry cleaner took on as his task to rejuvenate.

\*\*\*

*"Preacher."* Christine called out as the car came into the drive. My day had started early at six so that I was ready when they arrived at ten. I looked at my watch. She was an hour early.

*"Funny ten o clock,"* I said as she got out of the car.

*"Mum and Peter are on their way. She is so excited to be coming but please be careful, don't rush her. I need to see you on your own with Bob."*

Bob went to lock the car when I told him there was no real need, no one was going to use it.

*"I suppose you're right,"* he said. *"No one around for miles only where we live, it would be gone in five minutes."*

*"Hurry up Bob, they will soon be here,"* said his wife fussing to get him in the house. The three of us sat around the kitchen table while Christine explained that she thought the pair had rushed her mother into coming for the week and

the talk that she hoped to marry me was perhaps the only way she saw it pleasing her and Bob. For a long time now she had wanted to get out of the shop and let them run it on their own but as she lived above the place, they had no money to buy a home for her. Then the solution of living with me had come up, she was concerned that she had talked her mother into saying yes.

"Nonsense," I said. "If she wishes she can live here as my guest. I will not pressure her to do anything, and thanks for the tip." I felt gutted but would rather have her under my roof as a friend than never see her at all. Christine and I did an inspection of the three rooms upstairs that had beds with new sheets and pillowcases. She chose the one at the end of the long twisting passageway as the one her and Bob would like, the little one for Peter and the one with the blue sheets for her mother. The mention of my grandmother's large room did not enter our conversation. Bob had said nothing until then. He'd had his instructions to gather up the suitcases and take them to the rooms, and like a good little boy, he turned and did as bade.

***

Kay arrived with Peter to find the three of us having a pot of coffee. Peter ran up to me and threw his arms around my neck, ignoring his mother completely.

"Gran, gran, granddad!" he stammered, and his mother smiled at me.

"See what I mean?" she said, "Him too." I was trying to get him to let go so that I could take Kay into my arms to welcome her. Instead she sidetracked me and took a chair beside Bob and said,

"A cup of hot coffee, just what I need, he's been driving me crazy all the way down here." "How much further, are we nearly there?" The way Kay had sat down without greeting me in the way I had hoped made me realise that Christine's words of warning perhaps had some substance to them. Gently, gently was the way to go.

Although Peter had seen little of the farm other than the inside of the large barn, he insisted that he took his grandmother on a grand tour, leaving me behind with his parents. Poor old gran had to contend with him counting all the cows and sheep many times over. The pigs, she said, beat both of them, as they would not stay still long enough. Even the six wild rabbits were recorded by Peter to retell us over dinner that night!

Peter was tired that night and asked to be put to bed. His gran, he insisted, had to be the one to hold his hand until the sand man came and made him close his eyes. In many ways, other than his stature, he was still only a child.

***

While we waited for Kay to return Christine recounted the reason for his handicap. His birth had been a difficult one and his brain had been starved of oxygen. Bob now spoke up.

"No it wasn't. My brother was like him. It runs in the family."

"You only say that to hide the fact, tell Preacher the truth."

I saw a domestic approaching and quickly changed the subject.

"What are you doing tomorrow?"

"We hoped to go into town and look around, then on Tuesday pay a visit to the Romney Hythe Railway, and mum wants to go and look at the old house she used to live in."

"I can do better than that for her," I said. "I know the people that live there now, they would be thrilled for her to visit."

We heard the catch drop on Peter's door and waited for Kay to arrive. She did not come down and Christine suggested I go and find her. She was nowhere to be seen along the dimly lit corridor. My grandmother's bedroom door was open. She stood looking out of the window at the stars in the Heavens, crying softly to herself. I backed off and went downstairs.

"Well?" said Christine.

"You had better go up. She's in my grandmother's room crying." Christine ran up the steps and I heard them comforting each other from where I was standing at the open kitchen door, so shut it and sat beside Bob. He looked at me, and then put his hand on my shoulder.

"I'm sorry to bring all our troubles to you. You don't want the boy here with you all week, but really we must not stay for many days. The shop must open, we have a lot of clients that come from the continent to buy and on Wednesday we have a party of Germans, then Americans. We cannot really afford to let them arrive to find a piece of paper in the window saying 'closed.'

"Leave Kay and Peter here, I'm sure we can cope. Christ! I have a herd of pigs out there that don't know what manners are and we live together, OK?" With that, he took his hand off me and laughed. From that moment Bob and I became the best of friends.

The women appeared, wiping their faces and apologised. Kay said she was only too happy to have Peter for the week as it would let her daughter and Bob have a bit of time to themselves. Looking at me she said, *'Preacher and me could surely cope with him,'* and she stepped up to me and put her arm around me.

*"We will manage won't we?"* she said, tilting her head back to see into my face and looking at me with those lovely loving eyes.

*"We will be only too happy,"* I said and she tightened her arm around me.

"I am sorry about just now. I don't know what came over me but I had to see that bed again."

"Don't Kay, don't torture yourself. I have done enough of that in my time. Memories can be such nasty things at times." She smiled,

"I was only thinking ..." and I stopped her.

"Don't. You will make me cry," and she laughed.

"Always leaking you are!" The old clock chimed midnight and we all retired to our beds. Kay looked disappointed but said she understood why she was in the room across the passage on her own.

\*\*\*

On Sunday we all went to town and had lunch in the George Hotel. Then in the afternoon I took Peter fishing in the river where he caught a lot of Rudd on bread paste. The lad could not keep his eyes open that evening and Kay put him to bed early. Then we all sat and talked, mainly about what I had done in the years since Kay had last seen me. The fact that I had never had a real girlfriend seemed to upset Kay. Christine tried to steer her off the topic but she kept coming back to it. When the house was last decorated and did I get a girl to choose the colours? Things like that. The truth was I never had the notion that anything needed painting or cleaning. In fact the clothes I wore, I washed, as I did the dishes. The bedclothes got a good soak in the bath after I got out then went in the washing machine.

"Call that old Bendix a washing machine?" Kay said pointing to the paint chipped old thing under the sink. "That is really an antique along with all the other objects in this palace!" I was glad she chose the word palace to describe my home, for to me that is exactly what it was, the home of my family for over three hundred years.

***

Today Christine and Bob left for the shop, leaving Peter happily with his gran and me. Yesterday the little railway had entertained us for the whole day. Now today he wanted to go fishing again. The three of us sat on the riverbank and he landed dozens of little Rudd. Kay and I at last had the time alone to talk. She told me all about Australia and how over there they caught a little lobster type shellfish that they called Gabbies.

"Lovely to eat, do you find crayfish in this river?"

"Never heard of one being caught around here I said."

We talked of many things but never about the man she had lived with. I know that she had gone to Australia with a man but she did not let me know what she had done in the years she was absent, it was nothing to do with me. That is not the way she saw it. Everything I had done between the times she last saw me was eagerly sought. When did my parents die? Where were they buried? Who was the woman that cleaned my home? How often did she come? What did I pay her? And when I told her, she looked at me and put her arm around me.

"Perhaps you won't have that expense much longer." Our eyes made that sort of contact that spoke volumes. Our faces closed that little gap between us and our lips came into contact, at the same time our bodies lost their vertical positions and we lay locked together on the riverbank. Peter never showed any interest in the way we cuddled each other, only to shout,

"Look a big one!" as he pulled a four-ounce fish from the water. Her hands ran up around my waist under my shirt and caressed me. I followed like I had done forty years ago.

"You behave yourself," she said and like the fool I am, I thought I had gone too far and quickly withdrew them. "You are as green now as you always were," she said. "You really have never had a girlfriend have you?"

"You know I haven't?" I said. "Christine told you that."

"Don't you remember how I loved you doing that?" and she took my hand and placed it on her breast. "Have I got to tell you everything to do?"

"I don't know," I said. "I don't want to offend you."

*"There is truly Preacher, nothing you could do to me that would upset me,"* and her arms pulled me onto her. I was still not sure that I could to anything and not upset her. All my life I had respected women, now Kay was telling me that I could do anything I wanted to her! The sun was hot on our bodies and we dozed the noon away.

The chill of the evening made us call a halt to our cuddling and Peter was happy to wind up his line. Today Kay and I had talked and later over tea she agreed to take the place of the women that came once a week. In future she would do all the housework and washing. Her employment, she told me, came only with two conditions. First I had got to marry her and second was much more demanding, she wanted grandmother's room. I started to cry and she told me.

*"One more sob from you and I'll hit you with this,"* picking the teapot up from the table. When I said, *"as soon as possible, neither of us are getting any younger,"* she stuck her tongue out at me, *"but that doesn't mean we cannot start right away as we mean to go on,"* I see I will have to be boss, you are so slow. Now Peter, bedtime," and she said looking at me, *"don't you start doing anything because we are having an early night."* My feelings were out of this world had I heard right? To me that only meant one thing. I sat quietly listening to all the movement from the room above, hoping that Peter soon had his visit from the sand man. The old clock chimed seven and it was still daylight. Never had I gone to bed so early! The catch on his bedroom door made my pulse increase and Kay called out that she was having a bath and would be ready in ten minutes. I went to lock the back door and was startled by a sharp knock from the outside.

# CHAPTER TWENTYONE.

My hand slipped from the bolt to the handle and as the door swung open Abigail barged her way in.

"All right Preacher. Where is she? I know she's here."

"Abby! What do you want?"

"Her. Where is she? In bed I bet. You with your shirt undone looking like you two were at it. Heard me drive up did you? Going to lock the door on me were you? Kay Drew! Where are you?" she shouted."

"Ssh. You'll wake Peter, I said.

"Peter? Who the hell is Peter?"

"Her grandson."

"Him. You've got the whole family here? Didn't take her long did it? You fool. Can't you see that she's only using you? She has never liked me, always after you. I loved you first, then she got her grips into you, turned your head completely."

The door to the kitchen opened and Kay stood there in a beautiful long, frilly nightdress that one could see through.

"You bitch!" Abby said before I could utter a word of warning to Kay. She had not heard Abby come in while she had bathed. The look of utter amazement on Kay's face!

"Abigail! What are you doing here?"

"That's for me to ask you. Leave the poor man alone. Go back to where you belong and take that simple brat upstairs with you." The words Abby spat made Kay angry and she went to go for her. I stepped in between them.

"Abby. What do you want? Please stop this and go," I pleaded.

"I want you, you know that. You have not been to see me lately then Richard told me she was here."

"Richard?" said Kay. "I might have guessed he put you up to this."

"No he hasn't. He doesn't know I'm here."

"Then I suggest that you go home now and tell him that it's none of your business where I am or who I'm with. We're finished." Kay came up to me and put her arm around me. Her soft warm body made my pulse beat. This woman, Abby, was in the way again. Something really stirred in my heart for the woman holding me. With Abby it had been pure sex and she knew it.

"Abby. Please leave."

"And don't come back," Kay said.

"I'm not going until you pack your bags and scram! He's mine, you always spoil it."

"I spoil it! Who was it that had an affair with Richard when we were living happily together?"

"He was tired of you."

"No he wasn't. You lured him away with your lies."

"I never lured Preacher, he came to me and bedded me!" Kay was now looking at me to tell her it was all another of Abby's lies. *"Look,"* said Abby and from her handbag she took the sheet of paper that bore the council heading. *"Look, I can prove we lived together, he paid the rates for three years. He wouldn't do that would he, if he wasn't sleeping with me? Look."* Kay turned her head away. *"Look, his name is on the cheque,"* and I looked at the photocopy of my cheque for her rates given as a receipt in case the court case had come up before they could clear it. The damning evidence was there to see and Kay let my body go and ran out of the room crying.

"See. She believes me, now tell her to go."

"Abby. I don't believe you, coming here just to stir up trouble. Now I see what you are. You really have shown your true colours haven't you? First, a long time ago, you lied to me telling me you never heard from Kay. You know I never lived with you. Why tell Kay that and by the sounds of things you were responsible for Richard and her splitting up."

"She got what she wanted, the shop and all his money. He came to me with nothing but hate for her."

"Abby. I have heard enough now, we are no longer friends and please don't ever bother me again. I will never see you again. Now go and tell Richard that Kay is very happy, goodnight!"

"You don't get rid of me like that. She is the one to go," and she started towards the door that Kay had fled through.

"No you don't. That door," I said, pushing her gently towards the back door.

"Take your hands off me," she said.

"Get out then before I kick you out with my boot!" She was making me angry. As fast as she had come in she left, slamming the door behind her. I heard Peter scream and Kay's footsteps across the wooden boards as she rushed to comfort him. Abby left the yard, spinning the back wheels in the mud. Tonight she had really shown what sort of woman she truly was and I realised that grandmother's bed would not be in use for a day or two. Kay was up in Peter's room trying to calm him down. Abby's shouting had awoken him. I slowly walked up the stairs and listened at the door. Kay was telling him that it was nothing to worry about and that she and Preacher were still very good friends. The woman shouting did not mean what she said, none of it was true. Quietly I slipped into my room, not bothering to put the light on. I heard the latch of Peter's room drop and Kay go to her room.

I must have dozed off because the next thing I knew was the bedcovers moving and Kay slipping her body in alongside me. She put the flat of her hand on my face, turned my face to hers and passionately kissed me.

"Preacher. We have got to talk." I leaned over to put the bedside light on. "No, don't do that. Just lie here and cuddle me, please. What did Abby mean, you two lived together? You didn't did you?'

"Of course not I had not seen her for over thirty years, it was only when she met Josephine at Dover and I got news that you were still alive. Before that I didn't know if you were alive or not."

"Then what was she doing with that council paper that you paid?"

I could tell by the way Kay held me and talked that she was not one hundred per cent sure.

"I felt sorry for her. We were such good friends, then her husband dying and no money. I had the money to help her and no one to spend it on so Abby got her bill paid for her and yes, I suppose you have to know, I did spend the night there a couple of times, but that was all." Kay took my face in both her hands.

"She meant nothing to you did she? It was a man thing wasn't it? Any man would be a fool to refuse a woman with a body like hers, especially when she's on the hunt. Don't let it happen again. I believe you, she is a nasty bit of work," and with that she got out of my bed and wished me a good night. I lay on my back listening to her going to her room. At last, I thought, she understood Abby, but why had I told her of my nights with her? Up until then I really thought the pair of us were going to make my dreams come true. Again Kay and I had shared a bed but nothing had happened. Were we never going to make contact?

\*\*\*

Kay had my breakfast ready when I came downstairs in the morning. Coolly she said *"Good morning,"* looking out of the kitchen window as if expecting someone and kissed me on the side of my face.

Having finished my meal, I started work out in the yard feeding the animals. A car came into the yard and Kay ran out to meet Christine. The two hugged each other and I noticed Christine patting her mother on the back as they entered the house. The reason for my food being ready this morning became clear to me. Kay had been up early and phoned her, she had now come down to find out what was going on as her mother had been in tears on the phone. A few moments later the two came out the house and Kay called to me.

*"Look after Peter, he will be up in a moment. Give him his breakfast will you? See you later,"* and the pair of them left in the car heading for town.

Peter and I spent the best part of the day mucking out the pigs, and he loved riding on the tractor with the dung spreader, whisking the contents into the air. Sitting on my lap he steered a rather erratic course across the fields, leaving a trail for all to see. The sudden swerve from the path we were taking made me grab the wheel.

*"Peter, careful!"*

*"Mum, mumm, mummy,"* he stammered, and I then noticed a blue car travelling down the lane towards the house. Putting the spreader out of gear, we bounced across the field to the yard. Kay and her daughter were inside when we got there and Kay ran to me and slung her arms around me.

*"I love you,"* she said. *"Abby told us the truth. You really did only spend the two nights with her and now Richard knows he has packed his bags and left. She has got all she deserves. We girls fell out with her years ago for stealing our boyfriends. Now me and you must get married."* Her words were about to make me cry when Peter climbed on the chair beside us and leapt onto Kay.

*"Get married. Go on, now!"*

*"Soon,"* his grandmother told him. *"Now your mother wants you to go home*

171

with her, then we will have a big party and you can come and live here as much as you like."

"Live here forever and ever."

"We will see," I said, latching onto Christine's suggestion that we needed time to ourselves.

Christine helped Peter pack his things, then left. Kay and I stood with our arms around each other and waved them off. Turning to Kay, I asked if she really meant that she wanted to marry me.

"Yes," she said kissing me on the lips with those soft lips of hers. *"In that case I had better phone the vicar and arrange a meeting with him. There is also the church to book and the invites to sort out."* She put her fingers onto my lips to quieten me. *"First,"* she said. *"We ought to see if we can make it together. So often the pair of us have been there but never done it. Come on,"* and she tugged my arm by the hand. She grabbed me and we both ran to the door. *"Lock it,"* she said. *"We don't want any of your acquaintances walking in on us!"*

I bent to force the bottom bolt across, then reached up to slam the top bolt into place and turning the old key, went to follow. Kay was not in sight. The kitchen door was open and I closed it as I took my rubber boots off that were covered in pig dung. Reaching the landing I had no problem locating Kay. Her call of *"in here,"* made me open grandmother's bedroom door to see Kay slipping her jeans off to reveal a very skimp pair of knickers. She stood looking at me as I nearly fell over trying to get to her at the same time as dropping my trousers.

*"Steady boy,"* she said, teasing and pulling the blankets back to reveal the new white cotton sheets. I ripped all the buttons off my shirt in my frenzy to jump into bed with her. Together we went back in time. "Gently," she said as I lay with her in my arms. She kissed me and said, *"Take me into Wonderland!"*

\*\*\*

Neither us noticed the daylight leave the sky that night. Around two o'clock we both decided we needed food so slipping something on, we made our way downstairs. Like teenagers we fooled around with each other, then I chased her back up the old staircase and again we put creases in the cotton sheets, this time hidden under the old feather cover. Eventually I tired and Kay kissed me.

*"Now you can phone the vicar. We should have done that forty years ago. Why you never took me away, I will never understand, but then it was not as easy as it is today,"* and together we slept the night away to awaken to the sound of the pigs grunting through the open window for their breakfast. Kay stirred and sniffed the air. *"Those pigs stink!"* she said, then turned her head and smelt me. *"It's you,"* she said, *"you stink of pig shit,"* and she jokingly pushed me out of the bed.

I remembered Abby once saying, *'don't'* worry about that, it's you, when I had been cleaning the pigs out, and I felt guilty thinking of her so jumped back into bed and told Kay she hadn't complained last night.

\*\*\*

The pigs were really starving when at last we did surface and went down to a cooked breakfast. I had finished the feeding when I noticed Kay hanging a line of white sheets out on the line to dry. We waved to each other, and then I remembered the vicar and his white collar so hurried indoors to phone him.

Taking Kay in my arms, we looked into each other's eyes.

*"You did mean what you said, you will marry me?"* The joy on her face made me pick up the phone before she had answered. "Preacher, after last night I have done nothing else except wonder what I was thinking of, not to have told you that night of the party after I came back to find you so many years ago. I now know that your love is so strong, I was a fool ever to have doubted you."

***

The vicar's wife answered the phone and suggested we call round that afternoon to see her husband. The vicar had only lived in the town for eight months but as the place was small and everyone knew each other, gossip spread fast and he had heard much about me.

At three Kay and I stepped up to his front door and I rang the bell. The man in person opened it in a boisterous voice and way.]

"Come in. I understand you wish to marry in my church. Come in my love," he said, greeting Kay. *"My office is this way."* The attitude of the man in the dog collar reminded me of the last time I had sat in the man of the Parish's office. Then he had told me nothing I wanted to hear.

The way he fussed over Kay, I had that pleasant feeling that this man was going to tell me good news. He was so gushing thrilled that a couple wanted to marry in his church. *"So many don't bother today and who can blame them? Few stay together for long, but marriage is a sacred thing, not to be entered into without a thought and you two have had many years to think."* He then realised that he had presumed we had known each other for many years and became so apologetic. *"You I know as the Preacher, have never been married before and the women in the town say, have never had a girlfriend. You, my dear, they say have never been wed either. Is that correct?"*

*"The women seem to know a lot about us,"* Kay said.

*"They mean no harm, it's wild gossip only. They thought something was going on up the farm. First, a lot of traffic, then you,"* and he looked at me with a smile on his face, *"were seen in town buying new bed linen. Wendy, my daughter, spent some time up at your house cleaning didn't she?"* I smiled back at him as Kay sat looking up at me from the low armchair she had bagged on being shown into his room.

*"Your daughter?"*

*"Yes, she told me the house was beautiful."* As I was called the Preacher, he presumed I knew a lot of what the reasons were for getting married but did not mention the creation of children. I believe he thought we had missed the boat on that part of marriage.

The meeting went on for over two hours with the vicar's wife bringing tea and biscuits in and joining us. She told us that she came from a farm in Yorkshire where she had met her husband. Kay and her got on fine, as if they had known each other for years. Her husband was interested in pigs and had always wanted to keep a couple like his Archbishop did as pets for his hobby. He had a large garden with half an acre of old orchard.

That evening we left, with the promise that the bands would be read in church and I would supply him with half a dozen little pigs when he had the sty built and the ground fenced. Kay was so happy that at last she was to be married in a church. She took my arm as we walked down the path to the garden gate.

*"You are going to make me so happy. Now you can buy me an engagement ring."* I nearly stumbled over my feet. Where the hell was I? All this time talking to the vicar about weddings and the poor girl had no ring! Hugging her to me, I told her that first thing tomorrow it was the jewellers for her.

\*\*\*

The ring did not cost a fortune as Kay stated that I had once given her one and she foolishly had thrown it away in Australia, thinking that I did not love her anymore.

\*\*\*

We spent an idyllic month together. Never had I been so happy. The vicar had paid a couple of visits to view the pigs and purchase a load of straw to litter his new sty that a local lad had built for him. Kay's daughter, husband and Peter had stayed the odd weekend and the sun shone. The wedding was set for October after the harvest that Peter was coming to help with.

He was a willing lad and loved to help on the farm. His mother told me that since his visits to his grandmother, his whole attitude had changed. He stammered less and slept well. She did not have to give him a sleeping pill each night now. He would go for a couple of nights after his stays with us before he asked for one. After one of the weekend visits, the Monday post revealed a long brown envelope. Kay, who had taken over the task of reading the mail, and filing the bills to be paid, opened the letter. She gave a gasp and slammed the letter down on the table.

*"The wicked woman"* I will kill her! I very nearly choked on the fried bread I had in my mouth when she said, *"It's from Abby's solicitor claiming you owe her a lot of money! Please sort it out darling and let's hear no more of the woman."*

"I don't owe her a penny."

"I don't want to know. Now if I am to marry you in a month's time, I don't want to hear her name again." Kay got up from the table and left the room. Today Abby had gone too far. She was now affecting Kay's happiness, to say nothing of mine.

Pushing my plate aside and screwing the letter up as I put it in my pocket, I left the house and farm to find the address at the top of the letter.

\*\*\*

The girl at the desk was most polite but as I had no appointment, said that the man I wanted was not available. While I had been unscrewing the letter, a man had entered a door that had the signature's name on it in gold letters.

\*\*\*

The gentleman had obviously missed his breakfast as he sat in an old leather chair eating a doughnut with a cup of coffee steaming on the huge desk.

"Yes?" he said as I sat opposite him. *"Can I help you?"*

"This," I said, slamming the letter down in my temper. *"What's this all about?"*

*"And you are?"* he said, glancing at the now rather tatty piece of paper.

"I'm him," I said, pointing my finger at my name at the top.

*"The Preacher,"* he said and extended his hand across the desk to take mine.

"No, I don't shake hands with people who send filthy lies through the post to me." He looked rather hurt.

*"Lies you claim?"*

"Yes, lies."

*"This woman came to see me and alleges you lived with her and paid to do so. You don't deny that do you?"*

"I most emphatically do," I said.

*"She has proof. You paid the rates for three years. Now why would you do that?"*

"Because she was an old friend and I felt sorry for her. She lost her husband a few years ago."

*"Yes, a year before you moved in."*

I did not like the tone of his voice. Abby had certainly made an impression on him, now he thought I was the guilty one. If I paid the council tax for the next year, he said he was sure the woman could be talked out of taking any further action. I left his office leaving him in no doubt that I would never pay her any monies. She, as far as I was concerned, *'could go and screw herself.'* To that remark he nearly knocked his cup of coffee over that was now cold. I don't think anyone had ever stormed like I had into his inner domain and talked to him like that.

The girl on the reception desk certainly had not expected that I did not know him and the way he was telling her to never let another person to pass her without warning him, made me feel better as I grabbed my jacket from the coat rack in the entrance hall.

***

The drive home took an hour. As I entered the house, Kay's belongings were laying in a heap by the door where she had hurriedly flung them. Calling out her name I went in search of her. She was lying on the big old four-poster bed crying her eyes out.

*"It's all gone wrong." "I wish I had never met you again. You broke my heart when I was young and now you and Abby are still at it,"* and she buried her head under the pillows we had found so comfortable and full of sweetness for the last month.

*"Go away,"* she told me. *"Leave me alone."* I did as she said, now was the wrong time to try and tell her the letter was a pack of lies.

The car drew up in the yard and Christine stamped into the house with the greeting of, *"Where is mother?"* giving me a nasty look. Like a coward, I fled the house in tears. Kay had been on the phone while I was away and I found Bob stretching his legs in the yard.

*"What's going on?"* he said, quite unaware from his wife what the emergency was, having only been told to stay where he was. I took him aside and showed him the bit of paper that had arrived only a couple of hours ago yet had done so much harm. I told him it was a pack of lies and had been to see the solicitor.

*"No good doing that old chap,"* he said. *"It's this woman you should see. Where does she live?"* There and then he decided it was his business to sort the mess out once and for all. *"Come on, let's go and see her. She won't argue with the two of us! I know her from old."*

Why I let him talk me into going with him, I don't know, but we left the house and yard without telling the girls. At least I thought we have the car so this way Kay was going nowhere fast.

***

Abby opened the door and nearly fell out into Bob's arms. Then she saw me cowering behind him. Bob was a big lad and had filled up the doorway with his body.

*"Preacher!"* She was only allowed to utter my name before Bob pushed her back inside.

*"Now my girl, what's all this nonsense about you and Preacher, and him owing you money?"* Abby stood no chance against a man like Bob. He stood for no nonsense. Abby flustered, saying she could not discuss it with him, as it was none of his business. The fact that it was affecting his wife and he had had to cancel a game of golf, *'made it very much his business,'* he said. *"Now,"* he said. *"Phone that solicitor chap of yours and tell him it is all a pack of lies, or whatever you have to do. We want to hear no more of it, understand?"*

Bob was excellent. I'm sure I would have submitted to her charms. He never let her get a word in edgeways.

*"Right, that's sorted. Come on, home and let's find the women."*

We left Abby half lying, half sitting on the couch shedding tears because she had lost the battle to split Kay and me up.

Reaching the car Bob said, *"I need a drink."*

For the next two hours we sat talking in the first pub we came to. *"Give them time to cool down,"* he said. *"Christine is convinced her mother loves you and a little thing like that woman wouldn't change her mind. You mark my words a pot of tea will be on the table when we get back and apologies all round."*

***

As we entered the back door a pile of black bin liners greeted us full of Kay's clothes. Bob and I looked at each other.

*"So much for the tea on the table,"* I said, and then noticed a note in the middle of the barren table, which had Kay's new engagement ring sitting on it. *"She's left me,"* I blubbered.

*"Don't be silly. We've got the car."* I looked up at the row of old nails in the

beam by the door. My Volvo car keys were absent.
   *"She's taken my car you fool. They've gone in the Volvo!"*

## CHAPTER TWENTYTWO.

That was the first time today that Bob had taken any of the proceedings seriously and he sat down with a thump in the old armchair.
"Bloody Abby she's always been a nuisance."
"You know her well?" I said.
"Of course, always up our place with her late husband."
"The bitch," I said. "She told me she only met your wife at the Dover Docks by chance."
"Met by chance?" We had been on a booze run together. She had too much to drink. "You do know she's an alcoholic don't you? And she uses drugs."
This was news to me.
"Drugs?"
"Yes, heroin mainly."
"She what, I would never have believed it."
"She's always done it," he said. "Started back in the days of the Hippies, smoking weed at school."

Suddenly the back door flew open and Christine rushed in and grabbed the ring from the table, then without a word made to go out. A voice I knew was Kay's shouted, *"don't forget the note,"* and she turned to grab it. Bob was by this time on his feet. I ran from the house to see Kay standing in the open car door. Seeing me she sat back in and locked the door. I pleaded with her and after a few minutes she agreed to come into the house. Christine offered her mother her ring and she put it on the table, refusing to place it on her finger.

The four of us got talking and the girls told us that they had started to load the car with the clothes when the vicar had called to look at the six piglets he was hoping I could deliver to him this week. When he had heard of the domestic, he had suggested Kay went up to the vicarage and talked to his wife. There they had met a couple of the vicar's wife's friends from the area. As far as they could ascertain, I had never looked at a girl of any age. As soon as she had spoken these words, Kay's hand took mine and she smiled at me.

"I'm, sorry." I was about to rise from my chair to kiss her when the phone rang. Kay's other hand leant behind her and she lifted the receiver. The expression on Kay's face made all three of us looking on wondering who the voice was on the other end. Kay's eyes closed and the smile that always seemed to be on her face vanished.

"No!" she said and slammed the hand piece down. *"You bastard!"* she spat at me. *"That was your daughter. Wanted to talk to her father!"* "My daughter? What are you on about?"

None of the party would stay long enough to explain. Kay was leaving and that was the end of it. All my pleading with Kay fell on deaf ears.

*"I will collect my clothes another day Preacher,"* she said and I watched as the three vanished up the lane. I returned to the house very despondent. Abby sprung to my mind. I took the phone in my hand to dial her number, ready to

give her what I thought of her petty little tricks, when the idea came to me to check the number that had rung me. Surely she would not have the nerve to use her own phone and had borrowed one of a friend's. I was interested to know of her pals for somehow she always seemed to know the right time to interfere.

I dialled the numbers, one, four, seven, one and sure enough the recorded voice told me the number of my last caller. The number was not Abby's so I pressed three and waited for a person to answer. After a few rings I was ready to hang up when a soft female voice said, *"Hello."*

*"Who's speaking?"* I asked.

*"Ann, that you Preacher, who was that just now who talked to me?"*

*"That was Kay,"* I said. *"What did you say?"*

*"Oh, I thought it was a young girl and asked to speak to her dad."*

*"Her dad, you fool. She was upset and surmised that you were my daughter."*

*"Ooops. I hope she laughed about it!"*

*"No, she didn't. In fact, she has left me. Now what did you want?"*

*"I wanted to know what was going on with my mother. She is in a terrible rage. Something about you and what you have done to her."*

*"I've done nothing, that's the problem, only she wanted me to pay her rates again for her."*

*"Why would she ask you to pay them, that's her boyfriend's job isn't it? He's living with her. You two haven't been seeing each other again have you?"* I needed the chair.

*"Of course not. Now I would appreciate it if you never phoned here again."*

*"Ok. Hold your horses,"* she said, and hung up.

If only I had answered the phone instead of Kay. The poor girl had missed the point. Ann had mistaken Kay's voice for a little girls! I had to wait until I judged they had arrived back at the shop before I phoned.

Meanwhile I took Kay's belongings back up to our room. As I took each garment out of the bin liner she had stuffed them into, I shook the creases out and smelt them. Her body odour lingered on the clothes along with her perfume. Tidily I hung them up in the dust covers and on the hangers and rail in the old wardrobe. All the time I was watching the clock and wishing my life away for the time to tell me the shop would be inhabited by Kay again. Christine at last answered my call and told me it was a bad time and to phone tomorrow.

\*\*\*

Next day I paid the vicar a visit and delivered his pigs. His wife invited me in for a talk as he was out at the moment but expected back soon. She told me all that had gone on yesterday, and then I told her about the phone call.

*"You poor man!"* she said. *"That is terrible. Kay was ready to forgive you. We had convinced her that there was no other woman, then that. She must feel so let down."*

*"The wedding is off I'm afraid,"* I said. *"I will leave the pigs and will you tell your husband the church service will no longer be required."*

*"Tell him yourself here he comes now,"* and looking out of the window I saw

him walking up the path smiling to himself. He had seen and heard the pigs in the trailer parked outside.

"*My good fellow!*" he said, hugging me. "*You've brought my little darlings!*" His wife's manner and look told him that it was not the time to be joyful. He stared at me. "*What's wrong?*"

"Kay," I said. "*She's left me.*" He sank into a chair.

"*Oh no! I thought all was OK.*"

"*It's a long story,*" his wife said.

"*Anything I can do to help?*" he said. "*Just ask. Now those pigs.*" He seemed more interested in them than one of his human flock.

***

That night before I went to bed, I listened to the message on the phone. Only one the voice had said, so I listened as Bob told me to expect him early tomorrow morning to collect Kay's things. It was too late now to phone them so I slept in fits and starts until daylight.

***

Dressing as the birds sang the morning chorus, I let the dog out and made a cup of tea. I then ventured out into a clear bright morning feeling very down, a night without Kay made me remember all those lonely years, in a daze I entered the yard to feed the pigs and sort out the cows. It was nearly eight by the time everything was finished and I sat down to the table to eat a bowl of cornflakes. My appetite was not there. No way could I face a plate of food this miserable morning, even though the sun was blazing down. I was deep in thought when Bob drew up in the yard and I noticed he was alone. Why I had hoped that Kay would be with him, I have no idea. Perhaps it had something to do with my heart telling me that I knew we were both in love.

***

Opening the back door as Bob approached, he bid me good morning and plonked himself down at the table.

"*Any tea going I'm parched.*" Pouring a tepid cup of brew from the pot, which was stewing, he said, "*What the hell is going on? Kay was in tears yesterday and last night, her and Christine were on the blessed phone for hours.*"

"*You tell me,*" I said.

"*Peter hardly had a wink of sleep last night, he knows something is up and is disturbed. Kay won't tell us who the person on the phone was that upset her, but we know it was that bloody Abby lying again.*"

"*No it wasn't,*" I said, and told him of my discovery later that night.

"*Look Preacher. You must tell Kay the truth. I tell you what, I'm going to leave her clothes here and you come up with me and talk to her. She'll listen to you, I'm sure.*"

I told Bob that today I had to be here as the vet was coming then some men from the Ministry and there was no way I could get out of it, but for him to return and tell Kay to expect me later on my white charger to carry her away and that all her clothes were safe. Bob left me and I heard nothing more from up the town.

***

The vet came and went, then the men in there black suits arrived to ask a lot of silly questions and pour over the farm accounts, I thought they would never leave, never being one to be any good with paper matters every thing was always in a muddle, but Kay taking over the last month had all in order. Eventually they left and I ran to the car and took the road north to find out from Kay just what she was thinking about. After all we had said and planned, a little phone call from a slip of a girl had made her flee and she knew of Abby and her nasty tricks. Why, why had she stormed out of my life?

***

I parked in a vacant gap between two vans delivering to the shops in the street and walked to the shop. The door was closed and a notice hanging in the window of the door by a piece of string told me they were closed. I rang the bell by the side and awaited an answer. Nothing, then thinking the bell did not work I hammered on the frame, rattling the pane of glass. Amazed at the place being closed when they had told me they hated losing a day's trade, I banged even harder.

I must have made quite a noise as a woman came across the road from a shop opposite and told me that she was sure she was in. Obviously Kay had seen me, I thought, and was just hiding from the inevitable so I walked up the road to the phone box to phone Christine's Mobil.

Her daughter on the other end told me that her mother was in the flat and why didn't I go round the back and let myself in? The key was under the brick by the door. Telling her I had no knowledge of a back door, she gave me directions of how to go up the road to an alleyway, and then half way along I would see a bright green door and a latch to open it by.

Thanking Christine, I made my way up to the end of the street and found the alley. The latch allowed the door to swing open into a yard full of familiar flowerpots and a lot more old junk. Lifting the brick I retrieved the key to what I hoped was going to be a heart-stopping encounter with my Kay.

Closing the door behind me, I heard a noise above my head and realised someone was upstairs. Up on the landing I heard sobbing from behind what turned out to be a locked door. No one answered my gentle rap so knowing it could only be Kay I charged my shoulder to the door. Crashing into the room Kay lunged at me.

"Go away. I hate you!" Then in the same breath she threw her arms around my neck. We kissed passionately before releasing each other.

"Kay. Whatever came over you?"

"That girl on the phone I'm sure she said she wanted to talk to her father."

"She did. She thought you were a little girl. Bob and I had been to see her mother, Abby, he told her a few home truths and that she was to stop bothering either of us. Ann, Abby's daughter phoned to find out what we had said as her mother was ranting and raving. I rang her back after you left to find out the reason you fled so readily and told her also never to ring me again. Honest darling, she is as bad as her mother."

"I know," she said "but I am frightened that I am only going along with you and my family. You must tell me I'm silly, please, because they keep telling me to marry you quickly. Even Peter goes on and on about the two of us and how you are his granddad and he is going to live with us."

"What's wrong with that?"

"You don't understand do you? I can't believe that after all these years you still find me attractive."

"Attractive is the wrong word love. You're gorgeous, desirable, beautiful, everything I have ever wanted and to top it all you are all mine and coming home with me to marry and live with me, me, me forever!"

\*\*\*

The sun shone through the little bedroom window and she sobbed on my shoulder as I caressed her slowly and gently up and down her back while she lay in my arms. We eventually flopped onto the crumpled bed and then heard the shop bell ringing. Someone that had a key came into the shop and we heard voices. .

"It's Christine and Bob." Kay said.

"They must be here." Bob said, *"Upstairs in bed I expect!"*

"Oh I do hope so life will be bliss if mother goes with him as planned."

"There I told you," Kay said, moving away from me on the bed. *"They have it all planned."*

"No we haven't, you have," Bob said, standing in the hole where the broken door should have been. Neither of us had heard him come up the stairs.

*"You have done nothing but tell us what you had planned for the pair of you and how happy you were and by the look of this damage, the Preacher is a man of his word. Earlier to-day he told me he was coming on his white charger to get you!"*

Christine appeared at his side and told her husband the best thing for them to do now they knew mother was safe was to leave them and go down to the farm till they sorted themselves out. Turning in the doorway she smiled at the two of us and told us. *"Take as long as we liked the farm would be ok."*

\*\*\*

That night Kay and I lay talking in her tiny bed with the broken door open. She told me that after marrying me, her next wish was to give the shop to her daughter and son-in-law but before she could do that, she had to pay Richard off. One of the conditions with the settlement between them both had been that she did not sell the place for a certain number of years, and that condition still had four years to go. I told her not to worry about it, I would get my solicitor to check it out tomorrow. Something could be worked out, of that I was sure.

\*\*\*

That night the phone rang at a very unappreciated time. Eventually, the second time it rang, Kay insisted on answering it. Peter could not sleep until his gran told him that he could always see the pigs because she was going to live next to them. I heard his shrieks of joy as I lay with my head alongside Kay's.

"*Preacher,*" she said, turning over to look at me. "*Tonight you have made two of us happy, and tomorrow I hope to make two more of my family glad that you came back to me.*" She would tell me no more and we fell asleep.

***

On waking, we had five minutes to open the shop and then concentrate on something to eat and drink. The kettle had not boiled before the old bell inside the door announced the first customer of the day. I made a pot of tea and had a bowl of flakes. The pot was nearly cold when Kay came back to the kitchen table looking rather pleased with her self.

"*That's it,*" she said, waving a cheque at me. "*All mine. The rest Christine can have.*"

Taking a sneak at the piece of paper as she put the kettle back on, I noticed the cheque was made out to her for three hundred pounds.

"*Sold something?*" I asked.

"*You bet!*" she said. "*My last item from now on it's all Christine's if she wants it.*"

"*What did you sell then?*"

"*Your old bee hive from the farm that stood in the window. That was the last one. Now there is nothing of yours here except a pile of old flower pots and me, and you my love are going to take me away and never let me come back. Please promise never let me run away again.*" I took her in my arms.

"*All mine till death do us part,*" I said.  Tears showed in her eyes and I kissed them dry.

"*I love the way you kiss my eyes,*" she said. "*Let me have something to eat then. Sussex, here we come! I've locked the past up, sod the shop! You can look after me now. Where's the car?*"

"*Around the corner,*" I said. "*See you in a moment out the front,*" and left to get the car. Like a fool I had forgotten this was town, you could not park anywhere for long and the windscreen had a parking ticket under the wiper. Removing the plastic wallet, I discovered yesterday's ticket. It appeared that the wardens went to work early in this town.

***

Together we left the houses behind and headed across Kent to her new home. Entering the yard, I was surprised to see the tractor had been moved and the muck spreader hitched on and parked alongside a pig run. Kay could not wait to meet her family so I went to investigate the meaning of the tractor being where it was. I was flabbergasted to find Peter loading the trailer with pig dung. With a fork he was busy cleaning the pigs out.

"*You drove the tractor!*"

"*You don't mind do you? Only every Wednesday when I was here you gave them a new bed,*" he said, tapping one of the old sows on the back with the fork handle.

"No. I'm just surprised you got it started!"

"I watched what you did," he said. "I learn quick."

"Of course you do," thinking what an improvement he showed from the first time he had visited the farm. Then one had to tell him what to do over and over again. Peter had found a niche in life that he enjoyed, and it satisfied him. I entered the house to be greeted by Christine with open arms. She too had been crying. Was this all this family did? Bob, she told me, had gone into town to see the vicar as he had phoned about something to do with the pigs. Why Bob had gone beat her as all he knew about pigs was that bacon came from them, even then he was not sure from which part of the animal that was!

Taking her to one side, I told her how I had broken into Kay's room and was sorry for the damage but would pay to have it repaired. Kay appeared down the stairs from checking her cloths I had placed back in the wardrobe after her rush to leave the last time, as Bob returned to the house. I was just going to ask him what the matter was with the vicar's pigs when Kay said that could wait. She was bursting to tell Christine and Bob something.

"Now we are all here," she said, "sit down." I realised that it had something to do with her remarks yesterday so sat down to listen. "Preacher and I are to get married so I will be leaving the flat. I don't want to have anything more to do with it. He," and she took my hand, "knows the circumstances with Richard and is going to look into it but my mind is made up. I'm giving you the shop and all the stock. This morning I sold my last piece, that old beehive, look" and she took the cheque from her jeans pocket to place on the table.

"Don't leave it there," said Christine with more tears in her eyes. She leaned over the table and hugged her mother. "You can't!" she said.

"Yes I can and as soon as I can, I'm getting the deeds changed into your name." Bob looked at me.

"She means it you know," he said. "God help you boy, taking her on. When she makes her mind up you look out!"

"Put that cheque away safely mum," and Kay picked it up. "Put it under the clock," Christine said, "then it won't blow away." Kay stepped across the room and lifted the edge of the timepiece, then asked what all the money was doing under it. I had forgotten all about it. She pulled out the pile of notes and started to count.

"That's what Josephine paid me the first time she came down. I had forgotten it was there."

"Don't you look after your money?" Christine said. "Mother, you will have to look after all his money for him!" and gave me a sly look. "It will serve you right if she spends it all," she said looking me straight in the eye. I got the impression from the look Bob gave me that it was not a wise move to let Kay have my purse strings.

"She can keep that," I said, pushing the piles of notes she had abstracted from under the old time piece over to her. "Buy something nice for yourself."

"You can't afford to give me all this," she said shuffling the paper into a neat pile.

"How do you know what I can or cannot afford?" I said, and Christine said, "She soon will!"

\*\*\*

The mood was happy and lunch was to be had in the best hotel in town as a sort of celebration. Peter was rounded up and made to bathe before putting clean clothes on, and then we all went to take our table, which we had booked earlier. Champagne was uncorked and Bob gave a toast in our honour. Peter up until now had been quiet, now his voice was to be heard above everyone else's.

"Gran, if you never come to the shop and live with Preacher, I will never see you again" "and I love you!" His words, so simple and spoken by nothing but a child's voice made all us adults feel for him. Kay got up from her chair and cuddled him to her.

"Silly Peter! I will never leave you. You can come and stay whenever you like can't he Preacher?"

I now had Kay, so why not I thought?

"Live with you forever? I could look after the pig's granddad can grow me the grain to feed them on." This lad was way ahead of me. From staying the odd week, it now looked like he had changed. He was abandoning his mother and father to the shop! The look as Kay looked at me for guidance was lost on me.

"Hell. Why not" I said. "He can live with us." She nearly knocked the poor lad over in her haste to hug me. Christine and Bob were happy with the situation. Peter was ecstatic with joy. Even the staff of the hotel got in on the act by producing and giving us another bottle of bubbly!

\*\*\*

That night the house rang to the sound of joy. Never before could I remember the old home feeling as snug and peaceful as that night. Christine and Bob had been evicted from our room. Tomorrow they were to go home and open their shop.

\*\*\*

I paid the vicar a visit to ascertain the trouble of his pigs.

"It was trivial," he said. Bob had told him what he wanted to know.

"Bob?" I said puzzled that he knew anything after what his wife had told me.

"Only wanted to know if there was room for half a dozen more," he said, pointing to the half acre of tall grass that practically hid the six little pigs. "He reckons I could keep a dozen more with no problem. Told me you keep them in pens all their lives. Only I have had so many people ask if I would sell them a leg or two, I'm sure I could earn a little money."

I left the vicarage after telling him and his wife the wedding was back on but as the harvest was coming up we would leave it awhile. His wife suggested a spring one would be lovely.

\*\*\*

My solicitor was my next port of call and with a bunch of papers in my hand, he sat me down and started reading. Ten minutes of his time and he smiled at me.

"Don't know who drew this contact up. Obviously the office boy I should think! Easy way out Preacher, pay him off! Four years left to go, only fifteen thousand pounds. You have that don't you or have you spent all the money your mother left you?"

"No. Never touched it," I said.

"Good, then let me write to him today. I left a very happy man. Kay was so sure that the shop would never be hers to pass onto her daughter so soon. And the news that I had seen the vicar whose wife suggested the wedding should take place in six months time, in April just added to her joy." Kay said,

"Your birthday is four days after mine. Let's look to see if there is a Saturday between them."

"It doesn't have to be a Saturday," I said. "A day in the week is just as good."

"Heaven no! Only snobs get married then!" Kay said.

"Well mum, you are the lady of a big house, and marrying the squire"

"We could hold a big reception in the old barn, there's plenty of time to get it clean and empty," I said.

"You mean empty, then clean!" said her mother.

"All right you know what I mean."

\*\*\*

Peter got up at six every morning and fed the pigs before school. He was really good, he had found a niche in life and it suited him. Kay busied herself from dawn to dusk getting the house as she wanted, even down to finding and employing a window cleaner to come in every fortnight. The sunlight had never shone so fiercely into any room before. Even my mother had never cleaned the outside of the attic window. The large spare room downstairs was to be the last to tackle, she told me. Meanwhile it became the home for all the old things she found and which I told her she could dispose of.

\*\*\*

The days flew by and on Christmas Day the house was packed with the family I had inherited that year, along with my friends that over the years I had invited to lunch and which somehow had become the norm each Christmas. It had suited many that I had a large kitchen and plenty of room for kids. Two of my mates brought their aging mothers and they supervised while the wives cooked the turkey. To-day Kay was not the boss in her own kitchen but somehow the ladies got on fine. I believe they thought that this year would be the last time they would be invited back but late that afternoon Kay had said to me what a wonderful day we had had and she had asked them to come next year.

The young children that accompanied my guests really gave the place a Christmas feel and Peter had found many new friends. Never before had Kay had the opportunity of such luxury of so much space to entertain and she told me that in future dinner parties were on the agenda for the New Year. She said she planned parties to make the small town talk. Invites I learnt that night in bed had already gone out to some of the guests as they had left. The New Year,

Kay told me, was to be the start of our life, mine especially as now I had a woman for the first time in my life, and she gave me a hug.

\*\*\*

New Year's Eve saw the house once again full of people, this time including the vicar and his wife. Our wedding had been set for Valentine's Day. The rain we had been experiencing for the last four weeks had done nothing to stop the team Kay had assembled to clean out the old barn. All the missing tiles had been replaced and every cobweb in all the rafters had been swept away. I was worried that the council would pay a visit thinking I was converting it to a dwelling house without permission by the way the workers arrived in all their vans to clutter up the yard.

\*\*\*

Before Christmas Kay had sat down and designed her wedding dress and together she and Christine had sketched the Maid of Honour dress for Josephine and Peter's suit. Work was in hand, the vicar's wife informed me at the New Year's party, with a dressmaker in a distant town. This wedding, her husband told me, was to cost a fortune.

\*\*\*

A week into the New Year a letter arrived from my solicitor informing me that Richard had accepted the deal and to save any embarrassment on my part, he personally had paid. He asked that I reimburse him by return post. I left Peter to feed the pigs on his own, keeping an eye on how things were going. Kay told me that Peter had seemed a new lad since moving in with us. *"He's like the child we never had, you treat him so like your son."*

*"He is my son. He hates it when folk ask him if he is anything to do with us. He told the dustman he was our son and they believed him. If that is what people want to believe, it's fine with me."*

\*\*\*

Christine received the deeds to the shop as promised and immediately arrived on our doorstep to thank her mother.

The wedding was only three weeks away and Kay had insisted on no honeymoon. Instead Peter had got to have a holiday with his parents in a foreign country. I paid for them to have a ten-day break on the island of Cyprus. While they were gone, the shop was to have a visit from the decorators so she opened in her name with a completely new décor

Our honeymoon, Kay said, was to be in our own house, alone and with the doors locked. A firm of contractors had been hired to feed the pigs and do the arable that needed doing. There was no need for us to leave the house, she had thought of everything.

\*\*\*

I had spent the night at my mates as Kay insisted I was not to see her before she walked up the aisle. Christine and Josephine had made a marvellous job of getting her ready and the pageboy looked the real gentleman in his suit. The vicar's wife and daughter, along with the women of the town, had dressed the church in spring flowers. My soon to be son-in-law was acting as my best man and told me nothing could go wrong. My dream at last was only minutes away.

***

The church was full, *'The Old Squire,'* as all called me, was getting married. Kay took it all in her stride. The tears ran down my cheeks. Richard showed me the ring to demonstrate that all was in hand.

The vicar was half way through the service when he asked all those assembled whether any knew of why we should not be joined in Holy Matrimony.

Instantly a loud shrill voice shouted from the back near the door. All heads turned to see a woman in a green patterned dress and a large green brimmed hat standing and pointing her hand at the two of us. The vicar was quick off the mark and his voice boomed across the pews and congregation:

*"Your reasons my dear, please?"*

*"He loves me, not her."*

*"That is not a valid reason, let me remind you my dear you are in church, now let us carry on."*

All eyes other than Kay's had turned to look at this woman. I believe the vicar's wife was the first to reach Abby, I was more worried for Kay but a sly glance behind me confirmed that Abby's daughter and some of the girls I had secretly met in the pub in Ashford had the woman in green well in hand. Placing my arm firmly around Kay's slim waist I hugged her to me, the priest smiled at the two of us and whispered, *"Let's continue shall we."*

The noise at the back of the church subsided to a few chocking sobs and suggestions from young female voices of, *"be quiet,"* and all heads turned to face the front again

I held Kay by the waist to steady her, feeling her body stiffen to the woman's intrusion on our solemn affair.

***

The church bells rang out as the two of us walked arm in arm down the aisle as Mr and Mrs Tiltman. My dream had at last come true! Over fifty friends lined the pews to follow for the photographs.

As Kay laughed at the girl that caught the bouquet she tossed behind her, a friend asked her who the woman was in the green dress who had sat at the back of church. Now the poor woman was hurrying away down the path to the gate to leave the churchyard accompanied by her daughter. Kay tugged my arm.

*"Will she never go away"* she said nodding her head in the fleeing woman's direction. I looked up as the woman in green, wearing a large brimmed hat, stopped to take one last look at us. Kay's hand grabbed my arm and at the same time a shiver ran down my body.

*"It's OK,"* I said to Kay. *"She's leaving."* and I felt her tighten her grip on me.

*"She told me,"* Kay said, *"that last time she talked to me that she would be the one in church when you married."*

*"It seems she was right but got it wrong didn't she? It was you I married,"* and together we smiled at each other.

*"I love you,"* she said, *"take me home please to my wonderland."*
END